THE AMERICAN IMAGE OF RUSSIA · 1917–1977

THE AMERICAN IMAGE

WITH ILLUSTRATIONS

)F RUSSIA · 1917–1977

Edited with an Introduction and Comments by

Benson L. Grayson

FREDERICK UNGAR PUBLISHING CO. · NEW YORK

Copyright © 1978 by Frederick Ungar Publishing Co., Inc.

Printed in the United States of America

Designed by Irving Perkins

Library of Congress Cataloging in Publication Data
Main entry under title:

The American image of Russia, 1917-1977.

Includes bibliographical references and index.
1.   United States—Relations (general) with Russia.
2.   Russia—Relations (general) with the United States.
3.   Russia—Foreign opinion, American.   4.   Public
opinion—United States.   I.   Grayson, Benson Lee, 1932-
E183.8.R9A74   301.29′73′047   77-6972
ISBN 0-8044-1308-8

ACKNOWLEDGMENTS

The editor and publishers express their appreciation to the copyright owners by whose permission individual selections are included here, as follows:

American Federation of Labor and Congress of Industrial Organizations. For excerpts from January 1947 issue of *Free Trade Union News*, published by AFL-CIO Department of International Affairs.

The Atlantic. For excerpts from the comments of Albert Einstein as reported in "Atomic War or Peace," by Raymond Swing, Copyright © 1956, Estate of Albert Einstein.

The Chicago Tribune. For the cartoons "The Purpose of the Meeting Is to Take Measurements" and "Aren't We Having Enough Trouble with the Machinery Without Letting Somebody Throw a Monkey Wrench into It?" which appeared in 1961 and 1933 respectively.

The Devin-Adair Company. For "America's Retreat from Victory," by Joseph R. McCarthy, Copyright © 1951 by Joseph R. McCarthy.

Elizabeth H. (Mrs. John) Dos Passos. For excerpts from John Dos Passos's *The Best Times.*

Victor Fischer and George Fischer. For excerpts from Louis Fischer's *Men and Politics.*

Foreign Affairs. For excerpts from "The Sources of Soviet Conduct," by George Kennan, in the July 1947 issue, Copyright 1947 by Council on Foreign Relations, Inc.; and for excerpts from "The Challenge to Americans," by Henry L. Stimson, in the October 1947 issue, Copyright 1947 by Council on Foreign Relations, Inc.

Harcourt Brace Jovanovich, Inc. For excerpts from *The Autobiography of Lincoln Steffens*, Copyright 1931 by Harcourt Brace Jovanovich, Inc., renewed 1959 by Peter Steffens.

Harper and Row. For excerpts from Anna Eleanor Roosevelt's *Autobiography*, Copyright 1949 by Anna Eleanor Roosevelt.

Harvard University Press. For excerpts from Dean Acheson's *Power and Diplomacy*, by permission of the publishers. Copyright © 1958 by The Fletcher School of Law and Diplomacy, Tufts University.

Hill and Wang and Harold Ober Associates Incorporated. For excerpts from *I Wonder As I Wander* by Langston Hughes, Copyright © 1956 by Langston Hughes.

The Herbert Hoover Foundation of New York City and Mr. Allan

Hoover. For excerpts from President Hoover's memorandum of March 28, 1919 to President Wilson.

Houghton Mifflin Company. For excerpts from Victor Reuther's *The Brothers Reuther.*

International Publishers. For excerpts from John Reed's *Ten Days That Shook The World* and Earl Browder's *The Peoples Front.*

Corliss Lamont. For excerpts from his book *Soviet Civilization,* published in 1952 by Philosophical Library.

The League for Industrial Democracy. For excerpts from *Russia, Democracy or Dictatorship?* by Norman Thomas and Joel Seidman.

Little, Brown and Co., in association with The Atlantic Monthly Press. For excerpts from Walter Lippmann's *U.S. War Aims,* Copyright 1944 by Walter Lippmann. Copyright © 1972 by Walter Lippmann.

The Los Angeles Times. For the cartoon "On the Threshold!" which appeared in 1920.

Macmillan Publishing Co., Inc. and Hodder & Stoughton Limited. For excerpts from *The Memoirs of Cordell Hull,* Copyright 1948 by Cordell Hull, copyright renewed.

The New Leader. For excerpts from "The Myth of Soviet Politics," by Hans J. Morgenthau, published in the October 26, 1964 issue, Copyright © The American Labor Conference on International Affairs, Inc.

W. W. Norton & Company, Inc. and to George Allen & Unwin Ltd. For excerpts from Max Eastman's *Stalin's Russia and the Crisis in Socialism,* Copyright renewed 1968 by Max Eastman.

S. G. Phillips, Inc. For excerpts from Sidney Hook's *Political Power and Personal Freedom,* published in 1959 by Criterion Books.

Random House. For excerpts from Emma Goldman's *Living My Life,* James Wechsler's *The Age of Suspicion,* I. F. Stone's *Polemics and Prophecies,* and J. W. Fulbright's *The Crippled Giant.*

The St. Louis Post-Dispatch. For the cartoon "What's the Difference?" by Fitzpatrick, which appeared in 1918.

Charles Scribner's Sons. For excerpts from *Reinhold Niebuhr on Politics,* edited by Harry R. Davis and Robert C. Good, Copyright © 1960 by Charles Scribner's Sons.

The University of Pennsylvania Press. For excerpts from *Letters of Theodore Dreiser, A Selection,* edited by Robert H. Elias, published in 1959.

Contents

List of Illustrations

Photograph Credits

Title pages: *Tass* from Sovfoto, *Novosti* from Sovfoto; 8, 9: Herbert Hoover Presidential Library; 21: Wide World Photos; 39: *Tass* from Sovfoto; 63: United Press International Photo; 89: Archives of Labor History and Urban Affairs, Wayne State University; 107: Sovfoto; 137, 179, 207: Wide World Photos; 241: *Tass* from Sovfoto; 339: Wide World Photos; 343: Greater New York Conference on Soviet Jewry.

Introduction

EVER SINCE the United States emerged as an independent nation, we have found it necessary to follow developments in Russia for their likely impact on events in this country. Our image of Russia has changed often. In the early years Russia was considered a distant but potentially friendly power that might provide support against the immediate enemy, Great Britain. Toward the end of the nineteenth century relations with Russia cooled, as a result of more friendly American attitudes toward Britain and increased United States distaste for the authoritarian rule of the tsarist government. Following a brief honeymoon in relations between the establishment of the liberal Russian Provisional Government in March 1917 and its overthrow by the Bolsheviks eight months later, the United States came to regard the Soviet regime as a threat to democratic institutions and to the peace of the world.

Notwithstanding brief interruptions, most Americans continue to look upon Russia with suspicion and concern to this very day. At the same time, the material accomplishments of the Soviets and the emergence of Russia and the United States as the two world superpowers after 1945 have made it essential for America to pay the closest attention to events in the Soviet Union. Indeed, much of world history since 1917, and particularly since the end of World War II, can be described in terms of Russian-American relations. For this reason, an appreciation of American views of Russia in the period 1917–1977 is basic not only to an understanding of international developments in the past, but also as a guide to predicting the future course of events.

The Fall of the Tsar

The United States image of Russia was drastically changed by the Revolution of March 1917, which brought about the abdica-

1

tion of the tsar and the establishment of the Provisional Government. The popular view of Russia as a cruel autocracy savagely repressing the rights of its citizens was quickly replaced by that of a fellow democracy sharing common goals and interests. Americans hailed the event as a harbinger of the democratic tide which was expected to sweep over Europe and the world. Secretary of State Robert Lansing reflected this view when he urged President Wilson to assist the new regime as rapidly as possible because of its liberal nature, and this country was the first to grant it diplomatic recognition on March 22, 1917.

American entry into World War I, which made us an ally of Russia in the struggle against Germany, further strengthened ties between the two countries. The formation of the Provisional Government was considered of such significance in the United States that President Wilson referred to it at length in his message to a joint session of Congress on April 2, 1917 calling for a declaration of war against Germany. In the months that followed, Wilson dispatched a high-powered mission to Russia (headed by former Secretary of State Elihu Root) to work out the best means of cooperation in the prosecution of the war, and Washington extended some $325 million in credit to help keep the Provisional Government in the struggle.

The Bolshevik Revolution

This favorable view of Russia was shattered in November 1917, when Nikolai Lenin's extremist Bolshevik faction of the Russian Social Democratic Party overthrew the Provisional Government. While the intentions of the new regime were at first in doubt, the more Washington learned of the Soviet government the more American attitude toward it hardened. The initial point of discord was Lenin's decision to make a separate peace with the Central Powers and take Russia out of the war, which resulted in the peace agreement signed with Germany at Brest-Litovsk on March 3, 1918.

Equally repugnant to the United States were the growing indications of the dictatorial nature of the Bolshevik government and

WHAT'S THE DIFFERENCE?

A 1918 cartoon, showing the swing of public opinion away from the first favorable reaction to the Russian revolution. (By Fitzpatrick, courtesy of the St. Louis Post-Dispatch)

its use of force to repress domestic opposition. The initial reports that the Soviets had launched a reign of terror against their opponents reached America almost immediately after the November Revolution, and word of similar reports multiplied geometrically following the execution of the former tsar and his family by the Bolsheviks in July 1918. By September 1918 feelings in the United States were running so high that the State Department asked all nations with whom we had diplomatic relations to join in condemning the "openly avowed campaign of mass terrorism" and the "indiscriminate slaughter of Russian citizens" by the Soviets.

Although hostile to the new Bolshevik government, America did not join with the other Allies in supporting militarily those elements in Russia seeking to overthrow the Soviets. In March 1918 the State Department informed the Japanese government that it considered inadvisable a proposed landing of Japanese troops in Siberia. The American objection to this move was that it would play into the hands of the enemies of the Russian Revolution, for which the United States "entertains the greatest sympathy, in spite of all the unhappiness and misfortune which has for the time being sprung out of it." In short, the United States regarded the Bolsheviks as a temporary aberration in Russia's expected maturation into a democratic state. Eventually, small American detachments participated in the Allied landings at Murmansk, to prevent munitions from falling into the hands of the Germans, and in Siberia, to aid the evacuation of Czech prisoners-of-war who wished to fight on the side of the Allies. While the other Allied governments may have had ulterior motives in urging the landings, insofar as Washington was concerned, the sole purpose of the operations was to bring about a rapid and successful conclusion to the war against Germany.

The end of the war in November 1918 effected little, if any, change in America's attitude toward Russia. The United States continued to adhere to the assumption that the Soviet regime was a temporary phenomenon and would be replaced by a representative government as soon as the Russian people could exercise their choice. Washington anticipated no great delay in this respect, expecting that the restoration of an elected govern-

ON THE THRESHOLD!

A typical cartoon expressing early views of the Soviet Union as a menace to civilization after the Russian Civil War. (Courtesy the Los Angeles *Times*)

ment would ensure a national program unlikely to come into conflict with that of America. In accordance with this view, the United States entertained a hands-off policy concerning various proposals geared to support anti-Bolshevik forces in Russia.

Not only did Washington not work actively against the Soviets, but the United States even made tentative gestures indicating its interest in better relations with the Bolsheviks. In November 1918 President Wilson suggested the possibility of inviting the various combating factions within Russia to the Versailles Peace Conference, only to be informed by the Secretary of State after consultation with the other Allies that rival political forces in Russia would be unable to agree on the organization of such a delegation.

During the course of the sessions at Versailles, Wilson sent William C. Bullitt, a member of the American delegation, to head an unofficial mission to Russia in March 1919. Its task was to sound out the Soviet leaders on their terms for cooperation with the Allies. The Bullitt group, which included the noted American journalist Lincoln Steffens, met with Lenin and brought back the Soviet proposals for a settlement. These included a cease fire in place for the Bolsheviks and their opponents in the Russian Civil War and repayment to the Allies by Russia of the tsarist war debts. Although these proposals came a long way toward meeting Allied demands, they were not seriously considered at the Versailles conference in light of an expected Bolshevik defeat.

The end of the Russian civil war in 1921 left the Soviets less than anxious to gain America's friendship. In the absence of assurances that diplomatic recognition of Russia would be reciprocated with repayment of Russian debts to the United States and an end to Moscow's support of revolutionary groups abroad, Washington continued its policy of waiting for a favorable turn in the Bolshevik administration. The Republican administration of President Harding, which succeeded Wilson's in 1921, saw no reason to recognize the Soviet Union. The United States remained anxious to alleviate the hardships of the Russian population, however, and during the great famine in the Soviet Union, in 1921–1923, Congress appropriated twenty million dollars for aid to

Russia. All told, over sixty-six million dollars was raised in the United States for humanitarian assistance to Russia, and American relief programs saved an estimated ten million Russian lives.

Friends of Russia

While most groups in America shared the government's critical opinion of the Bolshevik regime, there were some dissenters. Radical and liberal elements hailed the Soviet seizure of power as signaling the start of the global proletarian dictatorship envisioned by Karl Marx, which would allegedly end the exploitation of labor by capital and bring about the desired socialist millennium. Others, less diehard in their beliefs, acknowledged the repressive nature of the Soviet government but justified it as an acceptable price to pay for urgently needed economic and social reform, asserting that it would soon give way to a more equitable system. For a time—in the 1920s and 1930s—those favorably inclined to the Soviet Union included many, if not most of America's leading intellectuals, such as Theodore Dreiser, John Dos Passos, and Lincoln Steffens.

When the Soviet Union adopted the New Economic Policy in March 1921, a sympathetic stance toward Russia became easier to defend. The policy marked a retreat by Lenin from the harsher communist programs implemented during the Russian Civil War. It included a limited toleration of small private farms and businesses and the replacement of arbitrary seizure of farm surpluses from the peasants by a more orderly and restricted system of taxes. Lenin defended the new policy as constituting taking one step backward in order to take two steps forward. In fact, he had little choice; the Soviet agricultural policy was partly responsible for the great famine of 1921–23 and the hardship inflicted on the general population had resulted in a mutiny by the workers and sailors at the naval base at Kronstadt. Incidentally, these very mutineers had been among the most esteemed Soviet heroes of the Bolshevik Revolution.

In addition to those Americans urging better relations with

An American Relief truck at one of its warehouses, Kazan.

At an American Relief kitchen in Moscow.

the Soviets for ideological reasons, some business and financial circles viewed Russia as a large and potentially lucrative market for expanded trade. This attitude remained relatively submerged so long as the American economy remained prosperous, but came to the fore during the short-lived United States recession in 1921 and in greatly strengthened form following the start of the great world depression in 1929.

Meanwhile, during the twenties, conditions in Russia improved under the relatively benevolent policies of the New Economic Policy. Unlike Emma Goldman, the Russian-born anarchist, who was so disillusioned by conditions in Russia before and during the Kronstadt Revolt that she left the Soviet Union a bitter critic, most Americans who visited Russia later—during the years of the New Economic Policy, between 1921 and 1928—were favorably impressed by the toleration of limited dissent and by the social and educational reforms. At the same time, an easing of the repressive measures which had marked the early years of the Bolshevik regime led some observers in the United States and elsewhere to accept the prediction of Karl Marx that under the communist dictatorship the state would gradually wither away.

The Death of Lenin and the Rise of Stalin

In contrast to the small group of sympathizers, most Americans in the 1920s regarded Russia as a distant and bizarre country. If the image of Russia as typified by a bomb-throwing Bolshevik had faded, there was still no bounding enthusiasm for closer ties until Moscow agreed to adopt policies of human conduct resembling those of other nations. Washington continued to hold Russia at arm's length. Moscow was not invited to participate at the Paris ceremonies in August 1928 during which sixty-two nations adhered to the American-sponsored Kellogg-Briand Pact outlawing war, even though the previous year the Soviet Union had taken the lead in calling for a comprehensive program of international disarmament. One reason for the lack of United States interest in establishing diplomatic relations with Russia was the fact that it appeared to have no effect on trade between the two nations. By 1930 American exports to the Soviet Union had climbed to the point where they represented more than a quarter of all Russian purchases, making the United States the largest single supplier.

Beneath the quiet exterior, however, fundamental changes were under way in the Soviet Union. In January 1924 Nikolai Lenin, the architect of the Bolshevik system, succumbed to a stroke, having been largely incapacitated by a previous stroke almost two years earlier. Lenin had held the post of premier and was also the dominant figure in the Bolshevik Party; nonetheless, his position was more of a "first among equals" and he occasionally, if only temporarily, found his wishes blocked by a majority of his party colleagues. He also had spent much time as an exile in the West, as had most of his senior associates, and they were all familiar with the methods and objectives of democratic institutions.

Even before Lenin's death his lieutenants, G.E. Zinoviev and Lev Kamenev, joined forces to oppose the bid for leadership by Leon Trotsky, Soviet Commissar of War and, next to Lenin, the most charismatic of the Bolshevik chieftains. Trotsky's strategic ability and organizational efforts had been very important to the Soviet victory in the Civil War, but his ostentatious behavior and the fact that he had once sided against the Bolsheviks in disputes among the exiled Russian revolutionaries prior to the revolution made him anathema to the other Soviet leaders.

The third and most junior member of the triumvirate seeking to block Trotsky's succession to the Bolshevik leadership was party secretary Josef Stalin, then little known outside the party. Unlike Lenin, Trotsky and the other Soviet leaders, he had spent no time in the West and did not share their familiarity with Western culture and manners. Although his duties were primarily administrative in nature, Stalin had used the position to promote his supporters in the party to positions of influence. Lenin, who had become aware of the danger, warned unsuccessfully that Stalin be removed from his position.

Ignoring Lenin's advice, as presented by his widow, Krupskaya, the Bolshevik Party Congress, which met in the summer of 1924, excommunicated Trotsky from the party. The immediate danger thus averted, the triumvirate of Zinoviev, Kamenev and Stalin fell apart, and the party secretary skillfully isolated his rivals and rid them of their prestige and influence. Using first one faction within the party and then another, his control over the party by early 1929 approximated that which Lenin had attained. Stalin was well on his way toward establishing a one-man dictatorship over both the party and the Soviet state.

By October 1928, his domination of the party sufficiently secure, Stalin abandoned the moderate policies of the New Economic Policy and initiated the First Soviet Five-Year Plan. In theory, this was intended to move Russia along the road to rapid industrialization by restricting consumer expenditures so as to increase investment in heavy industry. In practice, however, it resulted in the rapid and forced collectivization of many small farms, causing a great decline in agricultural production, actual starvation, and a great loss in human life.

The Great Depression and American Diplomatic Recognition

Although the American view of Russia might have been expected to worsen as a result of Stalin's harsh new policies, this tendency was more than offset by the onset of the great world depression of the 1930s. At the very moment when declining sales elsewhere made the Russian market more important to United States exporters, American sales to the Soviet Union sharply declined. In desperation, American business figures, many of whom had deplored the political coloration of the Soviet Union, called for Moscow's recognition in the hope of expanding trade.

Businessmen were not the only group in the United States who began to look more favorably upon the Soviet Union. Many liberals and leftists sincerely believed that the world depression had revealed the ineffectiveness of capitalism and the basic superiority of communism. In 1938, when Earl Browder, Secretary of the American Communist Party, boasted that the rate of growth of the Soviet economy was five or six times that of the United States in its period of most rapid expansion, numerous non-communists were disposed to agree that Russia might have something to offer. This sentiment was particularly strong in American literary circles. The novelist and journalist Ben Hecht commented: "In the twenties and thirties most of the New Yorkers I met were full of purrs for the new Russia of Lenin and Stalin."

Finally, even those Americans most opposed to the Soviet system had to admit that the international balance of power resulting from the World War I peace settlements had begun to topple, eroding the underpinning of the United States policy of nonrecognition of the Soviet Union. In September 1931 Japan revealed its aggressive side when its troops attacked the city of Mukden and then overran Manchuria. An even more important threat to world peace occurred in January 1933, when Adolf Hitler was appointed Chancellor of Germany and began his efforts to restore German power.

When the new Democratic administration of President Franklin Roosevelt took office in March 1933, there was widespread belief that its first policy initiatives would include, among others, recognition of the Soviet Union. Secretary of State Cordell Hull favored it as he believed Russia would cooperate with the United States in resisting possible Japanese or German aggression. Hull was encouraged in this view by William C. Bullitt, a close friend of the president who served as the secretary's special assistant. After hard bargaining in Washington with Soviet Foreign Minister Maxim Litvinov, the United States agreed to restore diplomatic relations with Russia in November 1933.

The Soviet Purges

The hopes and illusions that accompanied the United States' recognition were short-lived, and the American image of Russia deteriorated rather than improved after 1933. The proximate cause was Moscow's failure to honor the commitments given by Litvinov that the Soviet Union would cease propaganda efforts in the United States and would permit a measure of religious toleration in Russia. Similarly, the understanding that Moscow

A 1933 cartoon, reflecting the deep suspicions that accompanied proposals then current for diplomatic recognition of the Soviet Union. (Courtesy the Chicago *Tribune*)

would make satisfactory repayment of the Russian debts and in return receive favorable terms for American financial credits degenerated into a festering disagreement. Bullitt, who accepted an appointment as first American Ambassador to the Soviet Union and went off to his post in 1933 full of optimism, resigned in 1936 disillusioned and doubtful of any basic meeting of the minds between the United States and Russia.

Even more important in the failure to establish better relations between the two countries were the internal developments that were then taking place in the Soviet Union. By 1934 Stalin had consolidated his power and had become not only dictator over the country but also over the Communist Party. His former rivals who included Trotsky, Zinoviev, and Kamenev had been either silenced or exiled. Millions of Russian peasants had died during the 1929–1930 campaign to collectivize agriculture, but the entire story of these developments was not widely known both abroad and to most foreigners in Russia. In 1934, however, Stalin instituted a series of great purges in Russia; they were widely publicized abroad and caused many former sympathizers to view the regime with horror.

The incident which sparked the beginning of the purges was the assassination in December 1934 of Sergei Kirov, a close supporter of Stalin and head of the Leningrad Party organization. The definitive reason for the assassination was never established, nor could it ever be proven that Stalin, himself, was responsible for it. Whatever the cause, it was followed by the arrest of a large and growing number of former tsarist supporters, oppositionists, peasants, workers and many Soviet Party members and government officials. Most if not all were completely innocent, but they were accused of treason and executed or sent off to serve in forced labor camps. In August 1936 Zinoviev, Kamenev and fourteen others were found guilty of not only conspiring with Trotsky to assassinate Kirov, but of plotting the death of Stalin as well. They were promptly executed. In the following year Stalin turned his wrath against the Red Army, executing its commander-in-chief and purging approximately half of all army officers.

The reality of the purges could not be ignored because of their enormity and the fact that they were featured in Soviet propaganda as revealing the treasonous cooperation of the exiled Trotsky with Hitler and the West. Russian sympathizers could only assert that the defendants were guilty as charged, a position made easier by the fact that most admitted their guilt in open court. The reason for the confessions is not known, but they probably were prompted by the defendants' desire to protect their families and by a belief, described in *Darkness At Noon*, the fictionalized account by former communist Arthur Koestler, that such gestures would serve the cause of a revolution to which they had dedicated their lives.

The purges of the thirties caused many Americans to condemn, or at least to look with concern at the Soviet Union. John Dewey, the widely respected American educator and philosopher, headed a committee to investigate Soviet charges against Trotsky and found them to be spurious. Max Eastman, author and former admirer of the regime, concluded: "Aside from the punitive expeditions against peasants, the campaigns of state-planned starvation, the war of extermination against thinking people generally, he [Stalin] has put to death more sincere and loyal party-militants than ever died before with the death of a revolution. Even Joseph E. Davies, American Ambassador to Russia following Bullitt's departure and a partisan of the Soviet Union, was distressed by the purges although he believed most of the defendants to be guilty.

At the same time as the purges shook the fabric of Soviet society and impeded any improvement in Russian relations with the West, the international scene was becoming more tense. In 1935 Hitler renounced the Versailles settlement; the following year Germany signed the anti-Comintern pact with Japan, thereby directing its attack against the Soviet Union. In the Far East, Japanese troops moved to occupy China, seizing Peking in August 1937 and forcing the Chinese Nationalist government to retreat into the interior of the country. The third member of the new grouping of "revisionist" powers seeking to overturn the Versailles settlement, Italy, invaded Ethiopia in October 1935, joined with Germany to conclude the Berlin-Rome Axis in October 1936, and adhered to the anti-Comintern pact in November 1937.

In response to the formation of a German-Japanese-Italian coalition directed against it, the Soviet Union attempted to move closer to the West. Russia joined the League of Nations in September 1934, ending its isolation from the international community of nations. Soviet Foreign Minister Litvinov, who was Jewish and a firm opponent of Hitler, proclaimed Moscow's role as the leading foe of fascism. To reassure those suspicious of Soviet intent, Stalin went so far as to tell an American journalist in an interview printed in the *Pravda* of March 1936 that Russia had never harbored any plans to bring about a world revolution.

These Soviet efforts to build a better image in the West were largely unsuccessful, particularly in the United States. They could not overcome the feeling in America that Moscow had failed to live up to its prior commitments to cease support of communist groups abroad and to repay tsarist debts. Moreover, no Soviet posture of moderation could mitigate the many reports concerning the horrors of the purges and the police-type state that was prevalent there.

It is possible that, given more time, Moscow might have been able to convince the West that there had been a basic reorientation in Soviet policy. However, time ran out in September 1938, when Hitler threatened war unless Czechoslovakia yielded the Sudetenland to Germany. Although Moscow offered to join with Great Britain and France in resisting Hitler's demands upon Czechoslovakia, London and Paris capitulated. In the Munich agreement of September 30, 1938, Czechoslovakia was forced to relinquish the Sudeten borderlands and British Prime Minister Neville Chamberlain returned home with assurances of "peace in our time."

The refusal of Great Britain and France to accept Russia's proposals for a joint front at Munich, or even to invite Moscow to the conference, signaled a failure on Moscow's part in its attempts to build ties with the West. On May 3, 1939, Foreign Minister Litvinov, the spokesman for the policy of collective security, was dismissed. Three months later, Germany and Russia totally rearranged the diplomatic map of Europe by signing a nonaggression pact on August 23, 1939, thereby freeing Hitler's hands for an attack on Poland. The German invasion of Poland on September 1, 1939, was followed two days later by an Anglo-French declaration of war against Germany. World War II had begun.

Effect of the Nazi-Soviet Pact

Stalin's agreement to the nonaggression pact with Hitler had a disasterous impact upon the American image of Russia. The resulting wave of resentment against the Soviets equaled, if not exceeded, that which had followed the Bolshevik overthrow of the Provisional Government, and created an intense distrust of Russian intentions which has never ceased to exist. The effect was particularly strong among liberals and leftists, who had looked on Moscow as the arch-enemy of fascism. When conclusion of the agreement was announced, there was a moment of silence and disbelief. Although the American Communist Party recovered and attempted to defend the move as being forced upon Russia by the behavior of Britain and France, few except the hard core of the party believed them. Many party members, such as the noted scholar and author Granville Hicks, resigned, believing that there was no essential difference between fascist and communist dictatorships. Other Americans, who had never relinquished their suspicion of the Soviet Union, felt that the pact had revealed Moscow's true colors.

The number of Americans sympathetic to the Soviet Union was reduced still further on September 17, 1939, when the Red Army attacked Poland from the rear, occupying the eastern third of the country. Then on November 30, 1939, Russia invaded Finland, bringing Soviet-American relations to as low a level as prevailed in the inter-war period. Finland occupied a particularly warm spot in American sympathies, not only as a democracy but more importantly as the only nation during the depression to continue payments on debts owed the United States. President Roosevelt called for a moral embargo on the sale of airplanes or munitions to Russia which could be used in air attacks on Finnish cities; former President Hoover urged that the United States withdraw its ambassador from Moscow in protest over the Russian invasion; and the *New York Times*, in denouncing the attack, declared that "in the smoking ruins of the damage wrought in Finland lies what remained of the world's respect for the Government of Russia."

Throughout the duration of the war, and up until the Finns were forced to surrender to superior Soviet forces in March 1940, Americans hailed the initial Finnish victories and contributed generously to relief supplies for Finland. The strong anti-Soviet resentment provoked by the war in the United States also sparked a latent American suspicion that communist party members and sympathizers represented a threat to this nation's internal security. Although the House of Representatives Special Committee to Investigate Un-American Activities, under Chairman Martin Dies, was created primarily to investigate the subversive threat from American Nazis and fascists, it engendered considerable controversy in the press with its charges that the communists owed their first loyalty to Moscow and constituted a dangerous fifth column which was working to impose a Soviet-type dictatorship in the United States.

The defeat of France, and Germany's continued success in the war, was cause for a slight improvement in the American image of Russia, since Hitler came to be regarded as the immediate threat and the Soviet Union as a possible ally. After word reached Washington that Germany was planning to attack Russia, the United States in March 1941 passed on news of the impending threat to the Soviet ambassador in Washington. Stalin, suspicious of a Western trick, ignored both this and other warnings, with the result that the Red Army suffered great losses when Germany invaded Russia on June 22, 1941.

The Wartime Partnership

American perceptions of the Soviet Union changed quickly after the German attack, as Russia was now regarded as an ally in the struggle against Hitler. The first to react were the communists and their sympathizers. Having previously called for American neutrality in the war, they now shifted gears and stridently demanded Washington's participation in aiding Moscow. On pragmatic grounds many other Americans favored assistance for the Soviet Union to help defeat Germany, and in a significant decision on November 7, 1941, President Roosevelt authorized provision of one billion dollars in lend lease aid to Russia. His act was based on the determination that defense of the Soviet Union was vital to the defense of the United States.

American entry into the war against Germany following Pearl Harbor caused a great outpouring of expressions of friendship for Russia. Movies, newspapers and books praised the patriotism of the Russian people, their fierce struggle against Hitler, and the community of interest between the Soviet Union and the United States. In the full flush of this feeling, American media ignored or downplayed the many fundamental differences between the two nations and the totalitarian nature of the Soviet regime. Typical was the book *We're In This With Russia*, published by a journalist who briefly visited Russia after the German invasion. He concluded reassuringly that Moscow, "which originally believed that its interest lay in instability and revolution throughout the world, now knows it must join hands with the capitalist nations, great and small, to secure for itself that long period of peace which it cannot do without."

In support of the Russian war effort, the United States provided vast amounts of assistance, over nine and a half billion dollars worth by September 1945. Despite this aid, without which Moscow probably would have been unable to avoid defeat, the Soviet Union continued to display an attitude of suspicion and hostility toward Britain and America. The Anglo-American landings in North Africa in November 1942 were dismissed by Russia as minimally important in alleviating the German pressure, and Moscow charged that the opening of a second front in Europe was being delayed by the Allies in order to weaken the Soviet Union.

Western suspicion of Soviet intentions was, in turn, stimulated by the German announcement in April 1943 that the graves of

When Soviet-American friendship was at its height—the U.S. First Army meets Russian troops on a damaged bridge over the Elbe River in Germany.

several thousand Polish officers had been found at Katyn, near Smolensk. Moscow attempted to dismiss the story as mere Nazi propaganda, but it is now generally believed that the Russians deliberately executed thousands of Polish military personnel captured during the seizure of eastern Poland in September 1939 in an attempt to liquidate possible resistance to Soviet rule. In reaction to dissemination of these reports, the Soviet Union broke relations with the Polish government in exile in Britain, recognizing instead a puppet regime in Lublin.

Despite an attempt to more closely coordinate the war efforts of the United States, Great Britain and Russia through the meeting in Tehran in November 1943 of President Roosevelt, Prime Minister Churchill and Soviet leader Stalin, the frictions between the English-speaking democracies and Moscow could not be dissipated. Stalin continued to press urgently for the need of an Anglo-American landing in France and for even more military assistance to Russia, while at the same time adopting a harsh attitude toward the Polish government in London and toward the question of Poland's postwar frontiers. Although President Roosevelt continued his efforts to reassure Stalin that the United States and Britain sincerely desired friendly relations with Russia after the war and would accord Moscow an equal voice in the postwar settlement, an increasing number of American officials familiar with prewar Soviet policy began to warn that Russia might well seek to occupy the power vacuum which would result from Germany's defeat. Even the Allied landings in Normandy in June 1944, which signaled the approaching end of Hitler, failed to significantly improve relations between Moscow and Washington.

In February 1945 Roosevelt, Churchill and Stalin met again, at Yalta, a Russian resort on the Black Sea. This was probably the last opportunity for the United States and Britain to establish the basis for postwar cooperation with the Soviet Union. Although it was by then apparent that Germany would soon be defeated, Moscow still needed American aid and, even more, assurances that Soviet reconstruction would be assisted after the war. Roosevelt, who was in poor health at Yalta and was to die only two months later, was more widely respected and trusted by the Russians than any other Western leader, and could conceivably have persuaded Moscow on the wisdom of a policy of friendship with the West. However, the United States did not realize how close Japan was to being forced to surrender, and Roosevelt therefore devoted his energy to obtaining Stalin's agreement to enter the war against Japan. In this effort the president was successful; agreement was also reached at the conference that after its unconditional surrender Germany would be divided into zones under the control of the Allies, and that an international gathering would be held in San Francisco in April 1945 to create a new world organization—the United Nations.

When the Yalta conference broke up, it was clear to most of those who participated that relations between America and Russia were in for a stormy period. Stalin had agreed to participate in the war in the Far East, but his uncompromising stand concerning Poland raised fears that the Soviets intended to assume a position of dominance in Eastern Europe. Possibly even more important, Roosevelt's agreement to give Moscow three votes in the General Assembly of the United Nations, one each for the Soviet Union and the supposedly independent constituent republic of White Russia and the Ukraine, was bitterly attacked in the United States after the war as a "sell-out" to the Russians and as proof that appeasement of Stalin did not work.

The Cold War

American resentment over the attitudes adopted by the Soviet Union as the war came to a close caused a shift in the United States' image of Russia back to that which had existed prior to their wartime partnership. A tense and novel element was the growing fear that Moscow might unleash a surprise attack on America. As had been feared during the war, Moscow took advantage of the presence of the Red Army in Eastern Europe to establish regimes under Soviet control. Although initially they included some non-communist elements, this was a facade permitting the Russians and their local supporters to neutralize those individuals or institutions which could effectively oppose the ultimate communist takeover. The problem was addressed at the "Big Three" Summit Conference at Potsdam, Germany, in July 1945, the first such gathering attended by President Truman, and at a subsequent meeting of foreign ministers in London in September. To all Western requests that the Soviet Union agree to free elections in Eastern Europe, as had been promised at Yalta, Moscow turned a deaf ear. In response, the United States and Britain became less disposed than before to accommodate Russian wishes in areas of the world not under the control of the Red Army, such as Japan, Italy, and Greece.

Compounding the growing controversy between East and West was America's development and use of the atomic bomb. Although during the Potsdam meeting President Truman had informed Stalin of its existence in a manner deliberately intended to minimize appreciation of its importance, Moscow was quick to realize that it represented a drastic change in the relative military power of the Soviet Union and the United States. Quickly following the dropping of the first atomic bomb on Hiroshima, Japan on August 6, 1945, which overshadowed the Soviet declaration of war against Japan two days later, Stalin ordered all possible efforts to obtain the weapon.

As it became increasingly obvious in late 1945 and 1946 that the wartime partnership between the United States and the Soviet Union had given way to growing antagonism, America's monopoly over the atomic bomb gave little satisfaction. The rapid demobilization of the United States armed forces after 1945 in response to domestic political sentiment left many Americans feeling threatened by the vast Soviet conventional forces which had occupied Eastern and Central Europe and now showed no intention of withdrawing. The awesome nature of the atomic bomb, upon which American defense was forced to rely in the absence of sufficient conventional forces, was clearly recognized in the United States and efforts were being made to find some alternative solution.

Some Americans, such as the noted physicist Albert Einstein and Secretary of Commerce and former Vice President Henry Wallace, felt that Washington was at least partially responsible for the split by refusing to make sufficient allowance for Russia's great losses during the war or for its continuing and understandable suspicions of the West stemming from the cold shoulder accorded Moscow during the interwar period. The other point of view, which formed the basis for official United States policy and which most of the American people shared, was that Russia sought to establish by force communist regimes throughout the world and would attempt to do so unless prevented by the clear threat of superior military force. In the postwar world, with Germany and Japan defeated and occupied and Britain and France gravely weakened, only the United States had the strength to deter Soviet aggression.

The most forthright exposition of this position was made in a speech at Fulton, Missouri on March 5, 1946 by Winston Churchill, Britain's great wartime leader, who had been turned out of office in an election held during the Potsdam conference. His words on that occasion, delivered in the presence of President Truman and probably with his prior knowledge and approval, signaled the West's recognition of the existence of a "cold war" between the United States and Russia. In language reminiscent of that with which he unsuccessfully warned his nation of the rise of Hitler, Churchill declared: "From Stettin in the Baltic to Trieste in the Adriatic an iron curtain has descended across the Continent." He called for an Anglo-American alliance to bar the way to further Soviet expansion.

The hopes for close cooperation with Russia generated during the wartime partnership did not die quickly, however, and Churchill's comments produced considerable critical reaction in the United States. The speech was attacked by such persons as former Secretary of the Interior Harold Ickes, who called for President Truman to return to the late President Roosevelt's policies which included cooperation with Russia, and by Roosevelt's son James, who suggested that the Truman administration was not attempting to properly inform the American public of the true attitudes of the Soviet Union. President Truman's general agreement with the views expressed by Churchill accounted for the departure from the Cabinet of Secretary of Commerce Henry Wallace, who in a speech in New York on September 12, 1946 warned against adopting a "Get tough with Russia" policy on the grounds that "the tougher we get, the tougher the Russians will get." Eight days later, reacting to the speech and after consultation with Secretary of State James Byrnes, the President asked for and received Wallace's resignation.

In the months that followed, Russian-American relations became ever more tense. Moscow adamantly refused to permit free elections in the East European countries occupied by the Red Army and Washington became convinced that the Soviets were supporting communist subversion throughout the world. The formal announcement that the United States was in fact adopting the policy urged by Churchill came on March 12, 1947, when President Truman addressed a joint session of Congress. Although he did not mention the Soviet Union by name, his meaning was clear as he described Poland, Romania, and Bulgaria as countries in which totalitarian regimes had been imposed in violation of the Yalta agreements. The president called upon Congress to provide some four million dollars in aid to assist Greece and Turkey in resisting communist pressure, establishing the principle that the United States would seek to support nations resisting Soviet expansion or communist subversion. As a statement of American policy, the speech ranked in importance with the Monroe Doctrine or President Wilson's proposal for a League of Nations, and the position stated by the president has become known as the Truman Doctrine.

Most Americans approved of the president's speech and agreed with his estimate of the threat to this country from the Soviet Union. The influential *New York Times* reflected the views of most observers when it commented that the American people stood behind Truman's warning to Russia. The bill providing loans to Greece and Turkey, proposed by the president, was passed by over two-thirds majority in both the House and Senate. Although Wallace and a small minority continued to urge the need for conciliating Moscow, this position garnered little support; in the November 1948 elections, in which he ran as the presidential candidate of the Progressive Party, Wallace received scarcely more than a million votes, far behind Truman's twenty-four million and Dewey's almost twenty-two million and trailing even the States Rights candidate, Senator J. Strom Thurmond.

The theoretical basis for the Truman Doctrine was enunciated and explained in an important article entitled "The Sources of Soviet Conduct" in the July 1947 issue of the prestigious journal *Foreign Affairs*. Published anonymously, the article was eventually identified as the work of one of America's most brilliant Russian experts, George Kennan, then a senior official in the State Department. In the piece Kennan described the ideological and historical reasons for the basic incompatibility between the American and Soviet systems; stressed that in response to conciliation Moscow would only expand its demands; and recommended that the United States calmly and firmly bar any further Russian expansion in the hope that over the course of time the Soviet Union would evolve into a more democratic and less threatening regime. This policy, labeled "containment," has, in effect, been the one pursued by Washington toward Russia ever since.

Debate within the United States

While most Americans shared the image of Russia as a clearcut military and political threat to this country and supported the policy of containment, the issue became the subject of bitter attack from those individuals and groups who felt it did not go far enough. The communist takeover of Czechoslovakia through the threat of Soviet force in February 1948 convinced many Americans that no compromise with the Soviet Union was possible. It was followed on April 1, 1948, by the Russian imposition of a blockade on the Western-controlled sectors of Berlin, forcing the United States, Britain and France to transport essential supplies into that city by plane in the "Berlin airlift." Finally, throughout 1948 and most of the following year, the American-supported Nationalist Government of China was compelled by the Chinese communists to yield more and more territory and eventually to relinquish the mainland and seek refuge in Taiwan.

The vast communist territorial gains and the unmistakable realization that Soviet military might now constitute a threat to the survival of the United States were profoundly unsettling to many Americans. A strong feeling developed that this nation could not have so rapidly found itself in such peril without incredible stupidity or treason on the part of key government officials especially after the great victory in World War II. Concern over possible Soviet-controlled subversion by communists had existed in the United States almost from the time of the Bolshevik revolution in Russia, and it had been pointed to as an element of risk by the Dies Committee in the late 1930s. This sentiment was greatly strengthened in August 1948 when Whittaker Chambers, a former communist and a senior editor of *Time Magazine*, testified before the House Un-American Activities Committee that certain government officials had belonged to a secret group of communists prior to World War II. Prominent among them was Alger Hiss, then President of the Carnegie Endowment for International Peace in New York. He had previously served in the State Department as Director of Special Political Affairs, had accompanied President Roosevelt to the Yalta Conference and played an important role in the San Francisco Conference which established the United Nations.

After a hung jury in his first trial, Hiss was found guilty in January 21, 1950, of perjury for denying to the House Committee that he had ever passed secret documents to Chambers for transmittal to the Soviets. The humane but injudicious words of Secretary of State Dean Acheson following the conviction that he "would not turn his back" on Alger Hiss led to accusations that the Truman administration was infiltrated by communists and their supporters. This view was typified by the comments of Senator Styles Bridges, Republican from New Hampshire, who suggested the need for further investigations to determine if the "communist conspiracy" headed in the Kremlin still had agents working in the State Department. The charge that the American government was penetrated by Soviet agents was repeated in other quarters. Most prominent was the voice of Joseph R. McCarthy of Wisconsin, until that time a little-known member of the Senate, who went so far as to accuse Secretary of State Acheson and Secretary of Defense General George C. Marshall of facilitating Soviet efforts at expansion and subversion.

Although Senator McCarthy's charges were regarded as exaggerated, if not completely false, by many people, they none-theless created in the public an exaggerated sense of peril and fear that Moscow was on the brink of launching an attack against the United States. This fear was compounded by the Soviet nuclear explosion in September 1949, which revealed that America had lost its monopoly over nuclear weapons, and by the communist takeover in China in October 1949, which brought the most populous nation in the world under communist control. Indicative of this dislike and distrust of Russia was the widespread public support in the United States for the creation of the North Atlantic Treaty Organization in March 1949. It was designed to assure the protection of Western Europe from Soviet attack, and utilized for the conviction after a nine-month trial in New York in October 1949 of eleven leaders of the American Communist Party on grounds of advocating the violent overthrow of the American government.

The Korean War

The North Korean attack on South Korea in June 1950 and the resulting American involvement in the war strengthened the view in the United States that Russia was preparing to attack this country. It was generally assumed that the North Koreans, and subsequently the Chinese when they entered the war in November 1950, were acting as agents of Moscow, and Secretary of State Acheson publicly denounced Russia for its aggression. Symptomatic of the state of concern in the United States over the Russian threat was a series of accounts, both fictional and non-fictional, dealing with the theme of a future Soviet-American conflict. Representative of the type was a special edition of the popular magazine *Colliers* in October 1951 entitled "Russia's Defeat and Occupation 1952–1960, Preview of the War We Do Not Want," which postulated a Soviet invasion of Yugoslavia in May 1952 unleashing a third World War.

The widespread fear over a possible Russian attack—linked in the public's mind with resentment that the United States had failed to obtain a decisive victory in the Korean War and that the Truman administration had mishandled communist expansion in the Far East—all contributed to the victory in the November 1952 elections of the Republican presidential candidate, General Dwight D. Eisenhower. The victorious candidate not only promised to end the conflict in Korea satisfactorily, but his campaign stressed that the passive United States policy of containment toward Russia would be replaced by an active one aimed to achieve the "liberation" of the people in the Soviet-dominated countries of Eastern Europe. Officially, however, the new administration largely followed the policy set forth in the Truman Doctrine and in George F. Kennan's containment article in *Foreign Affairs,* and no American assistance was given the workers of East Berlin in June 1953, when their anticommunist demonstrations were halted by Soviet troops. Even Secretary of State John Foster Dulles, who came to be regarded as the arch-prototype of an American "cold warrior," did nothing more than repeat the pattern established by the North Atlantic Treaty Organization when setting up corresponding international security arrangements in the Middle East (Bagdad Pact) and Far East (Southeast Asian Treaty Organization).*

The death of the Soviet leader Josef Stalin, in March 1953, initially did not change the American image of Russia as a serious threat. Stalin had been the absolute ruler of the Soviet Union for over twenty-five years, and although he was widely disliked and distrusted in this country he was also a familiar figure. Many people feared that his death might result in Russia coming under the control of an individual or group more inclined to risk the chance of war with the United States. Reacting to the event, the "official condolences" transmitted by the State Department to Moscow were the minimum that diplomatic protocol permitted. Secretary Dulles told a press conference that the world was now freed from being dominated by the "malignant power of Stalin," and the *St. Louis Post Dispatch* warned that the "little-known

* The Bagdad Pact, concluded in April 1955, linked Turkey, Iran, Iraq, Britain, and Pakistan; the Southeast Asian Treaty Organization, formed in September 1954, included the U.S., Britain, France, Thailand, Pakistan, the Philippines, Australia, and New Zealand.

men" who assumed the vast authority that had been the Russian dictator's might be "more willing than he was to risk setting off World War II."

Khrushchev and "Peaceful Coexistence"

American fears over the imminence of a Soviet attack eased after the conclusion of a ceasefire in Korea and particularly as the post-Stalin leadership in Moscow did not appear any more anxious than Stalin to risk a hot war with the United States. In July 1955 the heads of the United States and the Soviet Union met face to face for the first time since the Potsdam Conference ten years earlier. President Eisenhower and Russian Premier Nikolai Bulganin met with British Prime Minister Anthony Eden and French Premier Edgar Faure at a summit conference in Geneva, Switzerland. The conference, which had been called in an effort to solve the long-standing problems of German reunification and disarmament in Europe, failed to reach agreement; nonetheless, the mere fact that East and West had thought it useful to get together for discussion caused a shift for the better in Russian-American relations.

This overall easing of tensions survived two interruptions in 1956 caused by a Soviet confession of Stalin's "crimes" and by the brutal Russian behavior in Hungary. In February Soviet Communist Party Secretary Nikita Khrushchev addressed the Twentieth Party Congress of the Soviet Party, the first since Stalin's death. Khrushchev, who had begun to overshadow other members of the collective Soviet leadership, emerged as Stalin's successor and the dominant figure in Russia. Carried away by his emotions during a speech describing the flaws and failures of the Stalinist years, he described in graphic language the tortures and executions the late dictator had conducted against the loyal members of the Party, and referred to Stalin's cowardice during the war. The period of "de-Stalinization" in Russia initiated by the speech had its counterpart in America, where many people, particularly those who had been sympathetic to Moscow, realized for the first time the enormity of Stalin's crimes. Reinhold

Niebuhr, the noted American theologian, voiced the public's reaction when he observed that "never have the evils of tyranny been so completely revealed from inside the realm of tyranny as at the 20th Congress."* More traumatic in nature was the response of disillusioned party members and supporters such as John Gates, Editor-in-Chief of the party newspaper *The Daily Worker.* Shocked by the revelations, he published the full text of the speech, and subsequently resigned from the party on the grounds that the Soviet Party and system could not be disassociated from Stalin's crimes.

Equally detrimental to the image of Russia in the United States was a second significant event which occurred in 1956—the suppression by Soviet troops of the independent communist government which came to power in Hungary in the fall of that year. Arrests resulting in the execution of the leaders of the ill-fated Hungarian uprising produced violent anti-Soviet demonstrations in the United States and elsewhere. American revulsion over the incident was reflected by William Henry Chamberlain's article in *The New Leader,* where he wrote: "The mask of the reformed, pacific Soviet Government, desiring peace with the West, has been ripped off. . . . There should be an end to all negotiations for agreements which would assume non-existent Soviet good faith."**

Although the resentment in America over events in Hungary was widespread, it did not prevent a resumption of the trend toward improved relations. Part of the reason was the stunning Soviet scientific success in October 1957, when Moscow announced that it had launched the first artificial earth satellite, the "sputnik." The fact that Russia had been able to outdistance the United States in space, if only temporarily, convinced many Americans that the Soviet Union had progressed technologically to the point where perhaps a *modus vivendi* in political issues was possible.

More important to the betterment of the American image of

* "The Tyrant as Symbol of Community," by Reinhold Niebuhr, in *The New Leader,* May 21, 1956.

**"The Murder of a People," by William Henry Chamberlain, in *The New Leader,* November 19, 1956.

Russia, however, was the personality of the Soviet leader, Nikita Khrushchev. While he was capable of flamboyant gestures and threatening speech directed against the United States, Khrushchev, unlike the remote and ominous Stalin, was generally liked in America for his openness and sense of humor, even by people who strongly opposed the Soviet regime. His emphasis on improving the living standards of the Russian people and his call for a policy of "peaceful coexistence" with the United States made him come across as someone with whom it was possible to reach a mutually beneficial understanding.

The high point in postwar Russian-American relations occurred in September 1959, when Khrushchev visited the United States at the invitation of President Eisenhower. The first Soviet head of government ever to visit this country (he had replaced Bulganin as Premier in March 1958), Khrushchev held discussions with President Eisenhower at Camp David and then traveled across the United States. His toast at a White House dinner mentioned the fact that the United States and the Soviet Union were "too strong to quarrel." The phrase was widely quoted in the press and stirred up favorable comment. When Khrushchev completed his visit and departed for Russia he left behind him in the United States a large measure of good will. *Time* magazine, after describing how Khrushchev had eaten and enjoyed his first hot dog in Des Moines, Iowa, noted that "each party was standing firmly on his own two feet, and not likely to be easily shaken in basic underpinnings."*

The U-2 Incident and the Cuban Missile Crisis

The warm feelings toward Russia engendered by the Khrushchev visit lasted less than a year, as American-Soviet relations entered a period of strain in the spring of 1960. On May 1, 1960, on the eve of the Big-Four Summit meeting in Paris, a U.S. high-altitude U-2 aircraft piloted by Francis Gary Powers was shot down over Russia while on a reconnaissance mission. President

* *Time*, October 5, 1959.

Eisenhower personally took responsibility for the flight, and his refusal to make what the Soviets regarded as sufficient apology led Khrushchev to bitterly denounce him. It also occasioned Khrushchev's walking out on the Paris conference. Many Americans believed the Eisenhower administration had blundered in continuing the flights on the eve of the summit and in publicly admitting to them, but the overwhelming majority in the country concluded that the Soviets had over-reacted to the event and were recklessly jeopardizing world peace when they aborted the Paris meeting.

Despite the increased tension following the U-2 incident, for which Moscow had held President Eisenhower responsible, no improvement in ties took place when President Kennedy's Democratic administration took office in March 1961. During the campaign of 1960, Khrushchev had indicated his low opinion of both Kennedy and the Republican candidate, Richard Nixon. Moreover, Kennedy's charges during a televised debate between the candidates on October 21, 1960, that the Eisenhower administration had let the Soviet Union achieve superiority in missiles over the United States and that Eastern Europe was Russia's most vulnerable area and one in which America should take the lead in challenging communism, undoubtedly raised fears in Moscow that Kennedy was as much of a "cold warrior" as John Foster Dulles had been.

Relations worsened further in April 1961, with the defeat in the "Bay of Pigs" of the American-supported landing of Cuban exiles seeking to overthrow the communist regime of Cuban Premier Fidel Castro. On the day after the abortive attempt, Soviet Premier Khrushchev warned that Moscow would give all necessary assistance to Cuba to repel an armed attack. Moreover, the first face-to-face meeting between Kennedy and Khrushchev, which took place in Vienna in June 1961, culminated in a disaster. The Soviet leader attempted to intimidate the youthful American President by threats to the very existence of West Berlin. On July 8, 1961, in support of public demands for a German peace treaty along the lines desired by Moscow, Khrushchev announced an increase in Russian military expenditures and withdrew plans to reduce the size of the Soviet Armed Forces.

Concern in the United States over a possible Soviet-American war, which had diminished since the dark days of the "cold war" in the early fifties, mounted, as the United States indicated it would not retreat in the face of Soviet pressure. On July 25, 1961, President Kennedy told the American people in a nationally televised address that "We cannot and will not permit the communists to drive us out of Berlin, either gradually or by force." As a token of America's resolve, the President called for a sharp increase in the defense effort and requested authority from Congress to call to active duty 250,000 members of the Army Reserve and units of the Air National Guard. The Soviet reaction on August 13, 1961, to prevent the continued flight of refugees from East to West Berlin by putting up the "Berlin Wall," added to the state of tension.

The low point in Russian-American relations in the postwar period came the following year, once again in a dispute over Cuba. In September 1962, after reports had reached Washington that the Soviets were establishing military bases on Cuba, Khrushchev warned publicly that any American attack on the island would mean war. President Kennedy was not intimidated, and, in what many people came to regard as his finest hour, he warned the nation on a nationally televised address on October 22, 1962, that Moscow had sought to upset the status quo by secretly sending strategic offensive missiles to Cuba. In ordering an embargo on the movement of offensive weapons to the island aboard Russian ships, the President accepted the risk of nuclear war with the Soviet Union. Fortunately for the preservation of world peace Khrushchev retreated, and on October 28, 1962, agreed to dismantle and remove Soviet offensive weapons from Cuba.

In the wake of the Cuban "missile crisis" there was a slight relaxation in tension between the United States and Russia, as both nations appeared shaken by the realization of how close they had come to war. In June 1963 Moscow and Washington agreed to establish a "hot line" linking the two capitals; its purpose was to insure instant communications in the event of any future crisis. However, no substantial improvement in relations took place until after the assassination of President Kennedy on November 22, 1963, and the entry into the White House of Lyndon Johnson.

Improved Relations and the Nuclear Non-Proliferation Treaty

The American image of Russia improved during the years of the Johnson administration. Despite frictions created by the Vietnam War, tensions between Washington and Moscow eased. Both nations were eager for a betterment in relations. The Russians, fearing that the United States might suspect them of involvement in the Kennedy assassination because of Lee Harvey Oswald's stay in the Soviet Union, sought to establish their innocence by turning over to America their files on the alleged assassin. Moscow also adopted a far less vituperative tone in its propaganda treatment of the United States following the assassination, probably reflecting Khrushchev's realization of how close the two nations had come to war during the missile crisis and the hope that he could establish a better relationship with Johnson than with Kennedy, for whom he had apparently harbored a personal resentment.

President Johnson similarly was anxious to reduce tensions with the Soviet Union and to reach agreement on mutual cooperation to reduce the threat of nuclear war. He took advantage of Soviet Deputy Premier Anastas Mikoyan's presence in Washington during the Kennedy funeral to inform Mikoyan of the administration's great interest in better relations with Russia. The improvement in ties between the nations which followed was not interrupted by Khrushchev's surprise ouster as Party First Secretary and Premier in October 1964, although the initial reaction of shock and concern in America was reminiscent to that which had followed Stalin's death.

Apprehension in the United States eased as it became clear that the new Soviet leaders, Party Secretary Leonid Brezhnev and Premier Aleksei Kosygin, intended no significant departures from the policies pursued by Khrushchev. Thus the American image of Russia continued its gradual improvement, facilitated by such agreements as the treaty signed in December 1966 to ban nuclear weapons (and arms of mass destruction from space.) In July 1968 relations between the Soviet Union and the United States took a giant step forward, as representatives of the two nations signed the Nuclear Non-Proliferation Treaty in the White House. The event marked the return of bilateral ties to the more cordial level which had existed prior to the collapse of the Paris Summit Conference in May 1960, and in the words of President Johnson represented "the most significant step we had taken yet to reduce the possibility of nuclear war."

Unfortunately, as so often had happened in the postwar history of relations between the two countries, Americans expecting a further moderation in Soviet behavior were disillusioned by Moscow. On the night of August 20, 1968, Soviet forces aided by their East European Allies invaded Czechoslovakia and crushed the liberal Czech communist regime of Alexander Dubcek. Reaction in the United States predictably paralleled the dismay and anger caused by the Soviet intervention in Hungary in 1956. The Senate refused to ratify the Nuclear Non-Proliferation Treaty until March 1969, and the momentum for a summit meeting with the Russian leaders and for further disarmament negotiations quickly receded.

Détente

Richard Nixon's victory in the 1968 presidential election might logically have been expected to produce a widening gulf with Moscow and a deterioration of the American image of Russia. He had been sharply criticized by the Soviets while Vice President under Eisenhower and when running as the Republican presidential candidate in 1960. Nixon's interest in revitalizing American foreign policy by building new bridges to Russia, however, coincided with Moscow's desire to pursue a policy of "détente" with the United States. Accordingly, relations between the two nations again improved, and negotiations for strategic arms limitations (SALT) opened in Helsinki, Finland in November 1969. The climax to this bilateral effort to achieve closer cooperation came in May 1972, when President Nixon visited Moscow and signed agreements with the Soviet Union to limit missile capabilities.

Although this development was generally welcomed in the United States as reducing the risk of nuclear war, ironically the image of Russia declined during the Nixon administration. The greatest area of concern was the Soviet's treatment of its political dissidents, including members of the Jewish minority who wished to emigrate. The issue came to the fore in January 1970, when American Jewish militants interrupted performances in the United States of Russian musicians and dancers to protest the treatment accorded Jews in the Soviet Union. Despite Moscow's efforts to dismiss or disprove the allegations, the Jewish question continued to impede any substantial improvement in relations. In December 1974, Congress overwhelmingly voted to make the extension of the most-favored nation status to Soviet imports contingent on Moscow's easing restrictions on the emigration of Jews and other dissidents from Russia. Predictably, the Soviet Union angrily responded by refusing to ratify the bilateral trade agreement between the two nations.

The Soviet Union's harsh treatment of non-Jewish dissidents aroused equal resentment in the United States. Virtually every segment of American society was appalled at the abuse heaped upon the famed Russian writer Aleksandr Solzhenitsyn (recipient of the Nobel Prize for Literature in 1970), who was subsequently deported and deprived of his Soviet citizenship in February 1974.

President Nixon's policy of détente with the Soviet Union came under attack from people such as Henry Jackson, the Democratic Senator from the state of Washington, and Ronald Reagan, the unsuccessful challenger for the Republican presidential nomination in 1976. They claimed that détente was being interpreted by the administration as giving substantial advantages to the Soviet Union vis-a-vis the United States. Not only were the arms limitation agreements criticized for giving Russia a military advantage, but the agreements entered into by the Nixon administration for the sale of one billion dollars' worth of grain to Moscow over a three-year period were denounced as contributing to greatly increased food costs in this country.

The joint Soviet-American communiqué is signed in Vladivostok on November 24, 1974 by President Gerald R. Ford and Soviet leader Leonid Brezhnev. In the background, center, Secretary of State Henry Kissinger and Soviet Foreign Minister Andrei Gromyko.

In the last years of the Nixon administration less attention in the United States was focused on Russia. Public gaze was drawn primarily to internal developments such as the economic slump and Watergate. Soviet Party Secretary Brezhnev's visit to America in June 1973 and Nixon's summit meeting with him in Moscow in late June and early July of the following year (during which additional arms limitation agreements were signed), were regarded as routine developments, or even as meaningless diplomatic meetings concocted by the President to ward off calls for his impeachment.

During the long Watergate crisis, Moscow seemed concerned that the political controversy raging within the United States would adversely affect progress made toward reaching détente. As a result, Moscow appeared eager to do whatever it could to keep Nixon in office. When Vice President Gerald Ford was elevated to the presidency in August 1974 as a result of the Nixon resignation, he took pains to assure Moscow that the policy of the United States toward Russia would remain unchanged. Ford's trip to the Soviet Union in November 1974 to meet with Brezhnev reassured Moscow that the new administration intended no break in the policy of détente. At the same time, there was no change in the American perception of Russia, with those critical of détente and of the Soviet treatment of dissidents continuing to harbor their suspicions of Moscow.

The Carter Administration and Human Rights

The victory of Jimmy Carter, the Democratic candidate in the November 1976 presidential election, had an almost immediate effect on the American image of Russia. The emphasis the new administration placed on human rights in the Soviet Union coincided with an apparent hardening in Moscow's policy toward its dissidents, leaving the United States more critical of Russia, and the Russians promising to rebuff any attempts at interference in its internal affairs.

In many respects the American view of Russia in 1977 was curiously similar to that which existed in 1917. Like President

Wilson, President Carter placed great stress on the need for the Soviet Government to enhance human rights. In the absence of any immediate threat to the United States, much of the American population seemed disposed to follow the president's lead. In the long run, however, the United States image of Russia will probably be determined primarily, as it has for the past sixty years, by the day-to-day and year-to-year actions of the Soviet Union and the responses of the United States Government.

1 THE PRESIDENT WELCOMES THE REVOLUTION

Woodrow Wilson (1856–1924)

Woodrow Wilson is widely acclaimed one of America's greatest presidents for his role in leading the country during the difficult years of World War I. Born in Staunton, Virginia, Wilson graduated from Princeton in 1879 and subsequently practiced law in Atlanta. After receiving his Ph.D. from Johns Hopkins in 1886, he taught at several universities prior to joining the faculty at Princeton, of which he became the president in 1902. Wilson was elected Governor of the State of New Jersey in 1911 and the following year was the successful Democratic candidate for the presidency.

An idealist who sought to make the world safe for democracy, Wilson hailed the overthrow of the Russian monarchy in 1917 and moved rapidly to provide American encouragement and support to the new Provisional Government. He attached such significance to the first Russian Revolution that he cited it in his speech to Congress on April 2, 1917, calling for a declaration of war against Germany; subsequently Wilson voiced his support for the Russian people, regretting that the United States could not do more to alleviate their suffering.

DOES NOT EVERY American feel that assurance has been added to our hope for the future peace of the world by the wonderful and heartening things that have been happening within the last few weeks in Russia? Russia was known by those who knew it best to have been always in fact democratic at heart, in all the vital habits of her thought, in all the intimate relationships of her people that spoke their natural instinct, their habitual attitude towards life. The autocracy that crowned the summit of her political structure, long as it had stood and terrible as was the reality of its power, was not in fact Russian in origin, character, or purpose; and now it has been shaken off and the great, generous Russian people have been added in all their naïve majesty and might to the forces that are fighting for freedom in the world, for justice, and for peace. Here is a fit partner for a league of honour.

(April 2, 1917, address to a Joint Session of Congress)

Although the Government of the United States is unhappily not now in a position to render the direct and effective aid it would wish to render, I beg to assure the people of Russia through the Congress that it will avail itself of every opportunity to secure for Russia once more complete sovereignty and independence in her own affairs and full restoration to her great role in the life of Europe and the modern world.

The whole heart of the people of the United States is with the people of Russia in the attempt to free themselves forever from autocratic government and become the masters of their own life.

(March 11, 1918, Message of Sympathy to the Russian People, from the "Official U.S. Bulletin, No. 255)

The other night in New York, at the opening of the campaign for funds for our Red Cross, I made an address. I had not intended to refer to Russia, but I was speaking without notes and in the course of what I said my thought was led to Russia, and I said that we meant to stand by Russia just as firmly as we would stand by France or England or any other of the Allies. The audience to which I was speaking was not an audience from which I would have expected an enthusiastic response to that. It was rather too well dressed. It was not an audience, in other words, made of the class of people whom you would suppose to have the most intimate feeling for the sufferings of the ordinary man in Russia, but that audience jumped into the aisles, the whole audience rose to its feet, and nothing that I had said on that occasion aroused anything like the enthusiasm that that single sentence aroused. Now, there is a sample, gentlemen. We cannot make anything out of Russia. We cannot make anything out of standing by Russia at this time—the most remote of the European nations, so far as we are concerned, the one with which we have had the least connections in trade and advantage—and yet the people of the United States rose to that suggestion as to no other that I made in that address.

(June 7, 1918, comments to a party of Mexican editors, from the "Official U.S. Bulletin," No. 332)

2 TERROR, BLOODSHED, AND MURDER

Herbert Hoover (1874–1964)

As the thirty-first President of the United States, Herbert Hoover was in office during the great depression and devoted most of his attention to domestic problems. Prior to his entry into the White House in 1929, however, he had long and intensive experience in foreign affairs, first as an engineer in Asia, Africa, Australia, and Europe, and then as U.S. Commissioner for Relief in Belgium during World War I. Following the Russian Revolution, President Woodrow Wilson asked Hoover's views on developments in Russia. His response, dated March 28, 1919, outlined the policy subsequently adopted by the United States— nonrecognition of the Soviet regime but a humanitarian response to the needs of the Russian people.

As the result of Bolshevik economic concepts, the people of Russia are dying of hunger and disease at the rate of some hundreds of thousands monthly in a country that formerly supplied food to a large part of the world.

I feel it is my duty to lay before you in just as few words as possible my views as to the American relation to Bolshevism and its manifestations. These views at least have the merit of being an analysis of information and thought gleaned from my own experience and the independent sources which I now have over the whole of Europe, through our widespread relief organization.

It simply cannot be denied that this swinging of the social pendulum from the tyranny of the extreme right to the tyranny of the extreme left is based on a foundation of real social griev-ance. . . . This situation was thrown into bold relief by the war and the breakdown. . . .

The Bolshevik ascendency or even their strong attempts so far are confined to areas of former reactionary tyranny. Their courses represent the not unnatural violence of a mass of ignorant human-ity, who themselves have learned in grief of tyranny and vio-lence over generations. Our people, who enjoy so great liberty and general comfort, cannot fail to sympathize to some degree with these blind gropings for better social conditions. . . .

Politically the Bolsheviki most certainly represent a minority in every country where they are in control. The Bolsheviki . . . [have] resorted to terror, bloodshed and murder to a degree long since abandoned even amongst reactionary tyrannies. . . . [They have] embraced a large degree of emotionalism and . . . thereby given an impulse to [their] propaganda comparable only to the impulse of large spiritual movements. . . .

[There is danger] the Bolshevik centers now stirred by great emotional hopes will undertake large military crusades in an attempt to impose their doctrines on other defenseless people.

We have also to . . . [consider] what would actually happen if we undertook military intervention. We should probably be involved in years of police duty, and our first act would prob-ably in the nature of things make us a party with the Allies to re-establishing the reactionary classes. It also requires considera-tion as to whether or not our people at home would stand for our providing power by which such reactionaries held their position. Furthermore, we become a junior in this partnership of four. It is therefore inevitable that we would find ourselves subordinated and even committed to policies against our con-victions.

In all these lights, I have the following suggestions:

First: We cannot even remotely recognize this murderous tyr-anny without stimulating actionist radicalism in every country in Europe and without transgressing . . . every National ideal of our own.

Second: That some Neutral of international reputation for probity and ability should be allowed to create a second Belgian

Relief Commission for Russia. He should ask the Northern Neutrals, who are especially interested both politically and financially in the restoration of better conditions in Russia, to give to him diplomatic, financial and transportation support; . . . He should be told that we will raise no obstructions and that we would even help his humanitarian task if he gets assurances that the Bolsheviki will cease all militant action across certain defined boundaries and cease their subsidizing of disturbances abroad; . . . This plan does not involve any recognition or relationship by the Allies of the Bolshevik murderers now in control. . . . It would appear to me that such a proposal would at least test out whether this is a militant . . . [intent] upon world domination. If such an arrangement could be accomplished it might at least give a period of rest along the frontiers of Europe and would give some hope of stabilization. Time can thus be taken to determine whether or not this whole system is a world danger, and whether the Russian people will not themselves swing back to moderation and themselves bankrupt these ideas. This plan, if successful, would save an immensity of helpless human life and would save our country from further entanglements which today threaten . . . our national ideals. .

3 VIEW FROM THE LEFT
John Reed (1887–1920)

Not all Americans opposed the Soviet seizure of power in Russia. Some, like John Reed, saw it as the wave of the future. A graduate of Harvard College (1910), Reed became a journalist. During World War I, he served as a correspondent for *Metropolitan Magazine*, reporting on the Western Front. He grew more sympathetic toward socialism when he was arrested in 1913 while covering a textile strike organized by the radical Industrial Workers of the World.

Following the overthrow of the tsar, Reed traveled to Russia as a correspondent for the socialist newspaper *New York Call* and was in the Russian capital during the crucial days before and during the second Russian Revolution. Reed's account of that event in *Ten Days That Shook the World* (1919) was sympathetic to the Bolsheviks, as the following preface to the work suggests. Lenin praised the book highly, calling it a "truthful and most vivid exposition of the events" that ought to be "published in millions of copies and translated into all languages." In August 1919 Reed participated in the structuring of the communist movement in America. He later returned to Russia, where he died of typhus. The Soviets thought so highly of him that his body was accorded the honor of burial in the Kremlin wall.

THIS BOOK IS A SLICE OF INTENSIFIED HISTORY as I saw it. It does not pretend to be anything but a detailed account of the November Revolution, when the Bolsheviki, at the head of the workers and soldiers, seized the state of power of Russia and placed it in the hands of the Soviets.

Naturally most of it deals with "Red Petrograd," the capital and heart of the insurrection. But the reader must realize that what took place in Petrograd was almost exactly duplicated, with greater or lesser intensity, at different intervals of time, all over Russia.

In this book, the first of several which I am writing, I must confine myself to a chronicle of those events which I myself observed and experienced, and those supported by reliable evidence; preceded by two chapters briefly outlining the background and causes of the November Revolution. I am aware that these two chapters make difficult reading, but they are essential to an understanding of what follows.

Many questions will suggest themselves to the mind of the reader. What is Bolshevism? What kind of a governmental structure did the Bolsheviki set up? If the Bolsheviki championed the Constituent Assembly before the November Revolution, why did they disperse it by force of arms afterward? And if the bourgeoisie opposed the Constituent Assembly until the danger of Bolshevism became apparent, why did they champion it afterward?

These and many other questions cannot be answered here. In another volume, "Kornilov to Brest-Litovsk," I trace the course of the Revolution up to and including the German peace. There I explain the origin and functions of the Revolutionary organizations, the evolution of popular sentiment, the dissolution of the Constituent Assembly, the structure of the Soviet state, and the course and outcome of the Brest-Litovsk negotiations. . .

. . . Roughly, the Mensheviki and Socialist Revolutionaries believed that Russia was not economically ripe for a social revolution—that only a *political* revolution was possible. According to their interpretation, the Russian masses were not educated enough to take over the power; any attempt to do so would inevitably bring on a reaction, by means of which some ruthless opportunist might restore the old regime. And so it followed that when the "moderate" Socialists were forced to assume the power, they were afraid to use it.

АРМАНД Е.Ф. ИНЕССА 1875-1920
ДЖОН РИД 1887-1920
РУСАКОВ И.В. 1877-1921
ПЕКАЛОВ С.М. 1918

John Reed remains a hero to the Soviet Union. Here flowers are placed at his grave on the seventy-fifth anniversary of his birth in 1962.

They believed that Russia must pass through the stages of political and economic development known to Western Europe, and emerge at last, with the rest of the world, into full-fledged Socialism. Naturally, therefore, they agreed with the propertied classes that Russia must first be a parliamentary state—though with some improvements on the Western democracies. As a consequence, they insisted upon the collaboration of the propertied classes in the Government.

From this it was an easy step to supporting them. The "moderate" Socialists needed the bourgeoisie. But the bourgeoisie did not need the "moderate" Socialists. So it resulted in the Socialist Ministers being obliged to give way, little by little, on their entire program, while the propertied classes grew more and more insistent.

And at the end, when the Bolsheviki upset the whole hollow compromise, the Mensheviki and Socialist Revolutionaries found themselves fighting on the side of the propertied classes. . . . In almost every country in the world to-day the same phenomenon is visible.

Instead of being a destructive force, it seems to me that the Bolsheviki were the only party in Russia with a constructive program and the power to impose it on the country. If they had not succeeded to the Government when they did, there is little doubt in my mind that the armies of Imperial Germany would have been in Petrograd and Moscow in December, and Russia would again be ridden by a Tsar. . .

It is still fashionable, after a whole year of the Soviet Government, to speak of the Bolshevik insurrection as an "adventure". Adventure it was, and one of the most marvellous mankind ever embarked upon, sweeping into history at the head of the toiling masses, and staking everything on their vast and simple desires. Already the machinery had been set up by which the land of the great estates could be distributed among the peasants. The Factory-Shop Committees and the Trade Unions were there to put into operation workers' control of industry. In every village, town, city district and province there were Soviets of Workers', Soldiers' and Peasants' Deputies, prepared to assume the task of local administration.

No matter what one thinks of Bolshevism, it is undeniable that the Russian Revolution is one of the great events of human history, and the rise of the Bolsheviki—a phenomenon of world-wide importance. Just as historians search the records for the minutest details of the story of the Paris Commune, so they will want to know what happened in Petrograd in November, 1917, the spirit which animated the people, and how the leaders looked, talked and acted. It is with this in view that I have written this book.

In the struggle my sympathies were not neutral. But in telling the story of those great days I have tried to see events with the eye of a conscientious reporter, interested in setting down the truth.

4 NO RECOGNITION OF THE SOVIETS

Bainbridge Colby (1869–1950)

A lawyer and friend of Theodore Roosevelt and Woodrow Wilson, Bainbridge Colby was Secretary of State for less than a year in the closing days of the Wilson administration. He was born in St. Louis, Missouri, and graduated from Williams College and the New York Law School. In 1912 he helped Theodore Roosevelt found the Bull Moose Party, which was Roosevelt's unsuccessful vehicle in his third-party campaign for the presidency. Following the resignation of Robert Lansing as Secretary of State, President Wilson named Colby to the post in March 1920. It was in this capacity in August 1920 that Colby despatched a message to various governments outlining U.S. policy with regard to the Soviet Union. The gist of the policy was that he would not establish relations with the Bolshevik regime because of its dictatorial nature and support of subversion abroad, but that we would harbor a warm friendship for the Russian people (who were expected to eventually replace the Bolsheviks with a democratic government), and that in the interim we did not wish to see any seizure of Russian territory. This statement, which had been cleared with Wilson, remained the basis of American policy toward the Soviet Union until diplomatic ties were restored in 1933. As such, it was probably the most important enunciation of the American position toward Russia in the period between the wars. Following Wilson's departure from the presidency, he and Colby were law partners from 1921 to 1923.

From the beginning of the Russian Revolution, in March, 1917, to the present moment, the Government and the people of the United States have followed its development with friendly solicitude and with profound sympathy for the efforts of the Russian people to reconstruct their national life upon the broad basis of popular self-government. The Government of the United States, reflecting the spirit of its people, has at all times desired to help the Russian people. In that spirit all its relations with Russia, and with other nations in matters affecting the latter's interests, have been conceived and governed.

The Government of the United States was the first government to acknowledge the validity of the Revolution and to give recognition to the Provisional Government of Russia. Almost immediately thereafter it became necessary for the United States to enter the war against Germany and in that undertaking to become closely associated with the Allied Nations, including, of course, Russia. The war weariness of the masses of the Russian people was fully known to this Government and sympathetically comprehended. Prudence, self-interest and loyalty to our associates made it desirable that we should give moral and material support to the Provisional Government, which was struggling to accomplish a two-fold task, to carry on the war with vigor and, at the same time, to reorganize the life of the nation and establish a stable government based on popular sovereignty.

Quite independent of these motives, however, was the sincere friendship of the Government and the people of the United States for the great Russian nation. The friendship manifested by Russia toward this nation in a time of trial and distress has left us with an imperishable sense of gratitude. It was as a grateful friend that we sent to Russia an expert commission to aid in bringing about such a reorganization of the railroad transportation system of the country as would reinvigorate the whole of its economic life and so add to the well-being of the Russian people.

While deeply regretting the withdrawal of Russia from the war at a critical time, and the disastrous surrender at Brest-Litovsk, the United States has fully understood that the people of Russia were in no wise responsible.

The United States maintains unimpaired its faith in the Russian people, in their high character and their future. That they will overcome the existing anarchy, suffering and destitution we do not entertain the slightest doubt. The distressing character of Russia's transition has many historical parallels, and the United States is confident that restored, free and united Russia will again take a leading place in the world, joining with the other free nations in upholding peace and orderly justice.

Until that time shall arrive the United States feels that friendship and honor require that Russia's interests must be generously protected, and that, as far as possible, all decisions of vital importance to it, and especially those concerning its sovereignty over the territory of the former Russian Empire, be held in abeyance. By this feeling of friendship and honorable obligation to the great nation whose brave and heroic self-sacrifice contributed so much to the successful termination of the war, the Government of the United States was guided in its reply to the Lithuanian National Council, on October 15, 1919, and in its persistent refusal to recognize the Baltic States as separate nations independent of Russia. The same spirit was manifested in the note of this Government, of March 24, 1920, in which it was stated, with reference to certain proposed settlements in the Near East, that "no final decision should or can be made without the consent of Russia."

These illustrations show with what consistency the Government of the United States has been guided in its foreign policy by a loyal friendship for Russia. We are unwilling that while it is helpless in the grip of a non-representative government, whose only sanction is brutal force, Russia shall be weakened still further by a policy of dismemberment, conceived in other than Russian interests.

With the desire of the Allied Powers to bring about a peaceful solution of the existing difficulties in Europe, this Government is of course in hearty accord, and will support any justifiable steps to that end. It is unable to perceive, however, that a recognition of the Soviet regime would promote, much less accomplish this object, and it is therefore averse to any dealings with the Soviet regime beyond the most narrow boundaries to which a discussion of an armistice can be confined.

That the present rulers of Russia do not rule by the will or the consent of any considerable proportion of the Russian people is an incontestable fact. Although nearly two and a half years have passed since they seized the machinery of government, promising to protect the Constituent Assembly against alleged conspiracies against it, they have not yet permitted anything in the nature of a popular election. At the moment when the work of creating a popular representative government based upon universal suffrage was nearing completion the Bolsheviki, although, in number, an inconsiderable minority of the people, by force and cunning seized the powers and machinery of government and have continued to use them with savage oppression to maintain themselves in power.

Without any desire to interfere in the internal affairs of the Russian people, or to suggest what kind of government they should have, the Government of the United States does express the hope that they will soon find a way to set up a government representing their free will and purpose. When that time comes, the United States will consider the measures of practical assistance which can be taken to promote the restoration of Russia, provided Russia has not taken itself wholly out of the pale of the friendly interest of other nations, by the pillage and oppression of the Poles.

It is not possible for the Government of the United States to recognize the present rulers of Russia as a government with which the relations common to friendly governments can be maintained. This conviction has nothing to do with any particular political or social structure which the Russian people themselves may see fit to embrace. It rests upon a wholly different set of facts. These facts, which none dispute, have convinced the Government of the United States, against its will, that the existing regime in Russia is based upon the negation of every principle of honor and good faith, and every usage and convention, underlying the whole structure of international law; the negation, in short, of every principle upon which it is possible to base harmonious and trustful relations, whether of nations or of individuals. The responsible leaders of the regime have frequently and openly boasted that they are willing to sign agreements and undertakings with foreign Powers while not having the slightest intention of observing such undertakings or carrying out such agreements. This attitude of disregard of obligations voluntarily entered into, they base upon the theory that no compact or agreement made with a non-Bolshevist government can have any moral force for them. They have not only avowed this as a doctrine, but have exemplified it in practice. Indeed, upon numerous occasions the responsible spokesmen of this Power, and its official agencies, have declared that it is their understanding that the very existence of Bolshevism in Russia, the maintenance of their own rule, depends, and must continue to depend, upon the occurrence of revolutions in all other great civilized nations, including the United States, which will overthrow and destroy their governments and set up Bolshevist rule in their stead. They have made it quite plain that they intend to use every means, including, of course, diplomatic agencies, to promote such revolutionary movements in other countries.

It is true that they have in various ways expressed their willingness to give "assurances" and "guarantees" that they will not abuse the privileges and immunities of diplomatic agencies by using them for this purpose. In view of their own declarations, already referred to, such assurances and guarantees cannot be very seriously regarded. Moreover, it is within the knowledge of the Government of the United States that the Bolshevist Government is itself subject to the control of a political faction, with extensive international ramifications through the Third Internationale, and that this body, which is heavily subsidized by the Bolshevist Government from the public revenues of Russia, has for its openly avowed aim the promotion of Bolshevist revolutions throughout the world. The leaders of the Bolsheviki have boasted that their promises of non-interference with other nations would in no wise bind the agents of this body. There is no room for reasonable doubt that such agents would receive the support and protection of any diplomatic agencies the Bolsheviki might have in other countries. Inevitably, therefore, the diplomatic service of the Bolshevist Government would become a channel for intrigues and the propaganda of revolt against the institutions and laws of countries, with which it was at peace, which would be an abuse of friendship to which enlightened governments cannot subject themselves.

In the view of this Government, there cannot be any common ground upon which it can stand with a Power whose conceptions of international relations are so entirely alien to its own, so utterly repugnant to its moral sense. There can be no mutual confidence or trust, no respect even, if pledges are to be given and agreements made with a cynical repudiation of their obligations already in the mind of one of the parties. We cannot recognize, hold official relations with, or give friendly reception to the agents of a government which is determined and bound to conspire against our institutions; whose diplomats will be the agitators of dangerous revolt; whose spokesmen say that they sign agreements with no intention of keeping them.

5 HIDEOUS BLEMISHES IN REVOLUTIONARY RUSSIA

Emma Goldman (1869–1940)

No American could have arrived in Russia more joyously hoping to witness the accomplishments of the Soviet system than Emma Goldman when she went there in January 1920; nobody could have left, less than two years later, in December 1921, more disillusioned with it than she. Born in Russia into a Jewish family, she emigrated to the United States in 1886. She became an anarchist, and when the Soviets took power in Russia she hailed the event as the "promise and hope of the world." In 1917 her organization of anti-war rallies in America led to her arrest, conviction, and deportation to Russia.

In the land of her dreams, Emma Goldman's hopes dimmed shortly after she witnessed scenes of official brutality and stupidity, and betrayal of the ideals she had thought inseparable from the goals of the revolution. The final blow was the savagery with which the Soviets put down strikes by workers in Petrograd in March 1921. Supported by units of the Russian fleet in Kronstadt, the workers were seeking to win such demands as freedom of speech, election of deputies to the Soviets, and equal food rations. Following her departure from Russia, Emma Goldman lived in France and England; she died in Canada while trying to raise funds for the Spanish nationalists. The following description of her disillusionment in Russia is taken from her book *Living My Life* (1931).

ALL WAS READY. It was the twenty-eighth day of our journey, and at last we were on the threshold of Soviet Russia. My heart trembled with anticipation and fervent hope . . .

SOVIET RUSSIA! SACRED GROUND. MAGIC PEOPLE! You have come to symbolize humanity's hope, you alone are destined to redeem mankind. I have come to serve you, beloved *matushka*. Take me to your bosom, let me pour myself into you, mingle my blood with yours, find my place in your heroic struggle, and give to the uttermost to your needs!

At the border, on our way to Petrograd, and at the station there we were received like dear comrades. We who had been driven out of America as felons were welcomed on Soviet soil as brothers by her sons and daughters who had helped to set her free. Workers, soldiers and peasants surrounded us, took us by the hand, and made us feel akin to them. Pale-faced and hollow-cheeked they were, a light burning in their sunken eyes, and determination breathing from their ragged bodies. Danger and suffering had steeled their wills and made them stern. But underneath beat the old childlike, generous Russian heart and it went out to us without stint.

Music and song greeted us everywhere and wondrous tales of valour and never-failing fortitude in the face of hunger, cold and devastating disease. Tears of gratitude burned in my eyes and I felt great humility before those simple folk risen to greatness in the fire of the revolutionary struggle. . .

Nothing was of moment compared with the supreme need of giving one's all to safeguard the Revolution and its gains. The faith and fervour of our comrade swept me along to ecstatic heights. Yet I could not entirely free myself from an undercurrent of uneasiness one often feels when left alone in the dark. Resolutely I strove to drive it back, moving like a sleep-walker through enchanted space. Sometimes I would stumble back to earth only half-aroused by a harsh voice or an ugly sight. The gagging of free speech at the session of the Petro-Soviet that we had attended, the discovery that better and more plentiful food was served Party members at the Smolny dining-room and many similar injustices and evils attracted my attention. . .

The Bolsheviki, in common with other social rebels, had always stressed the potency of hunger as the cause of most of the evils in capitalist society. They never grew tired of condemning the system that punished the effects while leaving their sources intact. How could they now pursue the same stupid and incredible course, I wondered. True, the appalling hunger was not of their making. The blockade and the interventionists *were* chiefly responsible for that. More reason, then, it seemed to me, why the victims should not be hounded and punished. Witnessing such a raid, Sasha had been aroused by its cruelty and inhumanity. He had vigorously protested against the brutal manner in which the soldiers and the Chekists dispersed the crowd, and he had been himself saved from arrest only by the credential Chicherin had given him. Forthwith the Chekist had changed his tone and manner, offering profuse apologies to the "foreign *tovarishtch*." He was only doing his duty, he said, carrying out the orders of his superiors, and he could not be blamed.

It was evident that the new power in the Kremlin was feared no less than the old, and that its official seal had the same awesome effect. "Wherein is the change?" I asked Sasha. "You can't measure a gigantic upheaval by a few specks of dust," he replied. But were they mere specks, I wondered, for they seemed to me gusts that were threatening to pull down the entire revolutionary edifice I had constructed in America around the Bolsheviki. Yet my faith in their integrity was too strong to charge them with responsibility for the evils and wrongs I was witnessing at every step. These kept growing daily, ugly facts utterly at variance with what Soviet Russia had been proclaiming to the world. I tried to avoid facing them, but they lurked in every corner and would not be ignored. . .

The hideous sores on revolutionary Russia could not for long be ignored. The facts presented at the gathering of the Moscow anarchists, the analysis of the situation by leading Left Socialist Revolutionists, and my talks with simple people who claimed no political affiliations enabled me to look behind the scenes of the revolutionary drama and to behold the dictatorship without its stage make-up. Its role was somewhat different from the one proclaimed in public. It was forcible tax-collection at the point of guns, with its devastating effect on villages and towns. It was

Emma Goldman in Moscow, 1921.

the elimination from responsible positions of everyone who dared think aloud, and the spiritual death of the most militant elements whose intelligence, faith, and courage had really enabled the Bolsheviki to achieve their power. The anarchists and Left Socialist Revolutionists had been used as pawns by Lenin in the October days and were now doomed to extinction by his creed and policies. It was the system of taking hostages for political refugees, not exempting even old parents and children of tender age. The nightly *oblavas* (street and house raids) by the Cheka, the population frightened out of sleep, their few belongings turned upside down and ripped open for secret documents, the dragnet of soldiers left behind to haul in the crop of unsuspecting callers at the besieged house. The penalties for flimsy charges often amounted to long prison terms, exile to desolate parts of the country, and even execution. Shattering in its cumulative effect, the essence of the story was the same as told me by my Petrograd comrades. I had been too dazzled then by the public glare and glitter of Bolshevism to credit the veracity of the accusations. I had refused to trust their judgment and their viewpoint. But now Bolshevism was shorn of its pretence, its naked soul exposed to my gaze. Still I would not believe. I would not see with my inner eye the truth so evident to my outer sight. I was stunned, baffled, the ground pulled from under me. Yet I hung on, hung on by a thread, as a drowning man. In my anguish I cried: "Bolshevism is the *mene, tekel* over every throne, the menace of craven hearts, the hated enemy of organized wealth and power. Its path has been thorny, its obstacles many, its climb steep. How could it help falling behind at times, how could it help making mistakes? But to belie itself, to play Judas to the fervent hope of the disinherited and oppressed, to betray its own ultimate aims? No, never could it be guilty of such an eclipse of the world's most luminous star. . ."

It was the common feeling in Petrograd among non-Communist elements that the situation was very grave. The atmosphere was charged to the point of explosion. We decided of course to remain in the city. Not that we hoped to avert impending trouble, but we wanted to be on hand in case we could be of help to the people.

The storm broke out even before anyone expected it. It began with the strike of the millmen at the Troubetskoy works. Their demands were modest enough: an increase in their food rations, as had long ago been promised them, and also the distribution of the foot-gear on hand.

Into this tense and desperate situation there was presently introduced a new factor that held out the hope of some settlement. It was the sailors of Kronstadt. True to their revolutionary traditions of solidarity with the workers, so loyally demonstrated in the revolution of 1905, and later in the March and October upheavals of 1917, they now again took up the cudgels in behalf of the harassed proletariat in Petrograd. . .

We felt elated over the splendid solidarity of the Kronstadt sailors and soldiers with their striking brothers in Petrograd . . .

Kronstadt was forsaken by Petrograd and cut off from the rest of Russia. It stood alone. It could offer almost no resistance. "It will go down at the first shot," the Soviet press proclaimed. They were mistaken. Kronstadt had thought of nothing less than of mutiny or resistance to the Soviet Government. To the very last moment it was determined to shed no blood. It appealed all the time for understanding and amicable settlement. But, forced to defend itself against unprovoked military attack, it fought like a lion. During ten harrowing days and nights the sailors and workers of the besieged city held out against a continuous artillery fire from three sides and bombs hurled from aeroplanes upon the non-combatant community. Heroically they repulsed the repeated attempts of the Bolsheviki to storm the fortresses by special troops from Moscow. Trotsky and Tukhachevsky had every advantage over the men of Kronstadt. The entire machinery of the Communist State backed them, and the centralized press continued to spread venom against the alleged "mutineers and counter-revolutionists." They had unlimited supplies and men whom they had masked in white shrouds to blend with the snow of the frozen Finnish Gulf in order to camouflage the night attack against the unsuspecting men of Kronstadt. The latter had nothing but their unflinching courage and abiding faith in the justice of their cause and in the free soviets they championed as the saviour of Russia from the dictatorship. They lacked even an icebreaker to halt the onrush of the Communist enemy. They were exhausted by hunger and cold and sleepless nights of vigil. Yet they held their own, desperately fighting against overwhelming odds.

During the fearful suspense, the days and nights filled with the rumbling of heavy artillery, there sounded not a single voice amid the roar of guns to cry out against or call a halt to the terrible blood bath . . .

The intelligentsia, the men and women that had once been revolutionary torch-bearers, leaders of thought, writers and poets, were as helpless as we and paralysed by the futility of individual effort. Most of their comrades and friends were already in prison or exile; some had been executed. They felt too broken by the collapse of all human values.

I turned to the Communists of our acquaintance, imploring them to do something. Some of them realized the monstrous crime their party was committing against Kronstadt. They admitted that the charge of counter-revolution was a downright fabrication. The supposed leader, Kozlovsky, was a nonentity too frightened about his own fate to have anything to do with any protest of the sailors. The latter were of sterling quality, their sole aim the welfare of Russia. Far from making common cause with the tsarist generals, they had even declined the help offered them by Chernov, the leader of the Socialist-Revolutionists. They wanted no outside aid. They demanded the right to choose their own deputies in the forthcoming elections to the Kronstadt Soviet and justice for the strikers in Petrograd.

These Communist friends spent nights with us—talking, talking—but none of them dared raise his voice in open protest. We did not realize, they said, the consequences it would involve. They would be excluded from the party, they and their families deprived of work and rations and literally condemned to death by starvation. Or they would simply vanish and no one would ever know what had become of them. Yet it was not fear that numbed their will, they assured us. It was the utter uselessness of protest or appeal. Nothing, nothing could stop the chariot-wheel of the Communist State. It had rolled them flat and they had no vitality left, even to cry out against it.

I was beset by the terrible apprehension that we also—Sasha and I—might reach the same state and become as spinelessly acquiescent as these people. Anything else would be preferable to that. Prison, exile, even death. Or escape! Escape from the horrible revolutionary sham and pretence.

Belo-Ostrov, January 19, 1920. O radiant dream, O burning faith! O *Matushka Rossiya*, reborn in the travail of the Revolution, purged by it from hate and strife, liberated for true humanity and embracing all. I will dedicate myself to you, O Russia!

In the train, December 1, 1921! My dreams crushed, my faith broken, my heart like a stone. *Matushka Rossiya* bleeding from a thousand wounds, her soil strewn with the dead.

I clutch the bar at the frozen window-pane and grit my teeth to suppress my sobs.

6 SOCIAL PROGRESS BUT NO FREEDOM

John Dos Passos (1896–1970)

John Dos Passos was one of many American intellectuals who visited Russia in the late 1920s with the hope of finding solutions to social problems afflicting the United States. Widely regarded as one of America's major modern writers, he was born in Chicago and graduated from Harvard University. The outbreak of World War I found him in Spain studying to be an architect; he later enlisted in the U. S. Army medical corps and after the end of hostilities became a writer. Dos Passos was generally regarded as a liberal and was arrested in 1927 while picketing to protest the conviction of the anarchists Sacco and Vanzetti. His stay in Russia in 1928 revealed to him the imperfections in Soviet society, which he later described in his book *The Best Times* (1966).

SACCO AND VANZETTI WERE DEAD. The New Playwrights' Theatre, though not quite on the rocks, was proving to be one headache after another. Administration and moneyraising just weren't my dish. It occurred to me this might be a good time to visit the Soviet Union. There wasn't much sense in going just for the trip, but studying the Russian theater, obviously in its heyday, would be helpful in planning new productions, and might give me sidelights on how people lived in a socialist society. . .

The summer of 1928 was a good time for Americans in the Soviet Union. Russian governments since time immemorial, have tended, like the oyster, spasmodically to open and close. This was

68

the period of a receptive attitude toward foreigners. The relaxation of NEP was still noticeable. The war to the death between Stalin and Trotsky was at a stalemate. Trotsky was in exile but Stalin did not yet feel himself sufficiently entrenched in power to sweep out Trotsky's adherents. People still dared to mention Trotsky's name. American engineers had been making themselves useful to the regime. There was no anti-American propaganda; in fact individual Americans were more popular than not.

Everything in Leningrad moved against a background of vast Palladian colonnades set up like stage scenery at the end of every vista. Always I was conscious of the iceclear steelgray waters of the Neva pouring past into the Baltic. I stayed at the old Evropskaya Hotel where the rooms still had the air of Stanislavski's settings for the Chekov plays.

Kittin's Russian was a great help. We saw the sights together. At the Hermitage we got so interested in talking to a Kirgiz that we almost forgot to look at the pictures. He was a young fellow just a year out of the nomad tents on the steppe. His brother was a party member and was studying at the university for eastern peoples. He himself was still *byezpartini* [without a party] he said; he wanted to see the world and to decide for himself. He was working as a common laborer in a metallurgical plant, where he made just enough to live on. He was a great reader. It was only since the revolution that there had been any reading among the Kirgiz. He was reading Gorki. He wasn't planning to read anything else until he'd read everything Gorki ever wrote.

The things he liked about the revolution were reading and the new kind of marriage. Before, among the Kirgiz, a man couldn't marry until he had enough cattle or money to buy himself a wife. Here at the plant where he worked, if a girl liked a fellow she would take up with him. If they got very fond of each other or were going to have a baby, then they registered the marriage.

He couldn't wait for us to tell him everything about America. Did we have any nomads, what was our marriage like, how much did a metalworker make? He wanted to go to America, he wanted to see as much of the world as he could so that he could decide what kind of system would be best for his Kirgiz people.

We had hardly sopped up all we could from the Kirgiz before I found myself shaking hands with Etienne de Beaumont and his wife. "*Quelle collection! Epatant. Formidable.*" I'd met the Beaumonts as friends of the Murphys at Villa America at Antibes. They were patrons of the avantgarde arts; and *très américains* perhaps because an ancestor of the count's had accompanied Tocqueville on his famous American tour.

Falling in with the Kirgiz and the Beaumonts on the same afternoon caused me to underline Leningrad's cosmopolitan air in my notes. It was as a gateway between east and west that the Czar Peter built his northern capital. Russian writers I met of the Leningrad school strongly felt the European tie. They didn't conceal their scorn of Moscow.

Stenich, who came to see me at the hotel, was as avantgarde as the Beaumonts. He spoke excellent English. He had translated a novel of mine and was eager for news of the latest by Joyce and Eliot and Pound. His father had been a wealthy businessman of Czech origin but Stenich wrote and thought in Russian. Friends whispered in my ear that he was a firstrate poet. He had joined the Red Guards very young and had commanded a division during the civil war, but he had somehow gotten in wrong with the regime, had been expelled from the Party, and had spent a year in jail. Jokingly he called himself a counterrevolutionary.

Stenich and his friends took me for long walks about the city through the milky northern midnight. He showed us the vast square where the monument was to the October dead and told how it was made on one of Lenin's Saturday afternoons when soldiers and factory workers would tackle some particularly unsightly corner of the city and dig it up into a park. He showed us the streets where he had fought eleven years before, the place where they had held the barricade against a desperate attack from the Cadets. He recalled wistfully the enthusiasms and comradeships of those days.

On the embankment of the shimmering broad Neva opposite the spires of the Fortress of Saints Peter and Paul we came upon the huge black statue of a man on a prancing horse. "That's my favorite Russian in history," cried Stenich, "Peter the Great who brought order out of chaos, the first Bolshevik."

Everybody seemed a little shocked. Stenich ought to have said that Lenin was his favorite Russian. Somebody proclaimed that he preferred Pushkin. Someone else brought up the name of Edgar Allan Poe. Did I know that Pushkin and Poe might have met in St. Petersburg? Excitedly they told me the story. During the period when Poe followed the sea he had sailed up the Baltic on a merchant ship. Poe and Pushkin had met face to face, maybe on this very spot. I suggested that this was a myth based on one of Poe's equivocal statements about his early history. Stenich asked brusquely: How did I know? I didn't! They wanted so to believe the story that I began to believe it myself. I remembered Stenich as the most vivid of the Russians I met in Leningrad. Poor fellow, he did not have long to live. He was rubbed out early in Stalin's purge of Leningrad writers. . .

I learned a great deal about how Russian theater people lived from my actress friend. Like Stenich she was nostalgic about the period of war communism. Though actors like scientists had preferential treatment the Art Theatre people came near starving to death. She had never imagined potatoes could be so delicious as the potatoes they roasted over the coals when potatoes were all they could get to eat. Walking home to my hotel after the theater we would often pass a window of propaganda material with a picture of Stalin in the middle. If she was sure nobody was looking she would make a hurried little gesture of shaking her fist at it. . .

Back in Moscow in October I had trouble finding a room. Fadyeev and his wife kindly put me up in their large apartment. Fadyeev was then a youngish fellow with a crew cut and a pleasant breezy manner which at home we would have associated with the West. He came from far east—Siberia. He had written a successful novel and was enthusiastic for the regime. His wife was high up in the Gay Pay U. They had a cheerful comsomolska for a maid and lived simply but well. Their apartment was near a Red Army barracks. Every morning I was waked up by the magnificent deep singing of the regiment marching out to drill. In those days the Russian soldiers always sang as they marched.

Fadyeev's friends could speak freely about all sorts of topics. No danger of having what you said reported to the Gay Pay U. This was the Gay Pay U. I must say I liked Fadyeev. After I left

Russia he became a leading proponent of Stalinism in the literary world. When Khrushchev denounced the monster and pulled his corpse out of Lenin's tomb Fadyeev killed himself.

I enjoyed these autumnal weeks in Moscow. The drizzle and sleet were just beginning to give way to snow. I managed to keep warm because I had inherited several suits of magnificent fleece-lined underwear from a lively bunch of American explorers who came through on their way home from hunting Siberian tigers for the Museum of Natural History.

I saw a great deal of Sergei Alimov and his wife Masha. Alimov was a grand fellow who'd lived in Australia and made a name for himself by writing some songs that were favorites with the Red Army. His songs gave him a certain immunity. He could say things nobody else would dare to say. Though he was a fervently patriotic Russian I got the impression he couldn't care less about Marxist ideology. There was always plenty of smoked whitefish and good bread and wine and vodka at the Alimovs, and talk about everything under the sun. Before I left, Alimov and his friends tossed me in a blanket, which among the Russians, as among the Esquimaux, is considered a compliment.

It was the season in Moscow. There were marvelous concerts. Though it wasn't open to the public it was fairly easy to get in to the great collection of French impressionist paintings some Moscow merchant had made. More new plays were opening than I could possibly get around to. I visited kindergartens and schools, army theaters, amateur theaters, factory theaters, the theater in the institution for reeducating prostitutes.

It was hard not to catch fire from the enthusiasm for social betterment you found everywhere. Among people who sided with the regime there was a universal sense of participation. Many of the partyliners were dedicated people. I liked what I saw of the efforts to dispel anti-Jewish prejudice, to give cultural autonomy to the subject nationalities like the Sheshians and the Ossetines and all the various unimagined ethnic groups I had run into slogging through the Caucasus. And always there was the stimulus, in spite of the painful difficulty of the language, of the Russian mind. I got the feeling that, in spite of the destruction of so many talents in the liquidation of the old educated and governing classes, the

Great Russians still comprised one of the world's major reservoirs of brains.

Like most westerners I've known who stayed any length of time in the Soviet Union I had my jitters too. Days and weeks go by without your being conscious of the Terror and then suddenly the iron fist shows through. I spent an evening with an Englishman and his Russian wife in a stuffy apartment full of bricabrac and veneered furniture. He'd come to Russia to work for the Communist cause. Now he was desperate to get out. It had become a nightmare. They would never let his wife leave. She had the wrong class origins.

He talked about the way the Communists repressed the sailors' revolt at Kronstadt—the Kronstadt story had given me the creeps since I first got wind of it—the incorporation of everything worst in the old Okhrana into the Cheka. "There's no cruelty like Russian cruelty, not even Chinese," the Englishman said.

I tried to argue with him. My point was that the Terror was fading. Most of the old Chekists had been shot. I told him about how freely I'd been able to travel, how easily people talked. My theory then was that the Russian revolution was entering a liberal phase. My parallel was France under the Directorate and Consulate. Napoleon's rule was iron but there were no massacres like Robespierre's.

It was all right for me to talk that way, the Englishman said; I could get out. He and his wife were trapped. Sooner or later they would come for them. They always came at night, no arrests were ever seen, no one ever dared tell.

I've often wondered what happened to them. Within five years Stalin had proved him right and me wrong.

Before I left Moscow I had the wind up almost as badly as the Englishman. The Interior Department kept putting off returning my passport from day to day. In spite of the fact that I seemed to be approved of by the Communist publications and was being treated to enough farewell parties to keep my head spinning, I kept wondering whether I had dropped some injudicious remark that might have been reported.

At last the passport was produced. I procured a Polish visa, a railroad ticket to Warsaw.

My Art Theatre actress friend brought the whole company from the Sanitary Propaganda Theatre she coached in one of the big factories to see me off. These were fifteen- and sixteen-year-old boys and girls, blueeyed, friendly, curious. They grabbed your hand with a hard firm grasp. They put on little skits to show in the factories about the dangers of syphilis, about cleaning your teeth, about proper food for children. "Tell us," she asked me as I stood beside my sleeper in the steaming trainshed waiting with desperate impatience for the train to leave, "are you for us or against us? They want you to show your face."

How could I answer? The train was already moving. I jumped aboard.

How could I answer that question? I liked and admired the Russian people. I had enjoyed their enormous and varied country, but when next morning I crossed the Polish border—Poland was not Communist then—it was like being let out of jail.

7 PROS AND CONS OF THE SOVIET SYSTEM

Lincoln Steffens (1866–1936)

On the basis of several trips to Russia, both as a member of the semi-official Bullitt mission and as a journalist, Lincoln Steffens concluded that despite its toll in human suffering and deprivation of individual political freedom, the Russian Revolution was worth the sacrifice. Born in San Francisco, California, Steffens graduated from the University of California and became a journalist with the New York *Evening Post*. As managing editor of *McClures Magazine* from 1902 to 1906, he played a leading role in the "muckraker movement," which exposed political and economic corruption in American government and business circles.

In the period prior to World War I, Steffens became interested in radical movements and closely followed the Mexican Revolution. In 1917, following the overthrow of the tsar, he traveled to Russia with several journalists, and was enthusiastic about the pressures for social reform he found there. Although he had returned to the United States prior to the communist seizure of power, he was eager to view the workings of the new Soviet regime. The opportunity arose when, in 1919, he was invited to become a member of the Bullitt Mission that traveled to investigate the situation in Russia under President Wilson's directives. The following selection from the *Autobiography of Lincoln Steffens* (1931) reflects his view that communism in Russia was a positive force in human development.

THE GREAT LEADERS of the Russian revolutionary movement were not in Russia when the Russian Revolution began; they were in exile; and the lesser leaders who were there did not expect it to happen. Somebody did. On the roofs of buildings that commanded the main thoroughfares, the grand boulevards and squares, we found still standing the machine guns planted to deal with the revolution that the revolutionists did not know was going to happen. And we had a look at the plans drawn to put down mobs of people who did not know they were going to rise in revolt. Government blue prints. Government preparations. It was the government that anticipated, prepared for, started, the revolution in Russia, as in Mexico.

Getting to the scene so soon after the beginning, we had—Crane, Shepherd, and I—the opportunity I craved to find out exactly how a revolution is made. Shepherd also had been in Mexico. Crane had seen the world. We were not to be distracted by the outrages, the inefficiency, the confusion, of such a crisis. Crane had old friends to see; Shepherd, a regular correspondent, had to cover the news; I, unattached, was absolutely free to pursue any line of inquiry I pleased. . . .

The cultivated lady who read the Russian newspapers to us correspondents would not read the Bolshevik paper. Any other paper, any other party, but she would not let the Bolshevik sheet into her house. It was Bill Shepherd who discovered the Bolsheviks to us and to the American papers, and he, I think, was caught by the word. At the sound of it he was fascinated.

"Just the word," he shouted in glee. "Bolsheviki! It sounds like all that the world fears. Bolsheviki! We must find out enough about the Bolsheviki to carry the word. Can't you see it in the headlines? It will stick. It will crackle in everybody's mouth, ear, and brain. Bolsheviki!" He rejoiced in it, and he enabled it, with a story of the party. The word meant nothing—"majority"; the Bolshevik party was not a majority; it was a small minority party, but it was a left party that was most demandful. And that's what Bolshevik meant to the Russian lady and came to mean all over the world, the party that demanded the most, all, and would take nothing less. And Lenin personified the Bolsheviki, and his speech expressed the patience, determination, and wisdom, practical and ideal, of the small minority which won finally in October.

I could not stay to see the second, so-called real, revolution, but I grasped enough to hold the key to it and to what followed— "the seizure of power" by the Bolsheviki that saved the Russian Revolution from repeating the history of the Mexican and all the known revolutions. The milling herd of the All-Russian Soviet, both inside and out in the street, never had a majority in command. It legislated, as we have seen, well; but there was no other action. Its laws aimed deep, but nothing happened, and there was much to do. The pressure to act was acute, and it grew as the hunger and the threats of war and famine increased. But split up into parties to begin with, the divisions increased, and the inactivity. Men of liberal minds, radicals, socialists, democrats, have wondered since how that democracy happened to go so straight to a dictatorship. I think I understand, not only how that happened, but that it had to happen, that it always will happen.

Think of a herd of wild cattle, restless, troubled, sensing danger. They mill and mill, round and round, as those Russians did, looking for a direction in which to stampede. Because those people were in earnest and in fear, as they debated they could not compromise; they split their several minority parties or groups into smaller, not larger, groups, and went on milling. You could see—I mean that I could see—that there could be no majority and that some one minority had to win and lead the whole herd off in some one direction, adopt, all, one plan, and so throw up one minority government that would rule the whole.

Now the minority that decided which degree of the circle was to be taken, the Bolsheviki, was not a unit. They presented a united front; they appeared to be a unit; but those of us who were interested in them knew that they also had debates and disagreements that were intense and lasting. But they had a man, that man Lenin, who could and who did always, finally, close the debate and command action, united and planned. They had a dictator, and the dictator had a plan. That's why the Bolsheviki came into power, not because they were the nearest right (or, if you please, the nearest left), but because they were the nearest ready. Lenin's speech had the idea. He knew that a time would come when the mob would tire of indecision and not only let Kerenski fall, but themselves ask for the czar they were used to, a ruler; and he made his propaganda and prepared his organization and his plans for that day, which he, a mob psychologist, would choose, to "seize power" (his phrase). Lenin had studied; he knew his history. . .

Soviet Russia was a revolutionary government with an evolutionary plan. Their plan was, not by direct action to resist such evils as poverty and riches, graft, privilege, tyranny, and war, but to seek out and remove the causes of them. They were not practicing what we and they preached. They were not trying to establish political democracy, legal liberty, and negotiated peace—not now. They were at present only laying a basis for these good things. They had set up a dictatorship, supported by a small, trained minority, to make and maintain for a few generations a scientific rearrangement of economic forces which would result in economic democracy first and political democracy last.

It was a new culture, an economic, scientific, not a moral, culture. And the Russians we were conversing with, the heads of the Soviet government, were talking out of a new philosophy. No wonder it was confusing and difficult.

Bullitt steered his way through to an agreement with Lenin and Tchicherin. The seven points of Lloyd George's memorandum, and House's points as well, were accepted with very slight verbal modifications. Feeling that he had what we came for, a basis upon which the allies could treat with Russia, Bullitt decided to hurry back to Paris. He arranged for me an interview with Lenin, so that I could ask my undiplomatic questions and get a sense of the man. I had my questions at my finger tips when I was sent in to the great room where Lenin sat behind his desk at one end.

A quiet figure in old clothes, he rose, came around in front of his desk to greet me with a nod and a handshake. An open, inquiring face, with a slight droop in one eye that suggested irony or humor, looked into mine. I asked whether, in addition to the agreement with Bullitt, I could not take back some assurances: that, for example, if the borders were opened, Russian propagandists would be restrained from flocking over into Europe. . .

Lenin was impatient with my liberalism, but he had shown himself a liberal by instinct. He had defended liberty of speech, assembly, and the Russian press for some five to seven months after the October revolution which put him in power. The people had stopped talking; they were for action on the program. But the plottings of the whites, the distracting debates and criticisms of the various shades of reds, the wild conspiracies and the violence of the anarchists against Bolshevik socialism, developed an extreme left in Lenin's party which proposed to proceed directly to the terror which the people were ready for. Lenin held out against them till he was shot, and even then, when he was in hospital, he pleaded for the life of the woman who shot him.

I referred to this, and he acknowledged it and said: "It was no use. It is no use. There will be a terror. It hurts the revolution both inside and out, and we must find out how to avoid or control or direct it. But we have to know more about psychology than we do now to steer through that madness. And it serves a purpose that has to be served. There must be in a revolution, as in a war, unified action, and in a revolution more than in a war the contented people will scuttle your ship if you don't deal with them. There are white terrors, too, you know. Look at Finland and Hungary. We have to devise some way to get rid of the bourgeoisie, the upper classes. They won't let you make economic changes during a revolution any more than they will before one; so they must be driven out. I don't see, myself, why we can't scare them away without killing them. Of course they are a menace outside as well as in, but the émigrés are not so bad. The only solution I see is to have the threat of a red terror spread the fear and let them escape. But however it is done it has to be done. The absolute, instinctive opposition of the old conservatives and even of the fixed liberals has to be silenced if you are to carry through a revolution to its objective."

"So you've been over into Russia?" said Bernard Baruch, and I answered very literally, "I have been over into the future, and it works." This was in Jo Davidson's studio, where Mr. Baruch was sitting for a portrait bust. The sculptor asked if I wasn't glad to get back. I was. It was a mental change that we had experienced, not physical. Bullitt asked in surprise why it was that, having been so elated by the prospect of Russia, we were so glad to be back in Paris. I thought it was because, though we had been to heaven, we were so accustomed to our own civilization that we preferred hell. We were ruined; we could recognize salvation, but could not be saved.

And, by the way, it was harder on the real reds than it was on us liberals. Emma Goldman, the anarchist who was deported to that socialist heaven, came out and said it was hell. And the socialists, the American, English, the European socialists, they did not recognize their own heaven. As some wit put it, the trouble with them was that they were waiting at a station for a local train, and an express tore by and left them there. My summary of all our experiences was that it showed that heaven and hell are one place, and we all go there. To those who are prepared, it is heaven; to those who are not fit and ready, it is hell. . .

Over in Hungary they were exploding another, a liberal, theory: that you can have a revolution without a red terror. Lenin himself had thought that and said so: we might avoid the actual killings; and I heard in Buda-Pest that he was advising Bela Kun, who was the head in that city of the victorious red revolution in Hungary. Anyway Bela Kun suppressed the red terror there, both the slaughter and the fear, and he lost out. The reds let the whites stay in Hungary, and they wiggled and wangled, got help from abroad (Hoover, who was feeding the people, used his charity for the whites against the reds), and finally rose and conquered the red revolutionary government, driving Bela Kun to Moscow, where, by the way, having learned his lesson, he became so ruthless that the Bolsheviki themselves demoted him. The terror, red or white, is inevitable in a revolution or a civil war, just as outrage and death are unavoidable in a foreign war and as bribery and corruption are natural elements in a political conflict of economic forces. . .

I went to Russia again in 1923, with Senator Robert M. La-Follette, his son Bob Jr. (who succeeded him in the Senate), and Jo Davidson. That journey brought out the difference between an American liberal, called at home a radical, and a real radical.

Senator LaFollette was very friendly to the Russians, who liked him well, but he deplored their excesses, both in the terror and in the lengths to which they had gone to change the foundations of life and government. I heard him tell the Russians that they need not have gone so far; if they had only introduced into Russia the reforms he had carried through in Wisconsin they would have got what Wisconsin had; and he invited them to send a group or a committee to his State to learn what to do. Wisconsin! It's about the best we have to show, but the system is intact there, and his son, Senator Robert M. LaFollette Jr., still fights it, and he knows that his State has not so much to teach Russia as Russia has to teach Wisconsin. Young Bob is not a radical; he certainly is not a Russian radical, but there was a generation between him and his fine old father, and the present senator could see and learn on that journey.

But what interested me on that fascinating trip was to see that the Bolshevik government was making good, and without compromise, too. They retreated. Their so-called New Economic Policy was a backing up, but it was temporary, a step back for a moment along the line they would soon renew the advance upon. The peasants, taxed according to their production, had reduced their harvests, and the Bolsheviki, having no sense of the land problem as we know it, having no idea that they might tax the land and not the harvest, had been forced to let the peasants sell what they reaped over and above what they needed. This required the government to let private traders buy the surplus and sell at retail other things that the farmers wanted to buy or exchange. So there was free exchange and private business on a small scale—for a while. But the Bolsheviki explained that they intended later, when they were quite ready for it, to dispossess the kulaks (rich farmers) of their lands, establish and make understood the law, as it then stood, that all the land belonged to the state and that the peasants paid rent for it (not taxes). But also they proposed, next, to sweep all the peasants off their own holdings and put them to work as labor on the great Soviet farms to be managed on a grand scale by experts who would direct all operations, as in the industries, in syndicates under central control for the common good. In other words the Bolsheviki, who are socialists, who are psychologically the proletariat, intended to transform the farmers from proprietors into laborers and then solve the farm problem as a part of the labor problem. . .

What they were doing is another question, and it is important. Lenin and his successors, the Bolsheviki, were sweeping away a culture, an organization of society, which they named capitalism and hated as a failure which threw up a few rich, many poor, and all grasping, cowardly, mean. Their theory was that human nature can be, if not changed, then so cultivated and selected by economic conditions that the more desirable parts will survive, the undesirable instincts be discouraged. They were founding on the revolution, on the cleared bottom of society, a new system without any incentives to or possibilities of riches and poverty, graft, war, injustice, tyranny. They were abolishing private property and making labor the owner and governor of all things and all men. . .

The United States is making an experiment second in hopefulness only to Russia, a revelation of evolution as against revolution. Revolution has the advantage in that it clears the ground. It swept away in Russia one detected cause of what we call evil; it opened the door to such human intelligence as a few thoughtful, feeling individuals had developed to lay out consciously and carry through ruthlessly a plan so to arrange the conditions of social living and so to adjust the forces of economic life that not the cunning, grasping possessors of things but the generous, industrious producers and the brave, imaginative leaders of the race shall be the fit to survive. Russia is the land of conscious, willful hope.

But the United States of America, which the Russians recognize as their chief rival, is, however unconsciously, moving with mighty momentum on a course which seems not unlikely to carry our managing, investing, ruling masters of industry, politics, and art—by our blind method of trial and error—in the opposite direction around the world to the very same meeting-place, as they, some of them, are beginning to see and say. Our poets and muckrakers might well watch what they do, and sing or prattle the message of their acts.

8 THE ARGUMENT FOR DIPLOMATIC RELATIONS

William E. Borah (1865–1940)

In the 1920s and early 1930s, Senator William E. Borah of Idaho was one of the leading advocates of American recognition of the Soviet Union. Born in Fairfield, Illinois, he attended the University of Kansas and became one of the most successful lawyers in Idaho. First elected to the Senate in 1907, he served there until his death. After 1924, he held the influential post of Chairman of the Senate Foreign Relations Committee. A Republican, Borah strongly opposed United States entry into the League of Nations. He was widely known as an excellent speaker, as reflected in this speech made to the Senate in 1931 urging the establishment of relations with Russia.

I CAN SEE NO REAL PEACE IN EUROPE until the Russian problem is settled. It is my belief there can be no disarmament of any moment, particularly land disarmament, until Russia is brought into the family of nations and amicable relations and clear understanding with all other powers are established; that there can be no economic health or stability in Europe, or the world, so long as this gigantic power, stupendous and incalculable in her natural wealth and her man-power, is writhing and struggling to escape her thralldom; and this will last so long as she is treated as an outlaw and denied an opportunity to enjoy the ordinary methods of credit and trade. I feel that all efforts toward peace and better understanding among nations must be indefinitely retarded so long as one-sixth of the earth's surface, occupied by

83

the third largest population in the world, is estranged and afraid. . . .

I have listened over the radio to and read discussions on Russia much of late, and I have been interested in some of the reasons for inveighing against Russia; some of the arguments which are advanced as to why we should refuse to recognize Russia or to even trade with Russia. It is urged in the first place that Russia is governed by a cruel dictator, that only a few ruthless rulers hold control. Suppose that is true. . . . the people of Russia are far better off under the present government than they have ever been in their history. They are undergoing great hardships and are undoubtedly suffering greatly. But they at least have a future. . .

There can be no doubt, Mr. President, that a new life, a new existence has been given to the peasant of Russia. There can be no doubt that he is a different human being with a different outlook. They may inveigh and propagandize and falsify the facts, but the truth is, that the revolution has released the Russian people from the old, dead, hopeless past. . . .

It is also claimed that she has repudiated her debts and confiscated property. She did repudiate her debts and confiscate property. She has stood ready for eight years to pay her debts. She is willing to meet the United States at any time upon a basis of equality to compensate for the damages of confiscation if the United States will consider the damages of invasion. It is claimed also that Russia does not respect her contracts and her agreements. I have here upon my desk a list of some three or four hundred firms who have been, and still are, doing business in Russia. Has anyone heard of any violation of contract with these men? These firms have extended credit, they have made heavy contracts. Is not the very fact that they continue to do business with Russia a better evidence of Russia's keeping her contracts than the testimony of escapees and convicts and criminals . . . ?

Mr. President, the three great and, I believe, imperishable instincts of the human race are religion, family, and property— something to believe, something to love, something to possess. Let us admit that those who now govern and dominate Russia, not the people of Russia, stand against them all. We stand for them all. Let us admit that it is an irreconcilable conflict. Let us concede that those who govern Russia, not the people of Russia, would uproot and destroy them all. Let us admit that they would summon them all to the bar of public opinion and would exile them from human affairs, if they had the power. We would foster and strengthen them all. Our whole civilization is built around them. But how deep and strong is our faith? Do we fear that capitalism will fail, will cave in, if brought in contact with communism . . . ?

You can not put an embargo upon news or ideas in these days. The people do their own reading and their own thinking. I am glad it is so. The restlessness and the discontent in this country spring not at all from Russian literature or Russian teachings. We stand or fall not by what Russia does, but by what we do right here in our own country. We are slow about cleaning up our cities and making property safe and human life secure. We have failed to give work to those who are hungry and who would like to work. We have been unable to cleanse our system of corruption. We have tolerated a system which compels honest and clean business men to pay tribute to crooks and criminals for the protection which their government fails to give. These are the things which cause restlessness and discontent and discouragement among our own people. It is not Russian literature which is disturbing our people or which we need fear. It is not that which is happening in Russia nor what Russia is proposing that is bringing doubt and worry to our own people. It is the conditions here in our own land. These are the things which challenge the attention and arouse the anxiety of the American people.

Capitalism should turn its eyes inwardly and take an account of its own internal affairs. Capitalism must turn its eyes inwardly and take into consideration and solve its own internal problems. If we do not solve them, God only knows what will happen. If we do solve them, communism and all antagonistic "isms" will prove impotent in their tasks. We have in this country from five to seven million men and women unemployed, seeking something to do. What has communism to do with that, and what is our solution? There is in the capitalistic nations of the world some fifteen to sixteen million men and women unemployed. What has communism to do with that? The mechanization of modern industries has left millions of men and women in middle life, or later, to readjust their whole lives to wholly new conditions, to adapt themselves to wholly new environments. They want to know how. Capitalism has not answered. Communism has had nothing to do with that. Mass production, our boasted achievement, continues to pile up goods in the sight of those whose purchasing power is daily diminishing. What is capitalism's answer to that? And what had Communism to do with bringing on that condition? We can not answer such questions by assailing communism. We hear about a surplus of fuel, and yet we know there are millions who are unable to secure enough of this surplus to keep them from hunger and cold. What is capitalism's answer to that? Can we meet the problem by assailing communism? I am not in the least disturbed about communism of itself. I am, I confess, disturbed about the unsolved problems of capitalism, and I am almost equally disturbed over the fact that the time which we ought to devote to solving these questions and to bringing about conditions which would help to solve them, is devoted to attacking some other theory and agitating against some other government.

9 WORKING IN A RUSSIAN FACTORY

Victor G. Reuther (1912–   )

Victor G. Reuther was born in Wheeling, West Virginia, one of four brothers. He played a vital role in the history of the American labor movement. He helped his older brother Walter to organize the United Auto Workers Union, and assisted him later by becoming administrative assistant to the president of the United Auto Workers Union and assistant to the president of the CIO. During the depresssion of the 1930s, Victor and Walter traveled to the Soviet Union and worked with other foreign workers in the auto manufacturing plant at Gorky. In the following excerpt from his book *The Brothers Reuther*, Victor Reuther describes their stay in the Soviet Union and his feelings about the Russian people and the Soviet System.

––––––––––––

WE LEFT BERLIN with some relief on the evening of November 15, 1933, and stayed in Russia for almost two years, working eighteen months at the Gorky plant and for the balance of the time touring through the Ukraine and Black Sea area, Georgia, and the fabled cities, Samarkand and Tashkent. Then home via China and Japan. . .

Reaching Moscow on the seventeenth, we were struck at once by the bitter cold. Unfortunately, our heavy clothing had been checked in our footlockers, along with our cycles, and we did not see our baggage again until we reached Gorky. We had only our essential tools, a change of underclothing, and the clothes we had on—short knickers, thin wool stockings and low-cut shoes, light wool jackets. Snow everywhere and subzero temperatures kept us from doing any sightseeing. An Intourist agent transferred us to the other railway station, where we waited most of the day for our train to Gorky, along with thousands of other passengers, who were sprawled on benches or the floor, lending their animal warmth to the unheated building.

The train to Gorky was a far cry from the international train: the compartments were spartan, and there were frequent stops as we lurched our way 250 miles northeast to ancient Nizhni Novgorod on the Volga, often called the gateway to Siberia. The morning we arrived the temperature was thirty-five below. The station was full to bursting and the stench was indescribable. The peasants, many looking as lifeless as the bundles beside them, covered almost every inch of the floor. They were clad in heavy quilted clothing, the women's heads wrapped in coarse scarves, the men in great felt hats with long earflaps, and all wore pressed felt boots, called *volinkiis*. We struggled through the crowd, carrying our suitcases and heavy rucksacks, reached the information office, and pronounced the only Russian word we had learned: *avtozavod*, "auto factory." Somehow we learned how to find the street car that ran out to the Gorky plant, six miles away. . .

The settlement was known as the American Village because there were so many technicians from Detroit and other U.S. cities. It had twelve or so two-story barracks-type apartment buildings and a number of small, jerrybuilt single houses, some communal rooms, and a special store where only foreigners were allowed to shop. We were given a single room on the second floor of a barracks, a room so small that when our footlockers and bikes were delivered, we had to fasten hooks to the ceiling and hang them over our beds. There was a single-burner electric stove in an alcove, central heating, a lavatory with a cold water tap in the hall. The walls were made of sheets of plywood with six to eight inches of straw and manure packed tightly between them —an age-old kind of insulation, efficient, and also a perfect breeding-place for roaches and vermin of every variety.

About thirty technicians lived in the American Village. There was a large contingent of Finns from the American Northwest. Luckily for us, they had built a primitive sauna, and invited us

Walter Reuther (center) and his brother Victor (right) at the Gorky Auto Plant die shop, 1934.

to use it. There were some Italians who had fled from Mussolini, some British, Poles, Germans. Later Austrians would arrive, after their unsuccessful 1934 uprising. The American technicians had come for various reasons: a contractual arrangement with Ford, political idealism, or simple curiosity about a country in the initial stage of industrialization. . .

The thirties were difficult years for the Soviet Union. The cost of industrialization forced it to export an unconscionable amount of its national resources. The agricultural collectivization program was not going well, and all food and clothing were under strict rationing. Walter and I soon became aware of the privations, and though foreign workers were given a more generous allowance than the Russians, we did not feel we could take advantage of that arrangement, and surrendered our ration books to the general pool, thus providing the children of the community with a little more butter and meat than they otherwise would have had. We ate in the cooperative cafeteria instead of in the special restaurant for foreigners, where a better grade of food was offered at no higher price. Again, we did not want to abet that sort of caste discrimination. Usually there was a large bowl of *schtchi*, or cabbage soup, a big piece of moist black bread, and a cup of weak tea. Sometimes we could have a dish of kasha, buckwheat groats, with a little vegetable oil on it. One could get a glass of *kvass*, made of bread or fruit and slightly fermented. We had no butter for many months; fresh meat was an infrequent luxury, though occasionally there was some dried fish, and fresh fruits were nonexistent. Things improved by 1935 and during our last six months potatoes and vegetables were served fairly often. . .

In our foreign community, even before the big purge got underway, we saw the first flashes of the political storm that was brewing. Near the end of August, a knock on the door at midnight prefaced the arrest by the secret police of an Italian worker who had been at Gorky long enough to marry and have several children. The next day the rumor was carefully wafted around that he had been in league with the Trotskyites and would be sent to Siberia. In the tool room we had known him as a gentle, sensitive person who rarely talked politics. There was no trial, no defense.

It is hard to describe the foreboding felt by all of us in the Village, especially the Italian contingent.

The assassination of Kirov and its aftermath were even more alarming. Representing Leningrad in the Communist Party hierarchy, Kirov was the only leader with the qualities and stature to present a serious challenge to Stalin. He was a remarkable and unpretentious man who had established rapport with both intellectuals and workers. Leningraders, with a degree of elitist pride, felt themselves to be the heart and brains of the revolution, and Kirov was their great hope in Moscow—to them a backwater inhabited by country bumpkins.

After our experiences in Germany, Walter and I were not deceived when Stalin, Molotov, Beria, Khrushchev, and others hurried to Leningrad, with expressions of shock, sadness, and concern, to attribute the killing to a Trotskyist plot. Kirov was shot by a disgruntled party member named Nikolayev, and there seems to be no evidence linking him to Trotsky. But the assassination became the signal for the launching of an enormous purge by the Communist Party leadership of any possible challenge or opposition. When Khrushchev in later years began to expose the crimes of the thirties, he implied that Stalin himself had arranged for Kirov's murder.

Even in our factory, we felt the blast of the new wind when parts of Nikolayev's trial were broadcast over the public address system at every lunch break. Meetings were organized in every department to "review the evidence" and adopt resolutions calling for revenge against the traitors who were out to assassinate the leaders of the party. The lynching urge was encouraged in every factory in Russia. Anyone in the least suspect was placed on trial for conspiracy, and some workers were removed without any trial at all. Under these circumstances, political talk was taboo in the tool room, and it was only on those rare occasions when we were alone with friends on a walk through the woods or perhaps in a rowboat in the middle of the Oka that we could talk to any Russian worker about his opinion of the Stalin regime and the political oppression that was hanging like a sword over his head.

The majority of citizens in the Soviet Union had never known democracy; neither under Czarism nor Communism did they have the right of dissent, or true freedom of personal expression. Therefore, for most of them, Stalinism was at first no surprise. But as they became more literate and educated, and began to think and to analyze the political scene, they found it less easy to accept the Stalinist purge, which went on and on until it reached a crescendo of horror. There was, in fact, some question as to whether the workers were being told the whole truth by the official press. The great contribution of Nikita Khrushchev was his revelation of Stalin's intrigues and crimes. This is not to say that he replaced the Stalin years with an era of democracy. But from my own discussions, thirty years later, with workers I had known when I was at the Gorky plant, I can attest to a definite loosening of political constraint under Khrushchev. I even heard some humorous sallies at the expense of the party and the bureaucracy; in the thirties, this would have meant Siberia or worse.

Historians will probably debate for centuries whether so vast a country could have made the transition from feudalism to an industrial state without great sacrifice of individual freedom. But in the thirties, we were constantly disheartened at the price that was paid, while at the same time we were astonished at the progress manifest not only in factory production but in the rise of the standard of living.

By the time we left, young Soviet technicians, though not yet so skilled as the American toolmakers, had taken over the full responsibility of building replacement dies and designing new ones. Cars were rolling off the line in increasing numbers. Almost all the foreign workers were gone, and their special store had been abolished. Most of the essential consumer goods could be purchased in ordinary stores. What was perhaps even more gratifying was the sight of hundreds of thousands of peasants, from remote and primitive cultures, moving into the workers' flats, and enjoying, with their children, the kind of education, food, and health care they had never known before. One can measure a society by how it treats its children and its old people, and in some respects that still primitive Soviet economy seemed to do better than some of the advanced industrialized countries.

I do not mean that medical care was equal to what we could have found in Detroit, assuming we had the cash to pay for it, but at least there were health centers, crèches, kindergartens associated with every factory and collective farm. Women were freed from the isolation of the home to learn skills and receive equal recognition at work, knowing that their children were being cared for and fed. The most apolitical tourist visiting the Soviet Union in that period could not help noticing that the children seemed remarkably well nourished and happy. And none of them worked in mills or went down into dark mines.

The catch, of course, was the intensely authoritarian regime; the catch was, and evidently still is, repression, forced labor, death or imprisonment or exile, without fair trial.

10 THE EXPERIENCES OF A BLACK VISITOR

Langston Hughes (1920–1967)

One of America's most renowned black authors, Langston Hughes visited the Soviet Union during 1932–33 as part of a group invited to participate in filming a movie about black American life. Born in Joplin, Missouri, Hughes studied at Columbia University from 1921 to 1922 before traveling around the world as a seaman. Graduating from Lincoln University in 1929, he was the only black American correspondent to cover the Spanish Civil War, representing the Baltimore *Afro-American* in 1937. Among his many works is the book *I Wonder as I Wander*, which includes a description of his stay in Russia.

IN LOOKING BACK at the saga of the twenty-two American Negroes who spent their own money to go several thousand miles to make a picture with no contracts in front, and, on the other hand looking at a film concern that would bring to its studios such a group without exercising any sort of selectivity beforehand, I am amazed at the naïveté shown on both sides. But I must say there was never any temporizing regarding work or money. We arrived in Moscow ready to work, and we were promptly paid all monies due. Nevertheless, our expedition ended in an international scandal and front-page headlines around the world, with varying degrees of truth in the news stories depending on the politics of the home paper or its Moscow correspondent.

The script of the film we were to make consisted of an enormous number of pages when I first saw it—entirely in Russian! Just like my contract, it had to be translated. This took two or three weeks. Meanwhile, all of us "Negro-worker-comrades," as Muscovites called us, were almost nightly guests of one or another of the great theaters, the Moscow Art Theatre, the Vakhtangov, the Meyerhold, the Kamerm or the Opera, where we saw wonderful performances and met the distinguished actors. There was sight-seeing by day, or nude bathing in the Park of Rest and Culture on the banks of the Moscow River. Finally, after weeks of shows, parties and pleasure, I received an English version of the scenario and retired to my room in the Grande Hotel to read it.

At first I was astonished at what I read. Then I laughed until I cried. And I wasn't crying really because the script was in places so mistaken and so funny. I was crying because the writer meant well but knew so little about his subject and the result was a pathetic hodgepodge of good intentions and faulty facts. With his heart in the right place, the writer's concern for racial freedom and decency had tripped so completely on the stumps of ignorance that his work had fallen as flat as did Don Quixote's valor when good intentions led that slightly demented knight to do battle with he-knew-not-what.

Although the scenario concerned America, it was written by a famous Russian writer *who had never been in America.* At that time only a very few books about contemporary Negro life in our country had been translated into Russian. These the scenarist had studied, and from them he had put together what he thought was a highly dramatic story of labor and race relations in the United States. But the end result was a script improbable to the point of ludicrousness. It was so interwoven with major and minor impossibilities and improbabilities that it would have seemed like a burlesque on the screen. At times that night as I read, I could not keep from laughing out loud, to the astonishment of my two roommates, lying at that moment half asleep in their beds, dreaming about being movie actors. But the situation really wasn't funny when I started thinking about my companions and the others from Harlem who'd come so far to perform in a film. But, not wishing to upset them immediately, I said nothing about the absurd script, since I had no idea what position the studio might take concerning my report on it.

I simply took the scenario back to the Meschrabpom officials the next morning to tell them that, in my opinion, no plausible film could possibly be made from it since, in general, the script was so mistakenly conceived that it was beyond revision.

"It is just simply *not true* to American life," I said.

"But," they countered indignantly, "it's been approved by the Comintern."

The Comintern was, I knew, the top committee of the Communist Party concerned with international affairs.

"I'm sorry," I said, "but the Comintern must know very little about the United States."

"For example?" barked the Meschrabpom officials.

To convince them, I went through the scenario with the studio heads page by page, scene by scene, pointing out the minor nuances that were off tangent here, the major errors of factual possibility there, and in some spots the unintentional portrayal of what amounted to complete fantasy—the kind of fantasy that any European *merely* reading cursorily about the race problem in America, but knowing nothing of it at first hand, might easily conjure up. I made it clear that one could hardly blame the scenarist who had had, evidently, very meager facts available with which to work.

Having red-penciled all of the errors, I said, "Now what is left from which to make a picture?"

The Russians are in general a talkative people, very argumentative and often hard to convince. I had to go over and over it all again, not only with the first officials that day, but several other sets of officials in the studio on subsequent days. They in turn, no doubt, checked with their political higher-ups. These political higher-ups, so I heard, months later, fired about half of the studio executive staff for permitting the mistakes of the scenario to happen in the first place. Meanwhile, as the days went by, nothing was said to the cast concerning the script difficulties. I left up to the studio official announcement of its problems. So our twenty-one actors continued to enjoy the pleasures of Moscow, although most of them began to be a bit restive and a little bored. . .

Among the crowd of Russian actors and writers who greeted us at the station when we arrived in Moscow, there were also four Negroes: a very African-looking boy named Bob, a singer called Madam Arle Titz, a young man named Robinson who was a technician, and Emma Harris. Of the four, Emma is the one nobody can forget. She was a "character." Everybody in Moscow knew Emma, and Emma knew everybody. Stalin, I am sure, was aware of her presence in the capital. Emma was perhaps sixty, very dark, talkative and very much alive. She had been an actress, and wherever she was, she had the ability to hold center stage. As our train came slowly to a stop in Moscow that morning, the first person we heard on the platform was Emma.

"Bless God! Lord! I'm sure glad to see some Negroes!" she cried. "Welcome! Welcome! Welcome!"

It seemed she had been wanting to see a sizable number of Negroes for a long, long time. Emma was from Dixie, and she had been in Moscow almost forty years. Since I am always hankering to see more and more Negroes myself, right off I took a liking to Emma.

All of us on the train were glad to see her. Emma made us feel at home. For the next few weeks, while we waited for the studio to start filming, "Let's go see Emma," was the phrase heard most often among us. When we didn't go to see Emma, Emma came to see us. She was a frequent visitor at the Grand Hotel. Official guides were assigned to our group by the theatrical unions and our film studio—but what the guides did not show us, Emma could, including the after-hour spots of Moscow. As old as she was, she liked to stay up all night, and she had incredible energy. Yet, in the middle of the capital of the Workers' Republics, Emma did not work. And, although freedom of speech was felt to be lacking in the USSR, Emma said anything she wanted to say. It was Emma who first told us the joke about the man who saw a swimmer drowning in the Moscow River. The man jumped in and pulled the wretch out. When the rescued one was revived, the man asked, "Who is it that I have saved?"

The rescued answered, "Stalin."

Whereupon the man cried, "Oh, my God, how unfortunate!" and jumped into the river himself.

Emma had little use for the Soviet system as compared to Tzarist days. Nevertheless, she was a featured speaker at all of the big Scottsboro rallies then being held in Moscow on behalf of the unfortunate boys under sentence of death in faraway Alabama. Emma could make a fiery speech in Russian, denouncing American lynch law, then come off the platform and sigh, "I wish I was back home."

Emma said she was from Kentucky, but her last stopping place in the United States had been Brooklyn. She had come to Europe at the turn of the century with a theatrical troupe. In Russia she had attracted the attention of a Grand Duke, and there Emma had remained all these years, growing, as she claimed, ever more homesick for Dixie. Naturally, when the Tzar fell, the Duke fell, too. Emma was left with a mansion in Moscow. The Soviets cut up her mansion into a dozen apartments, but permitted her a sizable flat on the first floor, where she lived quite comfortably. Emma said she made her living as a translator, but I never observed her at work, never found her without the time to cook a feast, serve a drink, or talk. She had some of the best food in Moscow. Her table was the only one in Russia on which I ever saw an apple pie or, in a private home, a whole roast turkey. Yet she had only an ordinary citizen's ration card. But Emma knew all about black markets—and speak-easies. In a city where almost nothing was open after midnight, Emma could always find a place to buy a drink. One night she took me, at two A.M., to a cellar den, where vodka and brandy were only a little more expensive than at regulation cafés during legal hours. And the customers in the subrosa joint looked just like speak-easy patrons around the world. They all knew Emma and she knew them and, before dawn came, everybody got slightly bleary-eyed.

"I'm like a cat with nine lives, honey," Emma said. "I always land on my feet—been doing it all my life wherever I am. These Bolsheviks ain't gonna kill me. . ."

It was Emma who first told us that summer that there was a famine in the Ukraine where, she said, the peasants had refused to harvest the grain. Living in the Grand Hotel and eating well, or accepting Emma's black-market hospitality, I never would have known there was a hunger a few hundred miles South of Moscow. But Emma said, "Why down around Kharkov, people's so hungry they are slicing hams off each other's butts and eating them. That's no lie! A Russian I know just come from there; he told me folks is turned into cannibals."

Emma lived near one of the large Moscow railroad stations, so she met friends coming and going. She first told us about the many railroad wrecks that later that year were openly played up in the Soviet papers as an urgent problem to be remedied. Emma would say, "Man, last night there was a wreck in the depot— one train going out, another coming in, both on the same track. These thick-headed comrades don't know how to run no trains. Bang! Fifty people smashed-up-kilt in the railroad yard. Ambulances been going by my door all night long."

Not a word of these frequent catastrophies would appear as news in the Moscow papers. But sometimes journalists in a position to know confirmed Emma's tales. Since the Soviet papers concerned themselves mostly with details of the Five Year Plan or decrees on collective farming, Emma would often say, "I ain't read about a good murder in no paper here in years. And these train wrecks you *never* read about, but they sure upset my nerves. Don't you think we need a little of this here Georgia brandy?"...

Arthur Koestler asked me one day why in Moscow I did not join the Communist Party. I told him that what I had heard concerning the Party indicated that it was based on strict discipline and the acceptance of directives that I, as a writer, did not wish to accept. I did not believe political directives could be successfully applied to creative writing. They might well apply to the preparation of tracts and pamphlets, yes, but not to poetry or fiction, which to be valid, I felt, had to express as truthfully as possible the *individual* emotions and reactions of the writer, rather than mass directives issued to achieve practical and often temporary political objectives.

The train from Tashkent got to Moscow in the middle of the night, several hours late, on one of the coldest nights of the year, more than twenty below zero. There were only a few sleepy porters about and it took a long time to get all my belongings in a taxi, but at least I had no heavy records or victrola to lug. Fortunately the porter got me a taxi instead of an open *drosky* or a sleigh. I told the driver to take me to the Grand Hotel where I had asked the Writers Union in Tashkent to wire for a reservation. At the Grand the desk clerk, who recognized me, said that they had gotten no message concerning a reservation and anyway, unfortunately, were entirely filled. He suggested I try another hotel on Twerskaya. That hotel was filled, too. In desperation I decided to try the deluxe Metropol. It, too, was full.

Taxis were then very expensive in Moscow. It was getting later and later and colder and colder. The streets of the city were utterly deserted, and highways, buildings, earth and sky were white with snow. It looked as if it had been snowing all winter, and it was still snowing, delicate isinglass flakes. I decided to try the one other hotel I knew, a lush *valuta* (foreign money) hotel serving first-class tourists—although I did not intend to spend my remaining American dollars to stay there. I thought I might persuade them to permit me a night in exchange for rubles. No luck. The clerk was adamant. Twenty dollars a day, gold currency, or nothing. Meanwhile, my bags were still in the taxi outside. I said I had no foreign money. The clerk said simply, "*Nichevo!* Then try the new Moscow."

That was the big hotel across the Moscow River from the Kremlin where I knew many foreigners stayed at ruble rates—especially technicians waiting to go to their assignments in various parts of the country. But it was generally overcrowded. I asked if he would phone and see if there was a room available. He did so, and said they had rooms. I returned to my by-now-impatient taxi driver, and we went speeding off again over the hard-packed snow, through Red Square in the darkness, past Lenin's Tomb with its immobile sentinels, past the Kremlin gates with the old Mininskaya opposite, where I had lived in the summer, and over the river to the doors of the New Moscow Hotel. The clerk inside said yes, he could give me a room. So I went out and asked the taxi man to bring in my luggage.

While the desk clerk was examining my papers and permitting

me to register, the driver made three or four trips to the car for my baggage. He had just gotten it all inside the lobby when the desk clerk uttered a loud cry. From among the mass of my papers, he had just gotten down to my travel permit.

"This," he cried, "has run out!"

"What?" I said, recalling that the permit had been good for six months. I had been away from Moscow just about that long, and I had neglected to have it renewed in Central Asia.

"It expired the day before yesterday," said the desk clerk. With that he pushed all my papers back to me and crossed my name off the register.

"I can't sleep in the streets tonight," I said.

"*Nichevo*," shrugged the clerk, closing the guestbook with a bang.

"I'll have it renewed the first thing in the morning," I said.

"But you *cannot* stay here," said the clerk. "Without a valid permit, you cannot stay in any hotel." He called the taxi man to remove my baggage. The man reached for a valise.

I said, "Put my things down. I'm going to stay here."

The desk clerk said, "Take his things out. He will not stay here."

As the taxi man started toward the door with an armload of luggage, I cried in the strongest Russian I knew, "Stop! or I'll call the OGPU."*

It worked. The man dropped my bags as if he had been shot. Then I began to argue with the desk clerk again, but to no avail. He would not let me have a room. Twenty below zero outside, and I had no place to lay my head. I made, as the French say, a *scandale*. I threatened, I begged, I shouted. I called it a disgrace that a foreign visitor should be so treated in the Soviet Union. But I got no room. Meanwhile the taxi driver began to talk in a Moscow argot of which I understood nothing, but I gathered that he wanted to be paid and to leave, for which I could not blame him. I paid him his enormous price, and tipped him besides. As the desk clerk still demanded that he

---

* Then the name of the Soviet Secret Police.

should take me and my luggage with him, the taxi man disappeared in a hurry and all we heard was his motor speeding across the bridge.

I looked at the irate clerk and did not say another word. Leaving my bags piled against the wall where they were, I curled up in one of the big lobby chairs, hat and coat on, and slept until dawn. In the morning I went into the restaurant and had breakfast. And after breakfast I went to the Writers Union to see about getting my travel permit renewed. . .

I think most idealists expected too much of Russia in too short a time. The Soviet Union was then only fifteen years old. I kept thinking of what someone once said about the freed Negroes in America, "Don't try to measure the progress of the Negro by how far he has gone but rather by the distance from which he had to come." Maybe my having gone to Central Asia gave me a broader viewpoint on Soviet achievements. In Turkestan the new setup was only eight years old, dating from 1924— yet there they had already come from almost complete illiteracy to schools for *all* the children, from ancient feudal serfdom to wages and work for all, from veils and harems and marriage marts to women treated like human beings and not chattels, and from Jim Crow cars to a complete lack of segregation—all in less than a decade.

Maybe the fact that I was colored, too, made a difference. All the tourists I saw in the Soviet Union except John Hope were white. Most of the other travelers, such as the technicians and writers I saw there, were white, too. Some things irritated these people much more than they did me. Just as the dirt in Central Asia upset Koestler, so it upset me. Dirt without Jim Crow was bad—but dirt *with Jim Crow, for me*, would have been infinitely worse. In the old days, Koestler and I could not have stayed in the same hotels together in Turkestan, nor ridden in the same railway compartments. My segregated compartment would have been dirtier. As a white man before the revolution, Koestler could have ridden first-class—but not I. Koestler perhaps could not understand why I did not complain as often as he did, nor why I was not quite so impatient with the maid who refused to set our bags over the doorsill in Bokhara. Koestler had never lived as a Negro anywhere. Even with dirt, there was freedom for a Turkoman now to sit in Ashkabad's dusty park and not see the old signs FOR EUROPEANS ONLY that formerly kept him out. Even with eternal grime and continued famines, racial freedom was sweeter than the lack of it. To Grasdani, such freedom in Asia meant only tin cans in the toilets and dark guests in the best hotels. But to Nichan it was education and football and *his* brown statue over a new stadium.

11 RECOGNITION BROUGHT FEW RETURNS

Cordell Hull (1871–1955)

As Secretary of State in 1933—when the United States reestablished diplomatic relations with Russia—Cordell Hull was deeply involved in formulating United States policy toward the Soviet Union. A native of Overton County, Tennessee, he graduated from the Cumberland University Law School in 1891. After practicing law and serving as a judge, in 1907 he was elected as a Democrat to the House of Representatives, of which he was a member from 1907 to 1921 and again from 1923 to 1931. Elected to the Senate in 1931, he resigned two years later to assume the post of Secretary of State in Franklin D. Roosevelt's first administration. In the *Memoirs of Cordell Hull* (1948), Hull described the manner in which American recognition of Russia was decided in 1933, and the subsequent failure of relations to improve to the extent that had been anticipated.

IN A RIGHT-HAND DRAWER of my desk, letters began gathering from my first day in office, requesting us to—or not to—recognize Soviet Russia and establish diplomatic relations with her. For sixteen years we had had no formal ties with Moscow. The new Administration was confronted with a question that had many ramifications both at home and abroad.

I kept these letters close at hand because I felt that the subject itself was close at hand. I was receiving delegations from various organizations presenting compelling reasons why Russia should —or should not—be recognized. Many ambassadors and ministers, whose countries' policy might be determined by our action, questioned me on our intentions. The matter was under discussion in Congress. Previous Administrations had had it under consideration—but decided against it. . .

We had rich food for debate. The Communist International, under direction from Moscow, was spreading communistic propaganda in the United States, seeking to overthrow the Government. Soviet Russia had refused to honor debts incurred by the Czarist Government to the United States Government and American citizens. Foreign citizens in Russia had been thrown into jail on slight pretext. Religious freedom was denied. Other large nations, among them Britain, France, Germany, and Italy, had recognized Russia, but their relations with Moscow had not been wholly happy.

Certain conditions were arising, however, which were not fully present under previous Administrations. Russia, emerging from her seclusion showed signs of willingness to cooperate with the Western Powers. She attended the Disarmament Conference at Geneva, beginning in February, 1932. Her relations with Japan were strained, and it was simultaneously apparent to us both that Japan was on the highroad to conquest and aggrandizement. Russia indirectly indicated to us on numerous occasions that she desired a restoration of diplomatic relations between us. She badly needed American credits to assist in her industrial revolution. She had established a trading organization in New York and had an informal representative in Washington. . .

In some respects we stood to gain more than Russia by a restoration of diplomatic relations. Without relations, the Russians were probably much better informed about conditions in America than we were about the situation in Russia. The Soviets were in close touch with what was going on here through their Amtorg, or trading office, in New York, an Information Bureau in Washington, and the American Communist Party. . .

Moreover, it was easier for Russians to do business in the United States without diplomatic protection than it was for Americans to do business in Russia. With few American citizens and

no diplomatic officials to consult in Russia, the American businessman yielded too readily to Soviet demands. . .

William C. Bullitt, an intimate friend of the President and my
special assistant, was in close touch with the Soviet representatives here. A brilliant person, well versed in international affairs,
he was particularly friendly toward Russia and was an ardent
proponent of recognition. He so expressed himself to the President and to me. . .

During a visit I made to the President . . . he casually picked
up a sheaf of papers from his desk and handed them to me.
"These are letters and petitions, pro and con, on recognition of
Russia," he said. "Will you look them over and any others you
have and give me your opinion on what we should do?"

I did not tell him that my opinion was already virtually formed.
I took the papers and returned to the State Department. There
I completed examination of the great mass of material I had on
the same subject. A couple of days later I went back to the
President.

"I favor recognizing Russia," I said, "although our correspondence reveals that great numbers of people are opposed to it.
Russia and we had been traditional friends up to the end of the
World War. In general, Russia has been peacefully inclined. The
world is moving into a dangerous period both in Europe and in
Asia. Russia could be a great help in stabilizing this situation as
time goes on and peace becomes more and more threatened."

The President, without a moment's hesitation, replied, "I agree
entirely." He then added: "Two great nations like America and
Russia should be on speaking terms. It will be beneficial to both
countries to resume diplomatic relations. . ."

Litvinov was due to arrive November 7. The day before his
arrival, I met with the President, Secretary of the Treasury
Henry Morgenthau, Under Secretary of State Phillips, and William Bullitt in the White House. We went over the subjects to be
discussed with Litvinov, and agreed that the two most important
were precautions against Soviet propaganda and illegal activities
in the United States and freedom of worship for Americans in
Russia. . .

Our conversations gave promise of leading to results. Litvinov

Diplomatic ties—Maxim Litvinov (left) the first Soviet Ambassador to the United States, with Secretary of State Cordell Hull, 1933.

and I reached specific agreements to the entire satisfaction of this Government on religious protection in Russia and discontinuance of propaganda here by all Soviet agencies. I had made it perfectly plain to Litvinov that, unless he agreed to straighten out the differences existing between us, there would be no recognition and no diplomatic relations, and of course no loan or credits. . .

The discussions between the President and Litvinov on debt settlement had failed to reach an agreement, hence this was the first important subject I took up with the Ambassador. On our part we were ready to extend credits to the Soviet Union. An Export-Import Bank of Washington was incorporated on February 12 for this purpose, with a capital of $11,000,000. But it was soon evident that Russia was not equally ready to settle her debts. The conversations between the President and Litvinov had narrowed the debts down to between $75,000,000 and $150,000,-000, and Litvinov said his Government might be willing to pay as much as $100,000,000. It now developed, however, that there was a complete disagreement on the subject of interest on the debts, which had already run for twenty years. We wanted the interest paid; the Soviets wanted to ignore it. . .

An unbreakable deadlock ensued, despite months of patient negotiation. The Soviet Government knew that payment of its indebtedness was unpopular in Russia but had hoped to offset this unpopularity by the credits it would obtain here. No credits were forthcoming, and no agreement could be reached on the payment of interest on the Soviet debt. Hence the Soviets were never to make a debt payment, and the Export-Import Bank was never to function with regard to Russia. The Soviet Union was actually in a worse position than other countries. Private corporations and banks of other nations in default could obtain credits in the United States, but all corporations and banks in Russia were government-owned.

The effect on our relations with Russia was unfortunate. Instead of the friendship I expected, a large number of points of friction and suspicion developed in the years to follow. The beneficial influence I had expected Russo-American cooperation to have on the political situation both in Europe and in Asia did not materialize. I argued again and again with Soviet ambassadors that it was disastrous to let the comparatively small sum of Soviet indebtedness and other modest differences stand in the way of our thoroughgoing political relations. I pleaded with them again and again that if only the United States, Russia, Britain, and France could present a common moral front to the aggressor nations, Germany, Japan, and Italy, war might be prevented. I warned them again and again of the dangers threatening us all. But a common front did not come until long after war had begun.

In September, 1934, Russia joined the League of Nations, and in December Litvinov proposed to the President and me, through the Soviet Embassy, that the United States join with him in a project for a permanent disarmament organization to sit at Geneva. His point was that the Kellogg Antiwar Pact of 1928 provided no machinery for consultation in the event it were violated, and that such an agency as he proposed could provide such machinery, and could offer the United States, not a member of the League of Nations, a place in which to present her views. But the political implications were such that the isolationist sentiment in America would have been aroused. I regretfully had to tell him, No.

I still hoped that something might be salvaged in the way of increased trade between the two countries. After the Trade Agreements Act was enacted June 12, 1934, and trade agreements began to be concluded with a series of nations, I had to decide whether to extend the tariff reductions, under most-favored-nation treatment, to the Soviet Union, which exercised a government monopoly of foreign trade. There was no such thing as freedom of trade in Russia.

Desirous of doing everything possible to better our relations, I agreed in July, 1935, that Russia should enjoy the benefits of our tariff reductions granted to other nations. In exchange Russia agreed to purchase $30,000,000 worth of American products during the next twelve months, compared to the three-year average of $12,000,000 annually.

But our efforts toward closer relations were again to be negated. The Communist International, with headquarters in Moscow, continued to support Communist propaganda and activities in the United States. We made verbal complaints to Moscow, without result. Finally Russia permitted the holding of an All-World Congress of the Communist International in Moscow from July 25 to August 20, 1935. American Communists attended and took part in discussions and plans for the development of the Communist Party in the United States. Here was a flagrant violation of the pledge of noninterference given us on November 16, 1933, and we could not let it pass without protest. By agreement with the President, I sent through Ambassador Bullitt a strong note to the Soviet Government. . .

We were now back almost to where we had started. We had official relations with Moscow, but they rested on no bedrock of friendship and cooperation. Try as I might, I could not establish the sound relationship I deemed so necessary not only for the two countries but also as a counterweight for peace in the scales tipping more sharply toward war.

As long as I was in the State Department, however, I was never to relinquish efforts to promote two-way friendly relations with Russia. I did not abandon my original idea that Russia and the United States, especially after the agreements reached at the time of recognition, had no conflicting national aims, and that the two countries, working together and in harmony with other countries opposed to war, could have a beneficial influence on the world. I recalled the fact that, especially since our Civil War, Russia and the United States had enjoyed thoroughly friendly relations, without interruption, and also that Soviet Russia, at the time of our recognition, was pursuing a strong disarmament and peace policy as a member of the Disarmament Conference at Geneva.

But I knew that much time and more patience would be required. Russia had not yet forgotten that the nations of the West had strenuously opposed the Bolshevik Revolution. She remembered that, when the war ended, the troops of the Allies remained on her territory for many months thereafter. Long isolated in her northern snows, she did not have the knack of dealing with other nations on a basis of understanding, friendliness, and freedom from suspicion. The efforts of the Comintern to overthrow other governments and the fact that Stalin in effect controlled both the Comintern and the Soviet Government—however much his Government sought to make it appear that there was no connection between the two—doubled our difficulties in dealing with Moscow.

No nation has the right to send money and organizations into a country to undermine and overthrow its government. Every nation has the right to preach its ideas anywhere in the world and to convey information regarding its government and the basic ideas underlying it to other peoples or countries; but those peoples or countries must have the chance to decide independently on their own form of government. This doctrine applies to all nations as well as to Russia.

During the years following our recognition, Russia did not pursue a stable course based on fundamental policies. The comparatively new Soviet regime seemed at this stage not to have settled on a solid, permanent, straightforward course in the conduct of its foreign policies. We noticed a careless or indifferent observance by the Soviet Government of some of the agreements and understandings our two Governments had entered into. There was a disposition to haggle over little things and to debate seriously and interminably over wholly minor matters which developed numerous pinpricks. Some questions of major importance were also to arise on which Russia's attitude was difficult to understand.

Negotiating with Russia, therefore, was not like negotiating with other great powers. In every approach to Moscow I had to bear these facts in mind.

12 HOW TO HANDLE THE RUSSIANS

William C. Bullitt (1891–1967)

William C. Bullitt was born into a prominent Philadelphia family. A journalist by profession, he had the distinction of being appointed the first American Ambassador to the Soviet Union following the reestablishment of diplomatic relations in 1933. A graduate of Yale (1912) and of the Harvard Law School two years later, Bullitt served as Washington correspondent for the *Philadelphia Public Ledger* before entering government service following the outbreak of World War I. He was a member of the American delegation to the Versailles Peace Conference in 1918–19 and was sent by President Wilson as head of a special mission to look into matters in the Soviet Union in 1919. Bullitt met with Lenin and other Soviet leaders during his visit and came back relatively sympathetic to the new Russian regime.

Although his recommendations for closer American ties with the Soviet Union were not implemented by Wilson, Bullitt continued to favor establishing diplomatic relations with Moscow. He was instrumental in getting the Roosevelt administration to set up such relations in 1933. Serving as ambassador in Russia from 1933 to 1936, however, he rapidly became disillusioned with the Soviets. The following observations were made in a cable he sent to the State Department in April 1936. Bullitt, who subsequently served as Ambassador to France from 1936 to 1941, became even more opposed to the Soviet system in the late 1930s and 1940s.

TODAY STALIN CONSIDERS IT SOUND STRATEGY to support democratic forms of government in countries in which communism is still weak; but the meaning of that support was displayed by Dimitrov at the Comintern Congress in August, 1935, when he pointed out that at the moment the cause of communism could be promoted best by use of the tactics of the Trojan horse and warned his communist comrades that they were not good communists if they felt that it was indecent or unduly hypocritical to become the collaborators and pretended friends of democrats in order the better eventually to lead those democrats to the firing squad.

The problem of relations with the Government of the Soviet Union is, therefore, a subordinate part of the problem presented by communism as a militant faith determined to produce world revolution and the "liquidation", (that is to say, murder), of all non-believers.

There is no doubt whatsoever that all orthodox communist parties in all countries, including the United States, believe in mass murder. Moreover, the loyalty of a believing communist is not to the nation of which he is technically a citizen but to his faith and to the Caliph of that faith. To such men the most traitorous betrayals are the highest virtues.

In the history of the human race many nations have had to deal with citizens whose loyalty lay beyond the boundaries of their native land. To deal with such men by means of secret police and firing squads is traditional. But to deal with them while preserving the liberties which have been gained so painfully by western peoples since the Middle Ages is extraordinarily difficult. To adopt the methods of the Nazis is to sacrifice the freedom from fear of the State which is among the most precious conquests of civilization, and to slay our heritage in attempting to defend it.

Yet it must be recognized that communists are agents of a foreign power whose aim is not only to destroy the institutions and liberties of our country, but also to kill millions of Americans. Our relations with the Soviet Union, therefore, involve questions of domestic policy which can not be answered except on the basis of a careful estimate of the strength of world communism and the reality or unreality of its threat to our liberties and lives.

Moreover, the time is not distant when the Soviet Union will become a dangerous factor in the field of international trade. The Soviet Government has not the slightest intention of abandoning its monopoly of foreign trade. It is attempting to make itself as self-sufficient as possible and it will use its monopoly of trade ruthlessly to undersell and injure its enemies and to assist its friends. It will not, in good faith, enter into any international agreements which have as their object improvement of the general economic condition of the world. It will, on the contrary, try to produce as much chaos as possible in the economies of capitalist countries in the hope that misery may beget communist revolution.

The standard of living in the Soviet Union is still extraordinarily low, lower perhaps than that of any European country, including the Balkans. Nevertheless, the townsfolk of the Soviet Union have today a sense of well-being. They have suffered so horribly since 1914 from war, revolution, civil war, and famine that to have enough bread to eat, as they have today, seems almost a miracle. Moreover, in each of the past three years, the quantity and variety of their food has increased and many varieties of merchandise which have been missing from Russia for years are now making their appearance in the shops.

The condition of the peasants has been but little improved; indeed, physically it seems to be worse than their condition in 1914. There are, of course, certain showplaces: highly successful and well organized *kolkhozes** and *sovkhozes.*** But the peasants have not yet adjusted themselves to the system by which the leaders of the Soviet Union hope to "proletarianize" them. Moreover, all that is being done to improve conditions in the cities, to build up industries, communication and the war machine, is being done at the expense of the peasants. Eighty-one percent of the revenues of the Soviet Government in 1935 were taken from the peasants by the simple means of keeping the price paid them for their products atrociously low—the Government taking the resulting profit on sales. Nevertheless, the land itself is rich,

* collective farms
** state farms

the peasants have been given some education and have been encouraged to develop an interest in sports; and among the young, at least, there is hope. . .

Russia has always been a police state. It is a police state today. The authority of the Kremlin rests on the strength of its army and the omnipresence of its secret police, no less than on the fervor of the convinced communists.

The secret police and the army are better fed, housed, and entertained than any other portion of the population. Their loyalty to the Soviet regime is unquestionable. And there is no longer reasonable doubt as to the strength of the Red Army. It numbers today nearly a million and a half men. Its material equipment in artillery, airplanes, and tanks is abundant in quantity though deficient in quality. It cannot undertake offensive operations due to the fact that the railroads are still inadequate for the peace time needs of the country and to the equally important fact that there are literally no modern highways in the entire Soviet Union. But on the defensive, the Red Army would fight hard, well and long.

The only actual threat to the Soviet Union is the Japanese. All Litvinov's propaganda trumpetings to the contrary, the Soviet Government knows very well that Germany can not be in a position to make war on the Soviet Union for many years. Every feasible route for German attack leads across Polish territory and the whole basis of Polish policy is never to permit the foot of either a German or a Russian soldier to be placed on her soil.

The Japanese threat is actual. But the Japanese have so bungled their relations with the Mongols, and the strength of the Soviet Far Eastern Army has increased so fast, that the Russians today are confident that a Japanese attack would end in destruction of the Japanese Army.

The single real fear of the communists is that their bureaucratic machine might break down under the strain of war. Dread of the Kremlin is so great that all Russian officials, except the highest, hesitate or refuse to make decisions. The life of the entire Soviet Union might well be clogged hopelessly in time of war by unsigned papers.

The chief weakness of the Soviet State today is, indeed, the inefficiency of the bureaucracy. The communist form of State requires a bureaucracy of exceptional ability. The Russians have always been and are bad bureaucrats. In consequence, extraordinary numbers of Jews are employed in all the Commissariats. Only one out of each sixty-one inhabitants of the Soviet Union is a Jew; but twenty of the sixty-one Commissars and Vice-Commissars are Jews. . .

What then should be the policy of the United States with regard to the Soviet Government and the world communist movement?

We would not cherish for a moment the illusion that it is possible to establish really friendly relations with the Soviet Government or with any communist party or communist individual.

We should maintain diplomatic relations with the Soviet Union because it is now one of the Greatest Powers and its relations with Europe, China, and Japan are so important that we can not conduct our foreign relations intelligently if we do not know what is happening in Moscow. Moreover, in spite of all efforts to conceal the truth from foreigners, it is possible to obtain in Moscow considerable information as to the Soviet Union and the world communist movement.

We should use our influence quietly to oppose war in the Far East between the Soviet Union and Japan not only because of our moral opposition to war but also because, if there is a war, someone may win it. In case the Soviet Union should win, a Communist China would be inevitable. In case Japan should win, China would be completely subjected to Japan. If war comes between Japan and the Soviet Union, we should not intervene but should use our influence and power toward the end of the war to see to it that it ends without victory, that the balance between the Soviet Union and Japan in the Far East is not destroyed, and that China continues to have at least some opportunity for independent development.

We should instruct our diplomatic representatives in Europe to use all opportunities in personal conversations to point out the danger to Europe of the continuation of Franco-German enmity and to encourage reconciliation between France and Germany.

We should attempt to promote our trade with the Soviet Union by direct bargaining of the sort involved in our agreement of July 13, 1935. But we should have no illusion that our trade with the Soviet Union may ever be stable or permanent. It may be cut off for political reasons at any minute. Therefore, we should not make loans or give long-term credits to the Soviet Union and should advise American industrialists against putting in expensive machinery to produce for the Soviet market.

We should realize that with every year that passes the products of the Soviet Union and the United States will become less complementary and more competitive. Soviet oil and grain will compete increasingly with our oil and grain. The Russian market for our cotton will decrease as the new Soviet cotton plantations increase their productivity. The market for our machines may increase until Russian industry improves in quality and productivity and is able to produce complicated machines of the highest quality. For a few years we may be able to sell the Soviet Union more than we buy from her but in the long run a fairly even balance of trade will be insisted on by the communists, and if we are not ready to buy more than today we shall not be able to sell so much as we sell today.

Our Federal Government should inform itself as to the membership of the Communist Party in the United States and as to the relations between the American communists, the Soviet Diplomatic and Consular Representatives, and the other agents of the Soviet Government and the Communist Party in the United States. . .

The keynote of our immediate relations with the Soviet Union should be patience. The communist movement in the United States today constitutes a potential danger but not an actual threat. We do not need to get excited about it. Our political relations with the Soviet Union are negative; but our trade is increasing. It is difficult to conduct conversations with the Soviet Foreign Office because in that institution the lie is normal and the truth abnormal and one's intelligence is insulted by the happy assumption that one believes the lie. But patience and diplomats exist for just that sort of difficulty.

We should neither expect too much nor despair of getting anything at all. We should be as steady in our attitude as the Soviet

Union is fickle. We should take what we can get when the atmosphere is favorable and do our best to hold on to it when the wind blows the other way. We should remain unimpressed in the face of expansive professions of friendliness and unperturbed in the face of slights and underhand opposition. We should make the weight of our influence felt steadily over a long period of time in the directions which best suit our interests. We should never threaten. We should act and allow the Bolsheviks to draw their own conclusions as to the causes of our acts.

Above all, we should guard the reputation of Americans for businesslike efficiency, sincerity, and straightforwardness. We should never send a spy to the Soviet Union. There is no weapon at once so disarming and effective in relations with the communists as sheer honesty. They know very little about it.

13 SOVIET PERSECUTION OF LEON TROTSKY

John Dewey (1859–1952)

Because of his untarnished reputation as one of America's most outstanding educators and philosophers, John Dewey was asked in 1937 to head a committee looking into the validity of the charges the Soviet Union had made against Leon Trotsky. Trotsky, one-time Soviet Commissar (Minister) for Foreign Affairs and subsequently Soviet Commissar for War, was exiled from the Soviet Union in 1929 after losing a bid for the leadership of Russia to Josef Stalin.

Born in Burlington, Vermont, Dewey graduated from the University of Vermont and received a Ph.D. from Johns Hopkins University in 1884. After serving as professor of philosophy at the University of Minnesota, he became associated with the Columbia University School of Education in 1904. By the time he was asked to head the commission looking into the charges against Trotsky during the Moscow purge trials, Dewey had long since become internationally famous as the founder of progressive education in the United States and as a leading proponent of the school of philosophy known as pragmatism.

The falsity of the accusations made against Trotsky by Stalin—that Trotsky had plotted to betray the Soviet Union to Germany and Japan—was strongly implied by Dewey in the comments he made to a meeting held under the auspices of the American Committee for the Defense of Trotsky in New York City on May 9, 1937. Dewey's commission subsequently concluded that Trotsky was innocent of the crimes of which he had been accused in the Moscow trials. On August 20, 1940, Trotsky was assassinated at his place of exile in Mexico by a man strongly believed to have been in the employ of the Soviet secret police.

THE PUBLIC RECORD OF TROTSKY extending over a long period of years stands in striking contrast to the charges upon which he was convicted of plotting terrorism, assassination, industrial sabotage, wholesale wrecking, and selling out the U.S.S.R. to Hitler, Nazi Germany, and Imperial Japan. The official reports of the Moscow trials show the absence of cross-examination upon every vital point as well as many gaps, inconsistencies and contradictions. . .

There are many liberals, free from partisan commitments, who are supporting the Defense Committee and the Commission of Inquiry. There are, however, other liberals who have been, to say the least, luke-warm about the inquiry. They take the stand that in any case the U.S.S.R. is the one workers' republic in the whole world; the one successful attempt of all history to build a Socialist society. Even though not themselves Communist, they want the experiment which is going on in Russia to have a fair chance. They do not want its course made harder than it is. I can understand this attitude. It has been and is my own. But there is something more than this at work to move genuine liberals to become indifferent and even opposed to an inquiry into the truth of the charges upon which Trotsky was convicted.

As far as I can make out, the reason they take the attitude which they have assumed is that they believe that Trotsky's theories and policies are mistaken and that, in contrast, those which are controlling the U.S.S.R. are correct. Many of the liberals to whom I am referring are honest in this attitude. Hence they deserve a consideration which cannot be claimed by those blind and bitter partisans who stoop to any means to prevent knowledge of the truth from being brought to light. Nevertheless, while these persons are honest in their intentions, they suffer from the intellectual and moral confusion that is the great weakness of professed liberals. For Trotsky was not convicted upon charges of theoretical and political opposition to the regime which exists in the Soviet Union. He was convicted upon certain definite charges whose truth or falsity is a matter of objective fact.

Leon Trotsky's record of opposition to the present rulers of the Soviet Union is public, beyond dispute. For a long series of years, he has been an open and often bitter foe of the present regime, claiming that it is a bureaucracy engaged in betraying the revolution of 1917. His position on this point is displayed in hundreds of articles and scores of books and pamphlets. The correctness or incorrectness of his position in this respect is in no way the matter at issue for it is not that upon which he was convicted. He was convicted, in his absence, upon charges of conspiring to effect the assassination of all the leaders of the Communist Party and the Government of the Soviet Union; of plotting with the enemies of the country for betraying it to them both before and during a projected war; of planning to dismember the Soviet Union by making over to Germany and Japan important territories, huge concessions of mines, forest and trade privileges. He was convicted of doing all of these things in order, according to the official records, to destroy socialism and restore capitalism and all for the contemptible object that he and his followers might come to political power.

These are the charges upon which Leon Trotsky was convicted. These are the matters upon which he demanded his hearing. These are the matters the Commission of Inquiry has been investigating and is going to investigate until the end.

In the cases of Tom Mooney in San Francisco and Sacco-Vanzetti in Boston, we got used to hearing reactionaries say that these men were dangerous nuisances anyway, so that it was better to put them out of the way whether or not they were guilty of the things for which they were tried. I never thought I would live to see the day when professed liberals would resort to a similar argument. I am confident that it is not too late to appeal to some, at least, of these liberals, to join the hundreds of other liberals in the inquiry which is attempting to get at facts fairly and squarely. To hold Trotsky guilty of the specific charges upon which he was convicted because of his well-known opposition to the present rulers of the U.S.S.R. is not fair or square. It is even less so because his public record is that of unswerving, constant appeal for support of the Socialist revolution and the Socialist U.S.S.R. When confusion of two entirely different matters is manifested by professed liberals, it marks an intellectual shirking that is close to intellectual dishonesty. More than that, it is treachery to the very cause of liberalism. For if liberalism means anything, it means complete and courageous devotion to freedom of inquiry. . .

The intellectual level of American liberalism has fallen pretty low if it can accept this as an example of logical reasoning. Has it fallen so low? I don't think it has.

The Commission of Inquiry, I repeat, is not trying to discover who is right and who is wrong in their political ideas and policies, the "Trotskyites" or their opponents. It is engaged in trying to get at the truth as to the specific charges upon which Trotsky was convicted in the Moscow trials. This work is one of evidence and objective fact, not of weighing theories against each other. Either Leon Trotsky is guilty of plotting wholesale assassination, systematic wreckage with destruction of life and property; of treason of the basest sort in conspiring with political and economic enemies of the U.S.S.R. in order to destroy Socialism; or he is innocent. If he is guilty, no condemnation can be too severe. If he is innocent, there is no way in which the existing regime in Soviet Russia can be acquitted of deliberate, systematic persecution and falsification. These are unpleasant alternatives for those to face who are sympathetic with the efforts to build a Socialist State in Russia. The easier and lazier course is to avoid facing the alternatives. But unwillingness to face the unpleasant is the standing weakness of liberals. They are only too likely to be brave when affairs are going smoothly and then to shirk when unpleasant conditions demand decision and action. I cannot believe that a single genuine liberal would, if he once faced the alternatives, hold that persecution and falsification are a sound basis upon which to build an enduring Socialist society.

A little over two weeks ago, when the investigation in Mexico was only just concluded, when the sub-commission had made no report, Ambassador Troyanovsky met the National Press Club in Washington. He informed the newspapermen that the hearings in Mexico were a "flop," that the members of the Commission were prejudiced in favor of Trotsky and had only one aim: "to rehabilitate him." I might inquire if the Ambassador thought our hearings were a put-up job, why such pressure was brought to bear upon members of the Defense Committee and of the Commission of Inquiry to induce them to resign? Perhaps, however, it is more to the point that he continued the effort to confuse and mislead public opinion by quoting from Trotsky a statement of the latter's vigorous opposition to the Stalin regime in the Soviet Union—a passage that could be multiplied many times over from Mr. Trotsky's public statements. I am not surprised that Ambassador Troyanovsky should thus attempt to becloud the issue. It seems to be part of his official job. I am surprised when liberals permit their eyes to be blinded by the smokescreens so deliberately emitted.

Toward the close of his speech, Ambassador Troyanovsky, who by the way, was invited along with the Communist Party of the U.S., to send a representative to the hearings in Mexico City, uttered the following words: "I wish all of you not to be too cautious and too skeptical in recognition of the contemporary situation." Since the "contemporary situation" to which he devoted his speech was the case of Mr. Trotsky he thereby virtually invited the American public to be incautious and credulous in accepting his and Moscow's version of events. It is natural that Ambassador Troyanovsky should feel that way about the attitude he would like the American public to take. This is his great and perhaps his only hope. I am rather surprised that he should expose his hand so openly. For while we are not all from Missouri, most American citizens are close enough to its border to want to be shown when elementary human decency, justice and historic truth are at stake. We are here tonight to state that we propose to be just as "cautious and skeptical" in obtaining and weighing evidence as all searchers and fighters for truth have the right to expect and demand us to be.

We, members of the Defense Committee and of the Inquiry alike, do not suppose for a moment that we are alone in holding that friendship for truth comes before friendship for individuals and factions. We do not for a moment imagine that we possess a monopoly of will for truth. Consequently we feel confident that, as the investigation continues and more and more truth comes to light, countless others will be inspired to join actively in its pursuit. We are committed to one end and one end only: discovery of the truth as far as that is humanly possible. Lines are being drawn between devotion to justice and adherence to a faction, between fair play and a love of darkness that is reactionary in effect no matter what banner it flaunts.

It is in the name of justice and truth as the end that we ask for your support. We go on in confidence that we shall have it. As Zola said in the Dreyfus case: "Truth is on the march and nothing will stop it."

14 A COMMUNIST'S PRAISE OF RUSSIA

Earl Browder (1891–1973)

Earl Browder was General Secretary of the Communist Party of the United States from 1930 to 1944, and as such one of the most vocal defenders of the Soviet Union. Born in Wichita, Kansas, he became associated with radical causes as a young man and opposed American involvement in World War I. An early member of the Communist Party of the United States, he was twice its candidate for the presidency, running against Roosevelt in 1936 and 1940. Browder strongly urged American cooperation with Russia in a "United Front" to oppose fascism, only to be stunned by the Nazi-Soviet Pact in 1939. In 1944 Browder proposed the dissolution of the Communist Party and advised cooperation with the Roosevelt administration. In the Party in-fighting that followed, he was removed from positions of leadership, finally being ousted from the Party in 1946. The following eulogy on the Soviet system comes from a speech he delivered on October 10, 1937, to a convention of the Communist Party of Canada in Toronto and was reprinted in his book *The People's Front* (1938).

IN THE YEARS 1776 TO 1787, the United States won its independence as a nation, and fashioned a stable state power, within which the only serious obstacle to unfettered capitalist development was the compromise with slavery. The bourgeois-democratic revolution was completed, in its most essential aspects, by the Civil War of 1861–65, and the consequent abolition of slavery.

Canada won essentially the same level of historical development in the struggles of 1837.

In the tsarist empire, however, the enemy was much more stubborn and powerful. Although the same democratic forces were at work there, they could not break through; they were defeated again and again. The development of capitalism sapped and undermined the foundations of the old order; but at each period of crisis the feudal autocracy emerged triumphant through a combination of extreme repression, concessions and foreign alliances. The result for Russia was an extremely backward and distorted economic development, and the almost complete post-ponement of the democratic revolution until the twentieth century, when it merged with the socialist revolution.

Thus it was, in brief, that these two great sections of humanity, Russia and North America, so similarly equipped in natural resources and population, came to the world crisis of 1914–1918 at the opposite poles of economic and political development. Russia was the most backward in every important respect; North America was the most advanced. Russia emerged from the World War with an economy shattered and prostrate, racked by famine, its old political superstructure broken and scattered to the four winds, its new infant system, Soviet power, fighting against a hostile world with its back to the wall, and spoken of deprecatingly even by its friends as an "experiment." North America emerged from the World War with an enormously strengthened economy, the world's banker, holding the debts of the other powers, and with, at least for a time, predominant prestige and influence in world politics.

What a contrast this was! Every philistine, every shallow thinker and vulgarian, could and did tell the world that North America was the promised land, that it had found the way to "permanent prosperity," that with the "American system" poverty was being abolished and the millennium ushered in. Henry Ford and the belt-line system of mass production were the new God. And with God in his heaven, all was right with the capitalist world. As for that curious and disreputable "experiment," Soviet Russia, everyone knew that it was prostrate and starving. Lenin was announcing the New Economic Policy and offering concessions to foreign capitalists; soon Russia would be safely back in the capitalist family, as the poor relation, tending the kitchen and doing the dirty work. Herbert Hoover contemptuously sent over the American Relief Administration, with some superfluous war-stores of wheat, expecting the 140,000,000 Russians to follow this wisp of straw obediently back into the capitalist harness. For all sensible people, the issue was settled. North America owned and led the world! Soviet Russia was a starving beggar at the doorstep! Such was the appearance in the early 1920's.

Today we call for an accounting of what has been done with this inheritance by North America, which inherited half the world's wealth and its leadership, and by Soviet Russia, which inherited ruin and starvation. The day of reckoning is here. To deal with the results of this reckoning, we are tempted to turn to some of the old Hebrew prophets, who celebrated the humiliation of the mighty and exaltation of the humble. Only the passionate words of an Isaiah could celebrate worthily the emergence of that "hungry beggar" of the 1920's, as the "proud builder," who not only restored completely his ruined inheritance, but multiplied it five times over in the past ten years; or find scorn bitter enough to describe how the proud and mighty have squandered their inheritance and cast their people into the desolation of unemployment, labor camps, a declining standard of living and the threat of fascist destruction of civilization. . .

During this same period of the humiliation of once proud America, the starving beggar, as our arrogant American capitalists considered Soviet Russia, emerged as the most rapidly progressing land in all fields—economically, politically, culturally —ever recorded in the history of mankind. Surrounded by a hostile world, with nothing other than its natural resources *and its superior system of social organization*, the Soviet Union restored its wrecked economy, proceeded to multiply its wealth production to thirteen times that of the early 1920's, and more than four times that of 1929, advanced from last place in Europe to the first, and is now engaged in a race to catch up with and surpass the United States. The rate of growth of Soviet economy is five or six times that of the United States in its period of most rapid expansion.

In the period when the American standard of living fell on the average by 50 per cent, the standard of living in the Soviet Union was raised by 400 per cent. While America was throwing 13,000,000 workers onto the streets, unemployed, of whom seven or eight million are still dependent upon the relief dole, the Soviet Union was not only abolishing all unemployment, but doubling the size of the industrial working class by absorbing peasants into the factories. While American agriculture was saved from destruction only by gigantic subsidies, paying for the curtailment and destruction of crops and cattle, Soviet agriculture had been reorganized on a collective, socialist, basis and doubled its production, with an increase of living standards on the countryside of immeasurable proportions—bringing a life of culture and security to the agrarian population for the first time in human history.

Above all, at a moment when democracy and culture are destroyed in half of Europe by the barbarian hordes of fascism; when they fight for their life in the rest of Europe; when China, the greatest country of Asia, fights against odds for its very existence; when democracy is under fire and threatened even in North America—at this moment, Russia, so recently the synonym of backwardness, steps forward with its new Constitution, shaped under the guiding hand of Stalin, a Constitution which is a new high mark in the achievement of democracy, such as in the past only a few great spirits could dream of, but which now comes to life in the everyday activities of 170,000,000 people.

The Constitution of the United States was for generations the most democratic in the world. But compare it with that of the Soviet Union.

The United States Constitution tolerated for generations the disfranchisement of the great majority of the population; for eighty years it confirmed slavery for one-tenth of the population; its grant of suffrage to the Negroes is still largely unrealized today; for over 130 years it excluded half the population, the women, from suffrage; citizenship rights begin only at the age of twenty-one years.

The Soviet Constitution provides universal adult suffrage, the only exception being those adjudged by a court as insane or guilty of a major crime against the state; the right to vote begins at eighteen years. . .

The Soviet Union has been able, in a world where elsewhere democracy is on the defensive or destroyed, to make a great new democratic advance, precisely because it has taken both economic and political power out of the hands of the enemies of the people, precisely because it has given to democracy a full and complete economic foundation, one which will endure, which will not be undermined and disappear as did the individual private property. Every advance of science in the Soviet Union, every increase in production and productivity, strengthens Soviet democracy and strengthens its economic foundation.

The Soviet Union has shown the way to the final and complete guarantee of democracy, and its fullest development. And such a democracy is unconquerable. . .

Trotskyism is treachery reduced to a science. Defeated and driven out everywhere it shows its face openly. Trotskyism now works in a hidden manner, especially making use of confused liberals and Socialists like John Dewey and Norman Thomas, who have lost their bearings in the chaos of capitalist disintegration. In the struggle against this poisonous and wrecking influence, as in every other phase of the struggle for progress, workers and other progressives can learn much from the experience of the Soviet Union.

In putting into effect the new Stalin Constitution the Soviet Union has released the full forces of its vibrant democracy to cleanse its house of all the lingering anti-democratic and anti-socialist remnants that have hung on from the past and that have developed through the degeneration of weak elements. At this same moment the forces of world fascism, preparing for their supreme effort of war to conquer the world, made a big drive through their Trotskyite allies, fully to mobilize their spies and wreckers whom they recruited from among these rotten elements. The results of the clash between these two forces within the Soviet Union have not brought much comfort to Hitler, Mussolini or the Japanese militarists. With its house cleaned, the Soviet Union is driving ahead with its socialist construction, is completing its military defenses, and is holding out the hand of co-operation to all the democratic and peace-loving peoples of the world for organizing world peace.

The Soviet Union has defeated all its enemies, internal and external, and has successfully constructed its new socialist society, because it was guided by the genius of the greatest teachers of history, Marx, Engels, Lenin and Stalin. It will defeat all its enemies in the future.

The People's Front will be successfully formed and will defeat fascism, because its conception was in the same scientific understanding of the laws of history.

With the defeat of fascism in its warlike aggressions, the peoples of Italy, Germany and Japan, losing their fear of a terrorism that lives only by constant victories, will turn upon and destroy the nightmare monster that today disturbs the peace of all the world.

With fascism wiped off the face of the earth, with the glorious achievements of the Soviet Union as an example, the rest of the world will find the transition to socialism relatively rapid and painless.

These are the main thoughts that arise from an examination of twenty years of Soviet power, of the triumphant emergence of the new society, which is showing the road for the entire world, which today stands as the most reliable protector of democracy and peace.

15 DISILLUSIONMENT OF A SYMPATHIZER

James A. Wechsler (1915–   )

James A. Wechsler was born in New York and educated at Columbia University. After graduation he joined the staff of the *Nation*, and from 1949 to 1961 served as editor of the *New York Post*. Mr. Wechsler, who was a member of the American Civil Liberties Union and Americans for Democratic Action, generally espoused liberal causes. In 1937, as a member of the National Committee of the Young Communist League, he traveled with his wife to Russia. In the following excerpt from his book *The Age of Suspicion* (1953) Wechsler explains how the lack of freedom in the Soviet Union precipitated his disillusionment with the communist regime.

WE REACHED KIEV IN EARLY AUGUST. The days we spent in the USSR did not shake the world. We saw as much and as little as average tourists were permitted to see in that twilight of the Russian travel era. What we saw in that brief interim scarcely constituted material for an extensive exposure of despotism; neither did we see anything calculated to revive our fading faith. We made the usual visit to a collective farm, which evoked the comment from one of our student group that he didn't see anything he hadn't seen in South Jersey. We visited hospitals and factories and schools; we attended open-air concerts. All that we were shown was evidence of some tangible material accomplishment, much, I suppose, as visitors to Nazi Germany were invited to marvel at the broad highways Adolf Hitler had built.

But I had begun to see that the issue was freedom, and nothing we saw or heard encouraged the hope that there were any fresh winds bringing any freer air to Russia's multitudes. We had heard it said ten thousand times that liberty was an "abstract concept." But when one encountered the countless ikons of Stalin in every public place and the withdrawn, uneasy faces of guides when one asked them questions, and when one went through the Museum of the Revolution where history had been carefully revised to conform to the Stalin legend, there was no abstraction involved. This was the concrete triumph of the monolithic mind; this was the rigid pattern of the communist movement expanded into a whole society. In New York, after listening to "Max," one could go out in the street and seem to get away from it all. How did one escape here? How was one to know whether one's neighbor was a friend or an informer and whether's one's children were eavesdropping so that they might file a report on one's whispered deviations?

On the train from Kiev to Moscow our guide was a nice but nervous Russian professor of literature. He spoke English fluently and, after we had shared a bottle of vodka, he spoke almost freely. We were talking about the party line in fiction; how could men write creatively if they lived in hourly fear that their works might be damned for failure to conform to the unpredictable decrees of the cultural commissars? At first he defended the system with a kind of feverish gibberish, but after the vodka had been consumed, he began making admissions. There were difficulties, yes. There were times when he was troubled about what they were doing; perhaps the functioning of the mind should not be dealt with in the same terms as factory output. . . . I wondered how many others suffered from these anxieties in the privacy of their rooms, and how often the loose tongues produced by vodka led to the arrest of "fascist-Trotskyite wreckers." The next morning our guide had a hangover and a haunted look, as though pondering his indiscretions and wondering whether I would turn him in. I tried to reassure him by saying the evening had been so gay that I could barely remember what we had discussed.

In Moscow we were led about by an attractive blonde schoolteacher. She was friendly, gracious and communicative—until we tried to get her to talk about the trials. I asked her as casually as I could what the public reaction had been. Her face froze. She suddenly acquired a blank look, as though she had lost her ability to hear. I started to repeat the question and she walked slowly off, giving no sign that she knew I had said anything.

I had mentioned the unmentionable. I tried the same question on others; the response was identical. One didn't discuss the Moscow trials in Moscow unless one had an exit visa.

We were still resisting the ultimate conclusion. One morning one of the Yale students in our troupe told us he and a companion had walked the streets of Moscow late the previous night and, on a side street, had seen a man dragged screaming and protesting out of his house and hurled into a police wagon. What they had seen—we learned later—was just one of innumerable such scenes being enacted that summer. Although we didn't know it at the time, the quiet purge of helpless thousands of "deviationists" was reaching a fierce peak that August. Great demonstration trials had been staged for the luminaries; the lesser victims were hauled away without such public spectacles. But when the Yale boy, who had no political interests and simply seemed to enjoy taunting us, told his story we expressed total disbelief. Nancy and I warned him his imagination had run wild as a result of the anti-Soviet fiction to which he had been subjected so long, and that is what we tried to persuade ourselves.

Our efforts to uphold the virtues of the Soviet Union in the face of undergraduate derision were beset by comic interludes. Upon arrival in Kiev three of the co-eds were assigned to a lavish suite at the hotel. It had a royal flavor; they were really delighted and were beginning to look with new understanding on the Soviet experiment. But shortly after dawn the next morning they were awakened by loud pounding at their doors. Excited voices told them to pack and get out of the suite at once because there was a leak in a pipe and the flood was expected at any moment. They got dressed, packed and fled; as they were leaving, a Russian general was ushered into the suite amid great pomp and circumstance.

Despite my membership on the YCL National Committee, I was not given access to any inner-council meetings in Moscow.

Indeed, our only contact with any communist officials was an evening spent with several Young Communist League leaders. It was a stiff, austere gathering, and when one of the students tried to start a discussion of the Moscow trials, there was a hasty retreat into other topics.

So there we were in the workers' fatherland, living in a hotel room that overlooked Red Square, and in this majestic setting we felt a nervous desire to reach Finland. There were no really untoward incidents. The sightseeing proceeded on schedule; but the sense of imprisonment was inescapable. We were in the communist citadel, and in place of exhilaration we had only the depressing sense that we ought to watch our words, and that our room was probably wired.

Sixteen years later a Senator was to say that he suspected I had had a private audience with Joseph Stalin and that Stalin had ordered me to return to America, pose as an anti-communist and prepare for the great day of warfare against Joe McCarthy. And I was to swear solemnly that it didn't happen.

In a sense, of course, I did see Stalin—everywhere. He gazed at me from every billboard. I saw far too much of him. I had come to Russia as a communist but, once there, I had not the slightest sense of belonging to this gray, monolithic civilization. I remember thinking how close I was to full entrapment, and how I would have felt if I had been sent to Moscow for training, as some Young Communist League leaders were. What if I were there without the certain knowledge that I could and would leave within a few days?

Somewhere in Red Square lay the body of John Reed, the Harvard man who had cast his lot with what he thought were the legions of emancipation. What would he have thought of the iron oppression his dream had become? In a little more than a week one could scarcely find out everything. One could only say with certainty that the air was stifling on the coolest, clearest day. It was being said over and over again that the Russians did not care as long as they were eating. They were, one might have said more precisely, subsisting on a diet of bread and dread.

Four months after leaving Moscow Nancy and I were both out of the Young Communist League.

16 THE RUSSIANS ARE NOT FREE

Norman Thomas (1884–1968)

Although Norman Thomas never held public office, as leader of the Socialist Party in the United States and its "six-time" candidate for the presidency, he significantly influenced American political thought. Thomas was born in Marion, Ohio, and graduated from Princeton University in 1905. After serving as a Presbyterian minister, he joined the Socialist Party in 1918 and became its leader in the late 1920s after the death of Eugene Debs. Ironically, as a socialist Thomas strongly opposed the Soviet regime in Russia and attacked the lack of political freedom in that country. These views come across clearly in a pamphlet, which he authored jointly with Joel Seidman in 1939, published by the League for Industrial Democracy.

SOVIET EXPERIENCE DEMONSTRATES that real liberty is not likely to exist in a one-party state. When, as has happened in the U.S.S.R., democracy is crushed within that party, then liberty is surely dead. For what has happened to freedom and democracy in Soviet Russia, Stalin's regime cannot alone be held responsible. It would be more accurate to say that he carried to an extreme certain practices and methods inherent in Bolshevism itself.

Clearly the Russians are not free, if that term has any real meaning. The rights that they possess are vastly inferior to those possessed by citizens of the United States and the other western democracies. In the first "workers' state" the worker is permitted fewer liberties than in capitalist democracies. Rights of free speech, assembly, organization, and press are non-existent. The Russian worker enjoys the real advantage of employment and of a certain degree of security, provided he is not critical of the regime; but living standards are terribly low, even for the more fortunate skilled workers. Officially there can be no exploitation in Russia, and productive equipment and the national income are the property of all workers. Actually the workers have little to say as to distribution of the national income, and a very high percentage is drained off for capital investment, for armaments, or for the huge bureaucracy. The state can exploit, just as private capitalists can.

Certain rights that the Russians possessed even under the despotic Czars have been curtailed or lost under the Soviets. The Soviet citizen today, for example, has virtually lost the right to emigrate. There was greater freedom to speak under the Czars, and greater freedom to publish papers and books, hold meetings, and form organizations. Each of the Imperial Dumas or Parliaments elected in Czarist Russia had large numbers of opponents of the regime, including Bolsheviks, in its membership. The overwhelming majority in the 1906 Duma were opponents of the regime. Political offenders were better treated under the Czars, though ordinary criminals were treated worse. On living standards accurate comparison is difficult; but under the Czars hours of work were longer, employment less certain, and educational opportunities limited. Russia was less of a police state under the Czars, but perhaps merely because the Czarist secret police were less efficient than the G.P.U. and N.K.V.D. Soviet citizens are encouraged to complain if they do not receive fair treatment, but they are utterly helpless if their complaints, as frequently happens, are ignored by the bureaucracy.

In other fields, notably literacy, science, and the treatment of women and national minorities, the Soviets have made progress. Once the industrial machine has been fully constructed, the living standards of the masses should rise to levels unprecedented for Russia. Perhaps—although this is debatable—liberty should be regained more readily from a party bureaucracy than from landlords, capitalists, and a hereditary nobility. At least democracy is a stated goal in the U.S.S.R., whereas in fascist countries

Two views from the left—a 1935 debate between Norman Thomas (left) for the Socialists and Earl Browder for the Communists.

dictatorship is a permanent ideal; some day the Russian workers may make their stated democratic goal a reality.

It must be recognized that the Soviet regime has had to cope with enormous problems, in rebuilding the shattered economic life of Russia after the war, in transforming a primitive agricultural economy into a modern industrial state, and in eliminating the private capitalist. All this has had to be done in the face of hostile powers, with the danger of war forever present. For their many real achievements the Soviets deserve full credit.

Certainly communism, with all its denials of human rights and civil liberties, is far superior to fascism. In Germany and Italy the workers have lost civil rights without making any gains in the economic or in other fields. Capitalism with all its attending evils is retained under fascism, civil liberties and democratic rights disappear, nationalism and militarism are glorified, and minorities are crushed. Nothing there is hopeful; in the Soviet Union, on the other hand, though the average worker does not possess more civil rights than under fascism, private capitalism, the source of so much woe, has been eliminated. With regard to the lack of civil and democratic rights and the use of terror to crush all opposition, fascism and communism are similar. The word "totalitarian" may equally be applied to both.

17 THE GOOD OUTWEIGHS THE BAD

Theodore Dreiser (1871–1945)

An advocate of social reform in the United States, the famous American novelist Theodore Dreiser wrote sympathetically of developments in the Soviet Union. Dreiser was born in Terre Haute, Indiana, and attended Indiana University, eventually joining the staff of the *Chicago Globe* in 1891. He won public recognition for his first novel, *Sister Carrie*, published in 1900; his many subsequent works included the famous *An American Tragedy*, published in 1925. Dreiser's works, which depicted the imperfections in American society, were very popular in the Soviet Union, and he visited that country as an official guest in 1927. Dreiser voiced his appreciation for what he regarded as the objectives of the Soviet Union in many of his letters, from which the following excerpts have been selected.

June 9, 1932, Replying to Mr. Dallas McKown, who had asked Dreiser to participate in helping to organize an Intellectual Workers League:

As you know, it has long been my desire to organize into an ultimately effective group the American workers, professional people, etc. who may be designated by the broad term "intellectuals." You know as well that I am not a member of the Communist Party, that the Party would not accept me as a member, and that, while I have found Communism functioning admirably in the U.S.S.R., I am not at all convinced that its exact method there could effectively be transferred to the self-governing of the people of the United States, or accepted by them.

> October 28, 1932, to Evelyn Scott, inviting her to write articles for the *American Spectator*, which Dreiser helped edit:

In so far as radical orthodoxy is concerned, that is out. In this paper, you are allowed to say what you actually think. The last thing we want to do is to edit either the individuality or the conclusions of any person who is invited, as you are, to contribute to this paper. It is not a right-wing periodical.

As for my Communism, it is a very liberal thing. I am not an exact Marxian by any means, and while I was in Russia, I was constantly threatened with being thrown out for my bourgeois, capitalistic point of view. My quarrel is not so much with doctrines as conditions. Just now, conditions are extremely badly balanced, and I would like to see them more evenly levelled.

> May 26, 1933, to Max Eastman, who had asked Dreiser to join with other liberal Americans to assist Communists jailed in Russia on the charge of assisting Leon Trotsky:

I have meditated almost prayerfully on this Trotsky business. I sympathize very much with the position of his adherents, but it is a question of choice. Whatever the nature of the present dictatorship in Russia—unjust, or what you will—the victory of Russia is all-important. I hold with Lincoln: Never swap horses while crossing a stream.

Until this present war entanglement is adjusted, if there is any possibility of its being adjusted, and until the Japanese danger is at least clarified, I would not want to do anything that would in any way injure the position of Russia. And, heaven helping me, I will not.

> November 15, 1934, to Henri Barbusse,
> a French leftist who had asked Dreiser
> to join a group to aid leftists in Spain:

When Russia came along with its Dictatorship of the proletariat, I was cheered beyond measure. And my visit to Russia in 1927-1928, as you may recall, was made delightful by the vision of the workers and peasants actually arranging a life which was fair to all who were willing to work, and that held nothing in store for either idlers or wasters. Since that time though, I know, as you know, that things have gone amiss.

> January 11, 1939, to Bruce Crawford,
> editor of the Norton, Virginia *Craw-*
> *ford's Weekly*:

One nation that I feel will put up a great fight, and ultimately be much more democratic than it looks to be now, is Russia. I think that at heart the Russian people have always leaned toward socialistic democracy, and, that if they have to fight a war to protect that idea, when it is over and they have won, they will not endure an iron-clad dictatorship but insist on a real democracy. Under any circumstances, if I read the signs right, they will fight with us from the first if we will let them. And if we have truly democratic leadership at the time in this country. So much for so much.

18 WORSE THAN FASCISM

Max Eastman (1883–1969)

Max Eastman, the well-known writer and poet, was so shocked by the excesses of the Soviet regime in the late 1920s and 1930s that he turned from an admirer into a bitter critic. Born in Canandaigua, New York, he graduated from Williams College in 1905 and taught philosophy at Columbia University from 1907 to 1910. In 1910 he also organized the first Men's League for Woman Suffrage in the United States. Eastman was editor of the leftist magazine *The Masses* from 1913 to 1917. Briefly a member of the American Communist Party, he opposed American entry into World War I; he also visited the Soviet Union in 1923. Eastman's book *Stalin's Russia and the Crisis in Socialism* (1940) is among the many works he wrote attacking the Soviet system.

IT WAS A STRANGE EXPERIENCE, for one who had lived through these twenty-five years as a Marxian socialist, to see how in proportion as the Soviet regime dropped overboard one by one every vestige of socialism, the liberal scholars and littérateurs of the whole world, in so far as they were at all flexible, "came over" to socialism, and rallied with extreme emotion to the "defense of the USSR. . ."

It would have been clear long ago that the Russian revolution had failed were it not for Stalin's skill in manipulating public opinion. His counter-revolution has been the bloodiest in all history. Aside from the punitive expeditions against peasants, the campaign of state-planned starvation, the war of extermina-

142

tion against thinking people generally, he has put to death more sincere and loyal party-militants than ever died before with the death of a revolution. His work makes that of the guillotine after the arrest of Robespierre look pale indeed. And yet because of his crafty guidance of the steam-roller and the machine of publicity, it required an open pact with Hitler's Germany to wake the world up to the fact that Thermidor was ended, that he was the man on horseback.

Stalin was trained as a "professional revolutionist"; that is why his counter-revolution shows so few amateur defects. He knows all the moves that can be made against him; he knows all the moves to make. He has used every trick in the repertory of dema-gogism in his colossal task of proving all loyal Bolsheviks traitors to the cause, and selling his personal tyranny to the public as the super-scientific beginnings of a millennium. And he has used one trick never thought of before—that of making distinguished batches of the old revolutionists "confess" publicly and in the face of death that *they* are the counter-revolution, he the sole loyal leader of the Party. . .

When historians look back, I believe the fading of religious faith in this era will seem a chief explanatory factor of its madness. Men haven't got used yet to the emptiness of the sky, and so they worship gods of clay again—what crude and bloody ones!—and believe in myths and promises of heaven on earth. Soviet Russia was far enough away, and sufficiently insulated by the language barrier, to function wonderfully in the place of Kingdom Come. All you had to do was dismiss all the plain facts as atrocity stories—they are horrible enough to sound like it—and believe the whole state-owned propaganda, and you could be as tranquil amid the falling ruins of civilization as an infant in the arms of Jesus.

This state of religious felicity was so widespread among American liberals, and their piety is so profound, that even the Stalin-Hitler pact and the raining of hellfire on Finland have barely waked them from their pious dream. They are wistful now—it is after all a sad world—but they still cling to the belief that somewhere in the background angels hover over Stalin.

The fact is that the bombing of Finland, although it obtrudes so uncomfortably into our real world, is a polite and civilized gesture compared to the sustained content of Stalin's domestic policies. The pact with Hitler is very much easier to defend, especially for a Marxian, than the regime that Stalin is linking with Hitler's. Instead of being better, Stalinism is worse than fascism—more ruthless, barbarous, unjust, immoral, anti-democratic, unredeemed by any hope or scruple.

There is too much dispute over the connotation of fascism for one simple formula to hold. We can as yet only point to all those traits which are common to the regimes in Italy and Germany, and not to be found in even the most caste-ridden of democratic countries. I have counted twenty-two such traits, and I find that in all but two, the regime of Stalin equals or exceeds them. I wish the reader who still feels a devout anguish over Stalin as a saint betrayed to temporary sin would go over this list with me, and see if Stalin is not better to be described as a super-fascist. . .

1. Nationalistic emotion is hysterically exalted.

"Patriotism is the supreme law of life," was the way Stalin's *Pravda* expressed it in 1934, and he was then still hampered by relics of the old slogan of Marx and Lenin: "Workers have no fatherland." By now patriotism in Moscow must be pretty nearly the whole law of life.

2. A single party, disciplined, centrally controlled and having a monopoly of the political field, takes over the power of the state. The state is reduced to the position of a false front, whose function is to "ratify" the decisions of the party.

Needless to argue that this system exists in Russia, since it was there that Hitler and Mussolini learned it.

3. Dissenting opinion is coerced by means of patronage and intimidation to the point where the party and its leaders can assert themselves to *be* the nation as a totality. The regime is called totalitarian exactly because it is not so, but this is a threat, not a boast. It means that all disagreement or even indifference, where it cannot be bridled, will be ruthlessly stamped out.

In Russia they talk of the "monolithic party" instead of the "totalitarian state," but this only because the system is so perfect that the state can be ignored.

4. The religion of nationalism comes into conflict with super-

natural religion. The church, like the state, is permitted to exist, but its priests, and even its God, must recognize the superior authority of the party.

Under "Socialism in One Country"—which is emotionally, even more than logically, the same thing as "National Socialism" —not only religion, but *philosophy* is regimented by the party!

5. The new religion finds its focus of devotion in "the Leader," who becomes to all intents and purposes a God.

In Russia, less civilized to begin with, this return to primitive superstition has gone farther than in Italy and Germany. In many minds it has gone to the point of literal deification. The adulation of the *"Liubimii Vozhd,"* printed almost weekly in full-page headlines in the great metropolitan newspapers of Russia—"Our Beloved," "Our Infallible," "Our Incomparable Stalin," "Our Sensitive Stalin," "Our Teacher," "Our Father of Nations," "Our Sun," "Our Soul"—would provoke laughter in any Western metropolis.

6. Anti-intellectualism, in a degree heretofore found only among guttersnipes, becomes a public policy. It takes the form of flattery to the ignorant and lazyminded, persecution, jail, death, or exile to those who stand for strenuous and honest thought.

Because of Stalin's personal jealousy of the brainier lieutenants of Lenin, and because the prejudice so easily aroused against highbrows was useful to him in overwhelming them, this policy has been more deliberately put through in Russia than in Italy or Germany. Moreover, with one exception, Stalin has not exiled his highbrows, but locked them up or shot them.

7. Anti-intellectualism also takes the form of a physical destruction of books and records, a rewriting of history and revamping of science to make it fit the momentary needs of politics.

Hitler made a public bonfire, but what Stalin has done in his craftier way to Russian books and documents and films, and even spoken memories—to all recorded truth—makes Hitler's bonfire look like an Independence Day celebration.

8. Anti-intellectualism also takes the form of an attack on "pure science"—described by the Editors of the *New Republic* as "one of the weirdest aspects of the weird Nazi ideology."

Exactly the same attack on pure science was made, with Marxian flourishes and police assistance, by Stalin's Politburo.

9. The manipulation of public opinion is substituted for its enlightenment. Human minds are regarded as receptacles for official decreed opinions. It becomes the function of the press and radio to put over the Leader's ideas, and misrepresent those of his enemies. Debate is abolished, dogma enthroned. Whatever intellectual life survives consists of inferences from temporary pronunciamentos of the Leader.

Here Stalin beats Hitler because he is operating upon a more primitive people.

10. Cultural isolation of the country is essential to this operation. The population is taught to believe all sorts of fables about their own merits and prosperities and the desperate condition of the outside world.

In Russia this has gone so far that private citizens cannot travel abroad, and are afraid to have friendly relations with a foreign visitor. It is, as we have seen, a crime of treason, punishable by death, to "escape across the border."

11. Party control of "scientific fact" (except in the industrial and military spheres) is accompanied by a similar control of creative art. Mussolini decrees the size of women's hips in Italian painting; Hitler suppresses as degenerate all the experimental art-works of the period.

Both Hitler and Mussolini learned this from Stalin, who inaugurated his aesthetic Inquisition in 1930. (See my *Artists in Uniform.*)

12. Immoralism takes two forms. Political lying and governmental hypocrisy are adopted as a system. Libel and slander become civic virtues. Fake plebiscites, solemn caricatures of judicial procedure, parodies of representative government, are accepted as the normal course. "Fooling all the people all the time" becomes the essential function of the state apparatus.

Stalin's "most democratic constitution in history," with its joker guaranteeing the political monopoly of the communist party and this party's domination in every social organization in the country, is the incomparable climax of this system. It is the most insolent hoax in history. It not only fools the people all the time, but fools them with the same trick, and hands it to them hand-embossed on parchment as the fundamental law of the land.

13. Immoralism takes also the form of state-planned assassinations, frame-ups, blood-purges, Reichstag fires, piracies in the Mediterranean, etc. The worst crimes in the code of civilization become the daring virtues of the totalitarian state.

Stalin, with his deliberate starvation of four to six million peasants, his deportations of whole villages, his millions in concentration camps, his whole counties consecrated to forced labor, his execution of practically every man in the country who has occupied a prominent position within the last fifteen years, makes Hitler's little blood-purge and Mussolini's regimen of castor oil tempered with assassination, look like a sophomore hazing party. If the shed blood of innocent men were measured, Stalin's would be a lake, Hitler's a duck-pond; Mussolini's could be dipped up by the tank-carful.

14. Besides its own crimes, the state encourages the population to bait, torture and destroy some public enemy. The hate and persecution of this internal enemy serves as a peacetime substitute for war, which is necessary to keep the passion of tribal solidarity on which the whole thing is based at white heat.

What Hitler has done to the Jews compares palely with what Stalin has done to "Kulaks," and to prominent people generally. He has reversed Napoleon's maxim: "Careers are open to all men of talent." The place for men of talent in Russia, generally speaking, is the bloodstained cellar of the Lubianka prison. Still Stalin has not—as yet—overtly persecuted the Jews or other Russian national minorities. He belongs to one of them himself.

15. In baiting the Jews, Hitler revived—from the Old Testament!—the principle of tribal guilt for the crime of an individual.

Stalin has written this principle into the Criminal Code. As we have seen, his treason law holds guilty not only the family of the traitor, but everybody who lived, however innocently, in the same house with him.

16. Besides an object of hate, the tribal passion must have an object of love. There must be some real glory-work to consecrate oneself to. Accordingly, we find in all totalitarian regimes a process of economic revival or reconstruction. Absolute tyranny

and complete regimentation of a population does solve—temporarily, I think—one or two of the anxious problems of civilization, although at the cost of civilization itself. It is a great way of climbing out of a hole. And only in countries climbing out of a hole have such regimes been established.

Russia was in a deeper hole than Italy or Germany, and she has more abundant resources. She is a backward nation still to be industrialized. The real job to be done, the object of honest devotion, is bigger, more sure of success, more exciting.

17. The national revival is focused around and sustained by preparations for war. The war industries dominate, and the population is completely militarized from youngest childhood.

In this, Russia, Italy and Germany are alike, and Russia has now joined these other military despotisms in aggressions against peaceful neighbors.

18. Together with militarization goes a reckless campaign for increased population. Birth control is discouraged, abortions are outlawed, large families are boosted with state propaganda. Here Stalin was impeded by Lenin's extremely liberal and humanitarian legislation. He has repealed all that legislation, and Russia is now making cannon fodder with the best of them.

19. Woman is relegated to a subordinate position, and laws are passed against her independence. The totalitarian regimes are male regimes. Woman's business in them is to breed.

Here, too, Stalin has repealed the equalitarian decrees and proclamations of the October revolution. He is traveling in the anti-feminist direction. But he is still a good way behind Hitler and Mussolini.

20. All three totalitarian governments are characterized by a paternal concern for the welfare, or at least security, of the toiling masses—in so far as they are completely submissive. This fact about fascist regimes has been little appreciated in America, but it is the foundation of their success. It is the price at which the German and Italian masses sold their freedom. In Russia, notwithstanding the legends spread by Stalin's propagandists, this concern for the toilers is no more real, and is on the whole less effective, than in Germany. The Russian masses, accustomed as they were to slavery, have sold their freedom at a lower price.

In both countries all the unions are company unions, and the company is the state.

21. All totalitarian regimes make a liberal use of the phraseology of working-class revolution against capitalism. They call themselves "proletarian"; they denounce democratic nations as "capitalist"; Mussolini asserts that he is still a "revolutionary socialist"; Goebbels promises a "socialism of nations"; Hitler calls his party "National Socialist," denounces the "Jewish capitalist world"; Goering describes Germany as a "workers' and peasants' state."

Stalin uses this language more plausibly than the others, because he stems from a revolution that did involve a rising of the workers and peasants. In so far, however, as it implies that the workers and peasants run the government or receive a slice of the profits of industry, the language is as false in Russia as in Germany and Italy. The profits are disposed of by the new holders of totalitarian power, the class of bureaucrats, whose principal public expenditure is on militarizing the country mind and body.

22. In all totalitarian regimes, industry, commerce and agriculture are controlled by the state—that is, the party and its leader. . .

In Russia this state control is more neat and absolute, because private claims have been abolished altogether. Control extends to the point of ownership. No one doubts that in this matter Stalin stands at the extreme toward which the fascist states have traveled. It is indeed this very difference which seems so vast and beneficent—and so "economic"—to our semi-Marxian intellectuals that they forgive Stalin all his massacres. They think that he has built a "socialist state," and they dismiss a death-toll similar to that of the First World War with the remark that "You can't make an omelette without breaking eggs."

19 THE SOVIET UNION IS A DICTATORSHIP

Franklin D. Roosevelt (1882–1945)

Four times elected to the presidency, Franklin Roosevelt's years in the White House spanned one of the most traumatic periods in our history, one that included the great depression and World War II. Roosevelt was born in Hyde Park, New York, and graduated from Harvard in 1904. After practicing law in New York, he served as Assistant Secretary of the Navy in the Wilson administration from 1913 to 1920. After running unsuccessfully as the Democratic candidate for the vice presidency in 1920, he was elected Governor of New York in 1928 and 1930 and then president in 1932.

Although it was during his first term in office that the United States established diplomatic relations with the Soviet Union, Roosevelt was not unaware of the defects of the communist regime. One of his strongest public denunciations of Russia came on February 10, 1940, in a speech on the White House lawn to the American Youth Congress Councils. He strongly criticized the Russian attack against Finland and described the Soviet Union as a dictatorship.

ONE OF THE big local American Youth Congress Councils, I am told, took a decisive stand against the granting of some form of aid by loan or otherwise by America to Finland. Did that not on the ground that we are to spend the money here among our own unemployed but on the ground that such action was "an attempt to force America into an imperialistic war."

My friends, that reason was unadulterated twaddle, unadulterated twaddle, based perhaps on sincerity, but at the same time on 90 per cent ignorance of what they were talking about. I can say this to you with a smile because many of you will recognize the inherent wisdom and truth of what I am saying.

Here is a small republic in Northern Europe. A republic which without any question whatever wishes solely to maintain its own territorial and governmental integrity. Nobody with any pretense of common sense believes that Finland had any ulterior designs on the integrity or the safety of the Soviet Union.

That American sympathy is 98 per cent with the Finns in their effort to stave off invasion of their own soil. That American sympathy by now is axiomatic. That America wants to help them by lending or giving money to them to save their own lives is also axiomatic today. That the Soviet Union would, because of this, declare war on the United States, is about the silliest thought that I ever heard advanced in the fifty-eight years of my life, and that we are going to war ourselves with the Soviet Union is an equally silly thought . . .

More than twenty years ago, while most of you were pretty young children, I had the utmost sympathy for the Russian people. In the early days of Communism I recognized that many leaders in Russia were bringing education and better health and, above all, better opportunity to millions who had been kept in ignorance and serfdom under the imperial regime.

I disliked the regimentation of Communism. I abhorred the indiscriminate killings of thousands of innocent victims. I heartily deprecated the banishment of religion—though I knew that some day Russia would return to religion for the simple reason that four or five thousand years of recorded history have proved to mankind that mankind has always believed in God, in spite of many abortive attempts to exile God.

And I, with many of you, hoped that Russia would work out its own problems and their government would eventually become a peace-loving, popular government with free ballot, a government that would not interfere with the integrity of its neighbors.

That hope is today either shattered or is put away in storage against some better day. The Soviet Union, as a matter of practical fact, as everybody knows, who has got the courage to face the fact, the practical fact known to you and known to all the world, is run by a dictatorship, a dictatorship as absolute as any other dictatorship in the world.

It has allied itself with another dictatorship and it has invaded a neighbor so infinitesimally small that it could do no conceivable, possible harm to the Soviet Union, a small nation that seeks only to live at peace as a democracy and a liberal forward-looking democracy at that.

20 RUSSIA CLOSE UP

Louis Fischer (1896–1970)

A long-time foreign correspondent, writer, and expert on the Soviet Union, Louis Fischer spent approximately fourteen years in that country during the 1920s and 1930s. Born in Philadelphia, he taught in public schools there before serving in the British-sponsored Jewish Legion in Palestine during World War I. Fischer became a foreign correspondent after the war, and in 1921 was the Berlin correspondent for the *New York Evening Post*. Many of his approximately twenty books deal with Soviet affairs; one of them, *The Life of Lenin*, won the National Book Award in 1964. From 1961 until his death, Fischer was research associate and visiting lecturer at the Woodrow Wilson School in Princeton, New Jersey. The following excerpts from Fischer's autobiography, *Men and Politics* (1941), reveal his initial sympathy for the ideals of the Russian Revolution as viewed during his stay in Russia in the 1920s and his strong revulsion toward the Soviet system after the purges of the 1930s.

Russia had always fascinated me. In my youth I had read the great novels of Count Leo Tolstoy and Dostoevsky and many of the stories of Turgenev, Gogol, and Maxim Gorky in English translation. Russia emerged a land of mysticism and misery. At the age of twenty I avidly devoured Prince Peter Kropotkin's *Memoirs of a Revolutionist*. There seemed to be a wealth of ideas and art in poor, downtrodden Russia. Russia was large, empty, distant, eastern and apparently so civilized yet uncivilized.

From Berlin, in 1922, I saw Russia at closer range. A revolutionary regime had supplanted the world's symbol of reaction. Iconoclasts had taken over the country of the ikon. The strong brute groped for modern weapons. East was being dragged westward and the West feared it. Russia, ever visionary and missionary, talked about reshaping Europe. If Europe had needed no reshaping it would not have been so worried.

Bolshevism was a protest against the Europe that had made the first World War and the peace that followed. It was a protest too against the future war implicit in that peace. My vague sympathy for Soviet Russia was first of all a reaction against the chaos, disunity, dishonesty, and despair of the rest of Europe. I never thought of Soviet Russia as a Utopia. I knew, when I first went there in September, 1922, that I was going to a land of starvation. If I had mistakenly expected a paradise I would have been disillusioned after the first glance. In Lenin's Russia of 1922, I looked not for a better present but for a brighter future. I also expected clean politics and a foreign policy that rejected conquest, colonies, imperialism, and the lying that is often synonymous with diplomacy. I anticipated an equality between people and politicians. I had read the statements of Lenin, Trotzky, Chicherin, Litvinov, and other Soviet officials. They were frank and strong. The notes of Foreign Commissar Chicherin to foreign governments shot holes in the screen of hypocrisy behind which bourgeois statesman tried to hide their activities. They threw a searchlight of humor, logic, and truth into the blackness of world affairs. I suspected that Moscow would be fun.

Soviet Russia, moreover, was conceived by its creators as the kingdom of the underdog. Evolution is the survival of the fittest; civilization is the survival of the unfittest. The Bolsheviks undertook to serve civilization by aiding those handicapped by poor parents, inadequate education, bad health, and slave psychology. . .

Yet for some reason that I cannot explain to myself now, the two Russian Revolutions occurred without making the slightest impression on me. I do not remember the abdication of the last Czar in March, 1917. I was in the United States and must have been reading newspaper accounts of this historic change, but my memory did not register it. When the Bolshevik Revolution occurred on November 7, 1917, I was in Canada, a volunteer in the British army. During the "Ten Days that Shook the World," I was learning to form fours and fire a rifle. Lenin and Trotzky stirred no ripple in my calm existence.

But in Europe, in 1921 and 1922, Russia could not be ignored. . .

From 1918 to 1921, Soviet city people and the army lived on rations given to them by the government. The peasants had to sell their crops to the government. The government paid with paper rubles. Paper currency is good if you can buy something with it. But all the stores were closed. So the peasant did not want to sell his produce, and the Bolsheviks, faced with the possibility of starvation in the army and cities, sent troops into the villages to requisition food. This stifled the peasant's natural desire to plant. Coupled with a drought, the result was a famine in the Volga region and the Ukraine where millions died. The peasant planted less, hid his harvest, and sold it only to private individuals who slipped out of cities with sacks full of old clothing, shoes, tobacco, or interior decorations. Bigger objects too found their way into the countryside in exchange for food, and traveling through Russian farm regions in later years, I saw pianos, gramophones, books, paintings and rugs, which lowly muzhiks had received from hungry law-breaking city folk during that difficult period. But this bootleg business was a thin unsatisfactory trickle. It could not meet the needs of millions of urbanites nor offer a regular market to a hundred million peasants. In 1920 and 1921, peasants in many districts openly displayed their displeasure at the restrictions on the sale of their crops. Revolts broke out in several provinces and among Kronstadt sailors who were peasants' sons for the most part. Lenin quickly grasped the significance of this. In March, 1921, he readmitted capitalism into Soviet Russia; he introduced the New Economic Policy—NEP.

Lenin called the NEP a retreat. It superseded a system which was in part "military communism"—a war necessity—and in part militant communism: the state ran the munitions plants, railroads, banks, mines. In lesser degree, the same system had been tried in the United States during the first World War—with this difference: in capitalist countries the capitalists were temporarily denied complete supervision over their properties. In Soviet Russia they were permanently dispossessed and exiled or imprisoned or shot, thus leaving a clear field for socialism. Under "military communism," moreover, the peasants tilled nationalized soil, which they held in usufruct. And private business was proscribed. The NEP altered one situation; private business was legalized.

I saw private trade take its first faltering steps in Communist Russia. Here a red-faced woman in white headkerchief stood on the pavement holding five pairs of cotton gloves in one hand and half a dozen neck scarfs in another. She was launching a business career. A wrinkled veteran had managed to scrape together ten packets of cigarettes and a few boxes of matches. A board suspended by strings from his shoulders was his showcase—and there he stood, a capitalist. Perambulating bookstores, pushcarts filled with luscious fruit from southern regions, and cobblers repairing shoes and nailing on rubber heels in the autumn cold completed the picture of open-air capitalism. . . .

The historic struggle between Stalin and Trotzky had not yet commenced, and Trotzky was recognized as the organizer of the Red Army. But though still the head of the army, Trotzky had too much dynamic energy to make it a full-time job in peace. He had taken over the ruined railroads of the country and was trying to bring order out of their chaos. He wrote long, half-page reviews in the daily press on European and Russian books (he was one of Russia's outstanding literary critics), delivered numerous speeches, and, in addition, preached puritan morals. Urging "a new life," Trotzky attacked swearing and those three-ply Russian "mother" oaths which, incidentally, Lenin used on rare occasions and Stalin often, but Trotzky never. "Cursing," Trotzky thundered, "is a heritage of slavery."

A strong puritanical streak runs through Communism. It denies to the individual for the sake of the whole and the future. Loose living is discouraged not as sin but because it softens the soldier fighting the social war. Besides, the NEP was corroding morals as well as socialist economy, and puritan self-restraint seemed a necessary corrective. I attended a dance recital directed by Goleizovsky, former ballet impresario. It was crude pornography. The police would have been summoned if anybody had done horizontally what the performers executed under the guise of dance. A Soviet critic declared this "thickly erotic style" incongruous "in our harsh revolutionary epoch." But these things were an attempt to escape from harshness. . . .

In 1922 and 1923, nevertheless, the fires of Bolshevik idealism from which the 1917 revolution rose were still burning high. The Kremlin's task was to keep them so. The call to a better world came from leaders who shrank from personal adulation. The fifth birthday of the Soviet government was certainly cause for congratulation; the Bolsheviks had expected to be crushed long before that. Yet the press refrained from personal tributes. Victory was the achievement of all. I have read carefully the anniversary issue of the *Pravda* of November 7, 1922. On the first page is a facsimile quotation from Lenin but no other mention of Lenin or of any other Bolshevik. Half of the second page is devoted to a survey of the civil war by General S. Kamenev. Not a single personal name occurs in it. A calendar of five years of the regime contains two casual references to Lenin, one to Trotzky, and one to Krylenko. Then there is an article by S. Zorin in memory of the Mensheviks who died in making the Revolution. The Mensheviks were now sworn enemies of the Bolsheviks. They opposed dictatorship and Soviet principles. But the official *Pravda* gave them the credit they deserved. For "they too" says Zorin, "participated in the memorable days of the Revolution." Such an honest tribute became inconceivable in later years. . .

I had not seen my family for seven months, and so I went to Moscow in August, 1937.

Red had ceased to be the correct adjective for Moscow. It was black. . .

Despite the cheering sun, heavy gloom pervaded Moscow. Friends and acquaintances did not want to meet one another. How could anyone know who was under surveillance? You might be incriminated by associating with a person who was scheduled to be arrested in a fortnight and in the meantime was being shadowed. People withdrew into themselves and the family circle. But could you be sure about members of the family? The press reported denunciations of arrested husbands by their wives, and denunciations by children of their arrested parents. Then perhaps it would be better not to share all one's troubles, worries, and impressions with the wife or with one's grown-up son.

The newspapers were dull where they had always been exciting. They gave less attention to foreign news, and an endless amount of space to the names of tractor drivers, cow hands, beet harvesters, and locomotive drivers who had won decorations for distinguished services. The phenomenon of giving public praise to common men was highly laudable. But when several times a week one or two pages of an eight-page newspaper were devoted to these lists, citizens yawned and threw the paper away after a few minutes.

Reading had been a great Soviet pleasure. But some writers had been arrested, and the others felt that it was safer not to write. "Better not" become the rule of conduct. Bureaucratic fear of responsibility paralyzed initiative. When an official was asked his opinion of a project he most frequently refrained from a positive recommendation lest its failure be pinned on him. He would say, "I have no objection." That was the old formula of Czarist officials.

Into this deadening atmosphere of dread, the GPU threw a spy scare. The Soviet newspapers published an unending chain of articles by GPU "experts" on spies. Foreign governments, they explained, had innumerable spies in Russia. Many Russians had emigrated from Russia before the Revolution. The secret services of foreign countries had them in their grip. They wrote to their relatives in Soviet Russia and their relatives wrote back, and how did you know when you wrote back you had not revealed important information to the enemy? Russians stopped all communication with foreign countries and with foreigners inside. Foreign scientific journals were kept from Soviet universities. Soviet scientists were discouraged from attending international scientific congresses.

American Communists who had lived in Soviet Russia for a

long time were clearing out, first because the Bolsheviks did not want them to stay, and also because they themselves had had enough. By this time most Polish, Hungarian, and German Communists had been arrested. A German Communist friend of mine discussed this, informally, with a GPU official who was a friend of hers. He said, "If German Communists are ready to build socialism in Germany they can do it in Siberia too." The revolutionary attitude towards foreign Communists had given way to this ugly cynicism. Yet the Soviet Constitution gave "the right of asylum to foreign citizens persecuted for furthering the interest of workers." But then it also guaranteed the "inviolability of homes and the secrecy of correspondence," as well as the "inviolability of persons." The GPU spat on all these rights. If it wished to seize anyone it did. If it wished to enter a home it did so. Never in Soviet history had insecurity been greater than in the *summer* of 1937. . . .

Every trial, every purge, every arrest started a long chain of more purges and more arrests.

Russia had lived badly since 1916. It had made innumerable sacrifices in living conditions and health. Its spirit and nerves had been subjected to heavy strain. The Five Year Plan and agrarian collectivization, 1929 to 1932, redoubled the tension. The tension was not relaxed at the end of that hard period. It continued. By 1935, I had an almost physical sensation that the Soviet Union was simply very tired. It wanted to sit still. It wanted to eat better, live better, and be left alone. It did not wish to be bombarded each day with radical changes, new appeals, new demands. There was a great yearning for silence and peace. That is why the economic improvement of 1935 and 1936 and the Constitution of 1936 brought so much joy. The regime had turned a corner, people said. And that is why the purges, trials and intensified terror of 1937 and 1938 broke so many hearts. "Will it never end?" Soviet citizens asked. . . .

August, 1937—the month I spent in Moscow: Kraval, assistant chairman of the State Planning Commission, Troitzky, chief of the Financial Plan, and ten other heads of departments who worked with Valeri Mezhlauk, excoriated as "enemies of the people." A black shroud covers their fate. Seventy-two shot in Irkutsk,

Siberia, for train wrecks. Six shot in Minsk, White Russia, for feeding poisoned food to soldiers. Thirty-four more executed in Irkutsk. Eight shot in Leningrad for "counter-revolutionary acts." *Pravda* attacks Dibetz, the director of automobile and tractor industry of the entire country. Since then no more has been heard of him. Two women shot in Leningrad for feeding poisoned food to children in schools. Hundreds of other arrests reported in the papers and thousands not so reported.

But these gruesome facts are mere child's play compared with the bloody pogrom which blackened the face of Russia in the fall of 1937 and throughout 1938, and which continues to this day under a thick veil of secrecy lifted only occasionally by the Kremlin or penetrated by stray bits of information which reach outsiders. . . .

It was better not to call on Soviet friends and acquaintances. The visit of a foreigner might get them into trouble. Always, literally always in the past, our apartment was filled with Russians when I arrived from abroad. They came just to welcome me back, but also to get the latest news and impressions of the international scene. This time nobody came. I read Lenin, walked the streets, and played tennis.

21 THE NEED FOR POSTWAR COOPERATION

Walter Lippmann (1889–1974)

Walter Lippmann was for almost half a century the dean of American political journalists and the confidant of successive presidents. Born in New York City, he attended Harvard, where he was elected president of the Socialist Club. Graduating in 1910, he was among the founders of the liberal magazine *The New Republic* in 1914. After serving as assistant to the Secretary of War in 1917, Lippmann joined the army and became a captain in military intelligence. He was a member of the United States delegation to the Versailles Peace Conference, and subsequently a columnist for the *New York World*, writing regularly for that newspaper from 1923 to 1931 and, upon its demise, for the *New York Herald Tribune*.

Among Lippmann's many publications is his book *U.S. War Aims* (1944). Lippmann here describes the role Russia might play in the postwar world and the need for the United States to establish a basis for mutual cooperation with Moscow to prevent another global conflict.

IF WE ARE TO stabilize our relations with the Soviet Union, we must study its vital interests and our own, and establish a policy accordingly. But we must recognize at the outset that in the Western nations there are profound differences of opinion as to Russia's interests and intentions. There are those who hold that the Russians will for a long time to come be absorbed in the

161

internal development of their vast country, and that the Soviet Union will be very nearly as self-centered as was the United States during the nineteenth century. This is one hypothesis. There is no way of proving that it is correct.

The other view is, of course, that Soviet Russia is an aggressive state which in various combinations fuses the ambitions of the Czarist Empire with the projects of the Third International. There is no way of proving that this hypothesis is incorrect. . . .

A Russian-American war is, as such, a virtual impossibility. In the West the two countries cannot get at one another except by crossing Europe. They might wage border warfare where Siberia and Alaska meet. But Americans could not invade and occupy the Urals by way of Alaska, nor Russians the Mississippi Valley by way of Siberia. No competent soldier would contemplate seriously either project.

Aerial bombing across the Arctic will no doubt become technically feasible in the near future. But only uncritical speculation can suppose that air forces based on Russian and on American soil could in the foreseeable future be capable of deciding a Russian-American conflict. The notion is quite contrary to all technological experience: it assumes that while the offensive power of the bomber will grow without limits, the anti-aircraft defense will not grow correspondingly. In the foreseeable future, which is all that statesmen can deal with, a war waged directly between Russia and the United States is very nearly as impossible as a battle between an elephant and a whale.

War is possible, however, if it is a general war in which the other nations participate. This is the reality with which we must be concerned. Russia and the United States can fight one another in the East if Japan and China provide the striking points, the battlefields, the bridgeheads, the covering forces of the defense, the advanced echelons of the assault. They can fight one another in the West if all of Europe and Great Britain are involved first. Only by means of allies can Russia and the United States come to grips; and by a conflict begun among their allies they can be entangled in a war.

Thus Russia and America are in the position where the issue of war and peace between them will be determined by the policy they follow in respect to their alliances. I am using the word "alliance" to cover any agreement among governments, whether it be formal or informal, avowed or implicit, that makes them partners in the event of war. Russia and America can have peace if they use their alliances to stabilize the foreign policy of their allies. They will have war if either of them reaches out for allies within the orbit of the other, and if either of them seeks to incorporate Germany or Japan within its own strategical system. . . .

The Soviet Union's relations with the United States, and indeed with all other European and American countries, are beset by profound contradictions which inhibit confident collaboration. We encounter them first in the fact that diplomatic intercourse is not on an equal and reciprocal basis. The Soviet government maintains a quarantine against free intercourse with us. The outgoing censorship permits us to know about Russia only what the government deems expedient. The incoming censorship permits the Russian people to know about us, even about our official acts, only what the Soviet government deems expedient. Within the United States citizens may oppose the Administration on a policy dealing with Russia, and if they can muster enough popular support, the policy, or even the Administration, can be changed. But on a Soviet policy towards the United States there is no appeal from the decisions of the government.

The Soviet quarantine means that in foreign affairs the Soviet government can use secrecy and surprise to maneuver in ways which democratic governments cannot do. Our institutions are such that we could not, without destroying them, equalize intercourse by establishing our own quarantine. Unlike the Soviet's, our policies can be formed only after deliberation and debate which put the whole world on notice.

The Soviet Union does not tolerate the existence of any opposition party which could become the government. But we not only recognize opposition parties as inherent and necessary to our constitutional system; we also tolerate an opposition party, namely the communist, which if it gained power and followed the Soviet model would abolish all parties opposing it and establish the totalitarian rule of the one-party system. Thus, while Russia has insulated herself internally against the propaganda of the Western constitutional system, we are not insulated, because of our principles of toleration, against the totalitarian propaganda. The phenomenon of red-baiting has its roots in this inequality and disparity. It is a convulsive, instinctive, and often neurotic reaction of fear and inferiority in the presence of the fact that while the Soviet constitution is protected by its police against being subverted by democrats, the democracies are inhibited by their own principles from protecting themselves conclusively against being subverted by totalitarians.

As long as this inequality exists, there cannot be true collaboration between the Soviet Union and the Western World. There can be only a *modus vivendi*, only compromises, bargains, specific agreements, only a diplomacy of checks and counter-checks. . . .

We owe it to the Soviet people to say that however correct may be our diplomatic relations, they will not really be the good relations they need to be until the basic political and human liberties are established in the Soviet Union. Only then will there be full confidence, and a free intercourse on a basis of full equality. For between states that do not have free institutions and those that do have them, international relations must necessarily be special and restricted.

A world order under the reign of universal laws cannot be realized under these conditions. Without the full collaboration of the Soviet Union no universal society can be formed. For in all the critical areas of the world—critical with reference to a long peace or a third World War—the Soviet Union is a principal power. In Europe it is the nearest of the great powers to Germany. In Eastern Asia it is the nearest to China and Japan. In the Middle East it is potentially the nearest and most powerful neighbor of the emergent Moslem states. Second only to China, it is substantially the nearest to India. In the universal society, which the Moscow and Teheran agreements call for, there cannot be genuine consultation and, after deliberation, common action, if between the Soviet Union and the other nations there is not an equal and reciprocal exchange of public information, if all the governments which wield force are not publicly accountable to their peoples and to the opinions of the world. The world order cannot be half democratic and half totalitarian. . . .

So we must go to the Russians; the key to the door is in their hands. Speaking to them frankly as allies who mean to be their friends, we must ask them to commit the world of the future to the cause of democratic freedom. We may hope and we may believe they will not refuse. The proof that they have accepted they alone can give—in the measures they take when the war is over to validate their own constitutional promises, and to make free, equal, and reciprocal the exchange of news and opinion between their own people and their present allies.

If they refuse, we can still do our very best to get on with them, persisting through the ordinary channels of diplomacy in the effort to prevent a third World War. But if they refuse, it will be better not to deceive ourselves, and to become relaxed in the semblance, which will have little reality, of a universal society for the maintenance of peace. . . .

Though at first it may not seem so, it is in Russia's vital interest and our own that the profound issue which divides us be brought into the full light of day and settled boldly and conclusively. Between Russia and the Western World there is a distrust which is ancient and deep. It is at least as old as the great schism of the Dark Ages which divided Christendom between Rome and Byzantium. The distrust has persisted into the modern era—under kings and czars, in democracies and soviets. It will not disappear suddenly or easily. By one means alone can the distrust be in the end dissolved, and that is by the acceptance and avowal of the same ultimate standards of value. . . .

The Russians simply cannot expect the rest of the world to believe in the democratic principles of their new foreign policy if they do not then practise those principles at home. And if the world distrusts Russian foreign policy, there is no way in which the Russians can make their policy work. Nothing could be more fatal to the Russian policy than to let the fear of bolshevism engender anti-Russian policy and fascism in the rest of the world.

It is vital to Russia herself that this fear be dissolved. Actually it would serve the Russian interest not only to repudiate, as she has already done, international communism, but to look without disfavor upon the legal outlawry and suppression by democratic states of all revolutionary parties. Russia would be infinitely more secure in the world if all the Western democracies followed the Swiss example. Russia would be freer to pursue her immense social projects if there were no communist parties and factions in the Atlantic Community providing fuel for the fires of fascist hostility to Russia. . . .

22 PLANNED TOTALITARIANISM

W. Averell Harriman (1891–   )

W. Averell Harriman, one of the keenest American observers of
the Soviet Union, was intimately associated with United States
foreign affairs during his more than thirty years of government
service. Born in New York City and the son of railroad magnate
and financier Edward Harriman, young Harriman graduated
from Yale in 1913 and joined the staff of the Union Pacific Railroad, serving as Chairman of the Board from 1932 to 1934.
Although raised as a Republican, Harriman supported Al Smith's
bid for the Democratic Presidential nomination and later became
a member of that party. In 1934 President Roosevelt appointed
him to the National Recovery Administration. After working on
lend-lease matters during the early years of World War II, Harriman was sent to Moscow as American ambassador in 1943 and
served there for three years. He subsequently continued his long
government service as Ambassador to Great Britain in 1946,
Secretary of Commerce in the Truman administration from 1946
to 1948, Governor of New York from 1955 to 1958 and Assistant
Secretary and Under Secretary of State in the Kennedy and
Johnson administrations from 1961 to 1965. During 1968–69 he
played a key role as United States representative at the negotiations with the Vietnamese in Paris.

Harriman was one of the first Americans to recognize that the
Russian-American collaboration in World War II was beginning
to disintegrate in 1945, and to warn of the threat of Soviet imperialism. The following excerpts from messages he sent to the
State Department in 1945 from the Embassy in Moscow helped
alert the Truman administration to the developing danger.

April 4, 1945

TURNING TO THE matter of policy, we now have ample proof that the Soviet Government views all matters from the standpoint of their own selfish interests. They have publicized to their own political advantage the difficult food situation in areas liberated by our troops such as in France, Belgium and Italy, comparing it with the allegedly satisfactory conditions in areas which the Red Army has liberated. They have kept our newspaper correspondents under strict censorship to prevent the facts becoming known. They have sent token shipments to Poland of Lend-Lease items or those similar thereto in order to give the appearance of generosity on the part of the Soviet Union. The Communist Party or its associates everywhere are using economic difficulties in areas under our responsibilities to promote Soviet concepts and policies and to undermine the influence of the western Allies . . . if the Soviet Government had shown any willingness to deal with economic questions on their merits without political considerations, as we approach them, I would feel that we should make every effort to concert our plans with those of the Soviet Government. On the other hand our hopes in this direction have proved to be futile. Unless we and the British now adopt an independent line the people of the areas under our responsibility will suffer and the chances of Soviet domination in Europe will be enhanced. I thus regretfully come to the conclusion that we should be guided as a matter of principle by the policy of taking care of our western Allies and other areas under our responsibility first, allocating to Russia what may be left. I am in no sense suggesting that this policy should have as its objective the development of a political bloc or a sphere of influence by the British or ourselves, but that we should, through such economic aid as we can give to our western Allies, including Greece as well as Italy, reestablish a reasonable life for the people of these countries who have the same general outlook as we have on life and the development of the world. The Soviet Union and the minority governments that the Soviets are forcing on the people of eastern Europe have an entirely different objective. We must clearly recognize that the Soviet program is the establishment of totalitarianism, ending personal liberty and democracy as we know and respect it. In addition the Soviet Government is attempting to penetrate through the Communist parties supported by it the countries of western Europe with the hope of expanding Soviet influence in the internal and external affairs of these countries.

Since we under no circumstances are prepared to involve ourselves in the internal political affairs of other countries by such methods, our only hope of supporting the peoples of these countries who resent totalitarian minority dictatorships is to assist them to attain economic stability as soon as possible. Lack of sufficient food and employment are fertile grounds for the subtle false promises of Communist agents.

The Soviet Government will end this war with the largest gold reserve of any country except the United States, will have large quantities of Lend-Lease material and equipment not used or worn out in the war with which to assist their reconstruction, will ruthlessly strip the enemy countries they have occupied of everything they can move, will control the foreign trade of countries under their domination as far as practicable to the benefit of the Soviet Union, will use political and economic pressure on other countries including South America to force trade arrangements to their own advantage and at the same time they will demand from us every form of aid and assistance which they think they can get from us while using our assistance to promote their political aims to our disadvantage in other parts of the world. . . . The Soviet Government's selfish attitude must, in my opinion, force us if we are to protect American vital interests to adopt a more positive policy of using our economic influence to further our broad political ideas. Unless we are ready to live in a world dominated largely by Soviet influence, we must use our economic power to assist those countries that are naturally friendly to our concepts in so far as we can possibly do so. The only hope of stopping Soviet penetration is the development of sound economic conditions in these countries. I therefore recommend that we face the realities of the situation and orient our foreign economic policy accordingly. Our policy toward the Soviet Union should, of course, continue to be based on our earnest desire for the development of friendly relations and cooperation both political and economic, but always on a *quid pro quo* basis. This means tying our economic assistance directly into our political problems with the Soviet Union.

April 6, 1945

We have recognized for many months that the Soviets have three lines of foreign policy. (1.) Overall collaboration with us and the British in a World Security Organization; (2.) The creation of a unilateral security ring through domination of their border states; and (3.) The penetration of other countries through exploitation of democratic processes on the part of Communist controlled parties with strong Soviet backing to create political atmosphere favorable to Soviet policies.

We have been hopeful that the Soviets would, as we have, place number 1 as their primary policy and would modify their plans for 2 if they were satisfied with the efficacy of plan 1. It now seems evident that regardless of what they may expect from the World Security Organization they intend to go forward with unilateral action in the domination of their bordering states. It may well be that during and since the Moscow Conference they feel they have made this quite plain to us. You will recall that at the Moscow Conference Molotov indicated that although he would inform us of Soviet action in Eastern Europe he declined to be bound by consultation with us. It may be difficult for us to believe, but it still may be true that Stalin and Molotov considered at Yalta that by our willingness to accept a general wording of the declarations on Poland and liberated Europe, by our recognition of the need of the Red Army for security behind its lines, and of the predominant interest of Russia in Poland as a friendly neighbor and as a corridor to Germany, we understand and were ready to accept Soviet policies already known to us.

We must recognize that the words "independent but friendly neighbor" and in fact "democracy" itself have entirely different meanings to the Soviets than to us. Although they know of the meaning of these terms to us they undoubtedly feel that we should be aware of the meaning to them. We have been hopeful that the Soviets would accept our concepts whereas they on their side may have expected us to accept their own concepts, particularly in areas where their interests predominate. In any event, whatever may have been in their minds at Yalta, it now seems that they feel they can force us to acquiesce in their policies. Since we are resisting, they are using the usual Soviet tactics of retaliating in ways that they think will have the most effect, one of which is the decision not to send Molotov to the San Francisco Conference. They are fully aware of the importance we place on this Conference.

I have evidence which satisfies me that the Soviets have considered as a sign of weakness on our part our continued generous and considerate attitude towards them in spite of their disregard of our requests for cooperation in matters of interest to us.

I am further satisfied that the time has come when we must by our actions in each individual case make it plain to the Soviet Government that they cannot expect our continued cooperation on terms laid down by them. We have recognized that the Soviets have deep seated suspicions of all foreigners including ourselves. Our natural method of dealing with suspicion in others is to show our goodwill by generosity and consideration. We have earnestly attempted this policy and it has not been successful. This policy seems to have increased rather than diminished their suspicions as they evidently have misconstrued our motives. I feel that our relations would be on a much sounder basis if on the one hand we were firm and completely frank with them as to our position and motives and on the other hand they are made to understand specifically how lack of cooperation with our legitimate demands will adversely affect their interests.

I hope that I will not be misunderstood when I say that our relations with the Soviet Government will be on firmer ground as soon as we have adopted a policy which includes on the one hand at all times a full place for cooperation with the Soviet Union but on the other a readiness to go along without them if we can't obtain their cooperation. Up to recently the issues we have had with the Soviets have been relatively small compared to their contribution to the war but now we should begin to establish a new relationship. As you know I am a most earnest advocate of the closest possible understanding with the Soviet Union so that what I am saying only relates to how such understanding may be best attained.

. . . Although we should continue to approach all matters with an attitude of friendliness we should be firm and as far as practicable indicate our displeasure in ways that will definitely affect their interest in each case in which they fail to take our legitimate interests into consideration by their actions.

In the compass of this message I cannot list the almost daily affronts and total disregard which the Soviets evince in matters of interest to us. Whenever the United States does anything to which the Soviet take exception they do not hesitate to take retaliatory measures. I must with regret recommend that we begin in the near future with one or two cases where their actions are intolerable and make them realize that they cannot continue their present attitude except at great cost to themselves. We should recognize that if we adopt this policy we may have some adverse repercussions in the beginning. On the other hand we have evidence that in cases where they have been made to feel that their interests were being adversely affected we have obtained quick and favorable action. In any event I see no alternative as our present relations are clearly unsatisfactory.

. . . In spite of recent developments, I am still satisfied that if we deal with the Soviets on a realistic basis, we can in time attain a workable basis for our relations. There is ample evidence that the Soviets desire our help and collaboration but they now think they can have them on their own terms which in many cases are completely unacceptable to us. They do not understand that their present actions seriously jeopardize the attainment of satisfactory relations with us and unless they are made to understand this now, they will become increasingly difficult to deal with.

Nov. 15, 1945

. . . Certain manifestations of internal discontent . . . have been evident in the Soviet Union since the conclusion of the war.

In general, it may be said that this discontent is the product of (a) the economic deterioration and social maladjustments which in any country result from war and invasion and (*b*) the nature of Soviet bureaucracy.

The enclosures to this despatch suggest that the discontent is fairly widespread. For reasons to be discussed at the end of this despatch, it would be an error to deduce from the enclosures that it is also of such general intensity as to jeopardize the stability of the Soviet system. The current dissatisfaction does, nevertheless, probably result in impairment of the morale, efficiency and, consequently, strength of the Soviet Union.

The evidence of discontent may be divided into three categories: (1) that involving demobilized soldiers and sailors and troops transferred back to the Soviet Union from East and Central Europe; (2) that arising in trades union organizations; and (3) that prevailing among the general public. . . .

Having viewed in some detail the evidence of discontent in the Soviet Union, an attempt should be made to evaluate this dissatisfaction in broad perspective. Such an evaluation raises and answers the question why Soviet discontent finds expression in resignation rather than revolt.

A number of factors in the Soviet Union nullify whatever impulse there may be to revolt. One is the ubiquitous strength of the Soviet control and repression mechanisms. The group now in power in the Kremlin got there through conspiracy and revolt; they know better than anyone else in the U.S.S.R. the symptoms and course of revolutionary conspiracy. In these circumstances, there is slight chance of serious organized opposition making an appearance, much less surviving. Another factor is the capacity of the Russian masses for long-suffering submission to authority. A third factor is that the people of the U.S.S.R. are now in the Soviet groove. They have lived for 28 years in the Soviet system. They undoubtedly desire modifications within the Soviet system, but few of them can now construct in their thinking a practical alternative philosophy of government. Finally, Soviet propaganda is an omnipresent and powerful pressure in the direction of conformity to and acceptance of the Soviet system.

Realizing all of this, the shrewd, inexorable and pitiless men who rule the Soviet Union can, if they wish, afford to overlook much of the popular discontent. They undoubtedly recognize that discontent means a lowering of morale and, consequently, efficiency. But discontent is not likely to jeopardize the stability of the system unless it becomes so general and intense as to disaffect the personnel of the state control and repression mechanisms.

The rulers of the U.S.S.R. are therefore able to handle (and have generally had to handle, since their advent to power) a wide margin of discontent—perhaps the widest known in any contemporary state. In the vital sphere of state planning—blueprinting the portentous future of the Soviet Union—the breadth of this margin enables the men who rule the U.S.S.R. drastically to limit production of consumer's goods and in direct ratio, to augment capital and military production and construction. All indications are that this is exactly what is being done—individual wants are being sacrificed to the aggrandizement of the economic-military might of the Soviet Union.

Discontent will therefore probably continue. If it approaches the boiling point of serious disaffection or if efficiency is dangerously impaired, concessions can be made in the form of a slight increase in consumers' goods. Otherwise, discontent will be allowed to exist as a necessary evil attendant to the realization of towering ambition . . .

Nov. 27, 1945

I have been attempting to obtain some understanding of the real effect of the atomic bomb on Soviet attitude and have come to the following tentative general interpretations.

It must be borne in mind that high Soviet Governmental and party leaders have lived throughout their lives in almost constant state of fear or tension beginning with the days when they were conspirators in a revolutionary movement. They attained their objective through determination and aggressive tactics as well as intrigue and bluff. As they have never felt fully secure either for themselves personally or for the revolution they have been constantly on the alert and suspicious of all opposition. This atmosphere continued throughout the period when they seized control of the Government and faced internal and external forces attempting to expel them. They feared capitalistic encirclement and dissension within the ranks of the party, leading to two ruthless purges: and later when Hitler came to power they faced the menace of German aggression. The invasion came and all but destroyed them. When the tide of the war turned, there must have been a feeling of tremendous relief. With victory came confidence in the power of the Red Army and in their control at home, giving them for the first time a sense of security for themselves personally and for the revolution that they have never had before.

It will be recalled that in September 1941, Stalin told me that he was under no illusions, the Russian people were fighting as they always had "for their homeland, not for us," meaning the Communist Party. He would never make such a statement today. The war had assisted in the consolidation of the revolution in Russia. They determined the Red Army should be kept strong and industry developed to support it so that no power on earth could threaten the Soviet Union again. Political steps were taken to obtain defense in depth, disregarding the interests and desires of other peoples. The strength of the Red Army would ensure that these policies could be carried out regardless of opposition.

Suddenly the atomic bomb appeared and they recognized that it was an offset to the power of the Red Army. This must have revived their old feeling of insecurity. They could no longer be absolutely sure that they could obtain their objectives without interference. As a result it would seem that they have returned to their tactics of obtaining their objectives through aggressiveness and intrigue. It is revealing that in early September in the Bulgarian elections campaign the Communist Party used posters to the effect that "we are not afraid of the atomic bomb". This attitude partially explains Molotov's aggressiveness in London. I have confirmation of this from a former member of the Communist Party. It is not without significance that Molotov, in his November 7th [6th] speech bragged about bigger and better weapons. The Russian people have been aroused to feel that they must face again an antagonistic world. American imperialism is included as a threat to the Soviet Union.

23 THE IRON CURTAIN HAS DESCENDED

Winston Churchill (1874–1965)

Twice Prime Minister of Great Britain, a Nobel Prize winner in literature, and the leader who by his courage and determination kept his country in the war against Hitler, Sir Winston Churchill has been called the most famous figure in the first half of the twentieth century. His inclusion in a compilation of American views of Russia is justified by the fact that he was made an honorary citizen of the United States in 1963. Not only was his mother American but, more importantly, the speech he made in Fulton, Missouri, on March 5, 1946, was the first clear warning to the United States of our involvement in a cold war with Russia. The speech is also noteworthy as marking the first use of the term "iron curtain" to describe the boundaries of the Soviet bloc.

A SHADOW HAS FALLEN upon the scenes so lately lightened, lighted by the Allied victory. Nobody knows what Soviet Russia and its Communist international organization intends to do in the immediate future, or what are the limits, if any, to their expansive and proselytizing tendencies.

I have a strong admiration and regard for the valiant Russian people and for my wartime comrade, Marshal Stalin. There is deep sympathy and good-will in Britain—and I doubt not here also—toward the peoples of all the Russias and a resolve to persevere through many differences and rebuffs in establishing lasting friendships.

Winston Churchill speaks at Westminster College, Fulton, Missouri, 1946. This was the occasion for the famous "iron curtain" speech, which set the tone of American opinion for many years.

We understand the Russian need to be secure on her western frontiers from the removal, by the removal of all possibility of German aggression. We welcome Russia to her rightful place among the leading nations of the world. We welcome her flag upon the seas. Above all, we welcome or should welcome constant, frequent and growing contacts between the Russian people and our own peoples on both sides of the Atlantic.

It is my duty, however, and I am sure you would not wish me not to state the facts as I see them to you, it is my duty to place before you certain facts about the present position in Europe.

From Stettin in the Baltic to Trieste in the Adriatic an iron curtain has descended across the Continent. Behind that line lie all the capitals of the ancient states of central and eastern Europe. Warsaw, Berlin, Prague, Vienna, Budapest, Belgrade, Bucharest and Sofia, all these famous cities and the populations around them lie in what I might call the Soviet sphere, and all are subject, in one form or another, not only to Soviet influence but to a very high and in some cases increasing measure of control from Moscow.

Police governments are pervading from Moscow. But Athens alone, with its immortal glories, is free to decide its future at an election under British, American and French observation.

The Russian-dominated Polish Government has been encouraged to make enormous and wrongful inroads upon Germany, and mass expulsions of millions of Germans on a scale grievous and undreamed-of are now taking place. . . .

I do not believe that Soviet Russia desires war. What they desire is the fruits of war and the indefinite expansion of their power and doctrines.

But what we have to consider here today while time remains, is the permanent prevention of war and the establishment of conditions of freedom and democracy as rapidly as possible in all countries. Our difficulties and dangers will not be removed by closing our eyes to them. They will not be removed by mere waiting to see what happens; nor will they be removed by a policy of appeasement.

What is needed is a settlement, and the longer this is delayed, the more difficult it will be and the greater our dangers will become.

From what I have seen of our Russian friends and allies during the war, I am convinced that there is nothing they admire so much as strength, and there is nothing for which they have less respect than weakness, especially military weakness.

For that, for that reason the old doctrine of a balance of power is unsound. We can not afford, if we can help it, to work on narrow margins, offering temptations to a trial of strength.

If the Western democracies stand together in strict adherence to the principles of the United Nations Charter, their influence for furthering those principles will be immense and no one is likely to molest them. If, however, they become divided or falter in their duty, and if these all-important years are allowed to slip away, then indeed catastrophe may overwhelm us all.

24 WORLD GOVERNMENT NEEDS THE SOVIETS

Albert Einstein (1879–1958)

One of the greatest mathematical geniuses of all time, German-born Albert Einstein came to the United States in 1933 to avoid Nazi persecution. Professor Einstein, whose work in developing the theory of relativity won him a Nobel Prize in 1922, became associated with Princeton University and was naturalized as an American citizen in 1940. After the outbreak of World War II, he was one of the nuclear scientists on whose recommendation President Roosevelt decided that the United States should embark on a program to develop an atomic bomb. At the end of the war Einstein became one of the leading advocates of world government as the best means of assuring that nuclear weapons would never again be employed. While aware of the non-democratic aspects of the Soviet Union, Einstein, a socialist, was critical of what he regarded as America's failure to take sufficient steps to reach an accommodation with Russia. The comments which follow were made in an interview which appeared in *Atlantic Monthly* in November 1945 and November 1947.

THE RELEASE OF atomic energy has not created a new problem. It has merely made more urgent the necessity of solving an existing one. One could say that it has affected us quantitatively, not qualitatively. So long as there are sovereign nations possessing great power, war is inevitable. That is not an attempt to say when it will come, but only that it is sure to come. That was true before the atomic bomb was made. What has been changed is the destructiveness of war.

I do not believe that civilization will be wiped out in a war fought with the atomic bomb. Perhaps two-thirds of the people of the earth might be killed. But enough men capable of thinking, and enough books, would be left to start again, and civilization could be restored.

I do not believe that the secret of the bomb should be given to the United Nations Organization. I do not believe it should be given to the Soviet Union. Either course would be like a man with capital, and wishing another man to work with him on some enterprise, starting out by simply giving that man half of his money. The other man might choose to start a rival enterprise, when what is wanted is his cooperation. The secret of the bomb should be committed to a world government, and the United States should immediately announce its readiness to give it to a world government. This government should be founded by the United States, the Soviet Union, and Great Britain, the only three powers with great military strength. . . .

Since the United States and Great Britain have the secret of the atomic bomb and the Soviet Union does not, they should invite the Soviet Union to prepare and present the first draft of a constitution of the proposed world government. That will help dispel the distrust of the Russians, which they already feel because the bomb is being kept a secret chiefly to prevent their having it. Obviously the first draft would not be the final one, but the Russians should be made to feel that the world government will assure them their security. . . .

The establishment of this world government must not have to wait until the same conditions of freedom are to be found in all three of the great powers. While it is true that in the Soviet Union the minority rules, I do not consider that internal conditions there are of themselves a threat to world peace. One must bear in mind that the people in Russia did not have a long political education, and changes to improve Russian conditions had to be carried through by a minority for the reason that there was no majority capable of doing it. If I had been born a Russian, I believe I could have adjusted myself to this situation. . . .

I say that nothing has been done to avert war since the completion of the atomic bomb, despite the proposal for supranational control of atomic energy put forward by the United States in the United Nations. This country has made only a conditional proposal, and on conditions which the Soviet Union is now determined not to accept. This makes it possible to blame the failure on the Russians.

But in blaming the Russians the Americans should not ignore the fact that they themselves have not voluntarily renounced the use of the bomb as an ordinary weapon in the time before the achievement of supranational control, or if supranational control is not achieved. Thus they have fed the fear of other countries that they consider the bomb a legitimate part of their arsenal so long as other countries decline to accept their terms for supranational control. . . .

I do not suggest that the American failure to outlaw the use of the bomb except in retaliation is the only cause of the absence of an agreement with the Soviet Union over atomic control. The Russians have made it clear that they will do everything in their power to prevent a supranational regime from coming into existence. They not only reject it in the range of atomic energy: they reject it sharply on principle, and thus have spurned in advance any overture to join a limited world government.

Mr. Gromyko has rightly said that the essence of the American atomic proposal is that national sovereignty is not compatible with the atomic era. He declares that the Soviet Union cannot accept this thesis. The reasons he gives are obscure, for they quite obviously are pretexts. But what seems to be true is that the Soviet leaders believe they cannot preserve the social structure of the Soviet state in a supranational regime. The Soviet government is determined to maintain its present social structure, and the leaders of Russia, who hold their great power through the nature of that structure, will spare no effort to prevent a supranational regime from coming into existence, to control atomic energy or anything else.

The Russians may be partly right about the difficulty of retaining their present social structure in a supranational regime, though in time they may be brought to see that this is a far lesser loss than remaining isolated from a world of law. But at present they appear to be guided by their fears, and one must admit that the United States has made ample contributions to these fears, not only as to atomic energy but in many other respects. Indeed this country has conducted its Russian policy as though it were convinced that fear is the greatest of all diplomatic instruments.

That the Russians are striving to prevent the formation of a supranational security system is no reason why the rest of the world should not work to create one. It has been pointed out that the Russians have a way of resisting with all their arts what they do not wish to have happen; but once it happens, they can be flexible and accommodate themselves to it. So it would be well for the United States and other powers not to permit the Russians to veto an attempt to create supranational security. They can proceed with some hope that once the Russians see they cannot prevent such a regime they may join it.

So far the United States has shown no interest in preserving the security of the Soviet Union. It has been interested in its own security, which is characteristic of the competition which marks the conflict for power between sovereign states. But one cannot know in advance what would be the effect on Russian fears if the American people forced their leaders to pursue a policy of substituting law for the present anarchy of international relations. In a world of law, Russian security would be equal to our own, and for the American people to espouse this wholeheartedly, something that should be possible under the workings of democracy, might work a kind of miracle in Russian thinking.

At present the Russians have no evidence to convince them that the American people are not contentedly supporting a policy of military preparedness which they regard as a policy of deliberate intimidation. If they had evidences of a passionate desire by Americans to preserve peace in the one way it can be maintained, by a supranational regime of law, this would upset Russian calculations about the peril to Russian security in current trends of American thought. Not until a genuine, convincing offer is made to the Soviet Union, backed by an aroused American public, will one be entitled to say what the Russian response would be.

It may be that the first response would be to reject the world of law. But if from that moment it began to be clear to the Russians that such a world was coming into existence without them, and that their own security was being increased, their ideas necessarily would change.

I am in favor of inviting the Russians to join a world government authorized to provide security, and if they are unwilling to join, to proceed to establish supranational security without them. Let me admit quickly that I see great peril in such a course. If it is adopted it must be done in a way to make it utterly clear that the new regime is not a combination of power against Russia. It must be a combination that by its composite nature will greatly reduce the chances of war. It will be more diverse in its interests than any single state, thus less likely to resort to aggressive or preventive war. It will be larger, hence stronger than any single nation. It will be geographically much more extensive, and thus more difficult to defeat by military means. It will be dedicated to supranational security, and thus escape the emphasis on national supremacy which is so strong a factor in war.

If a supranational regime is set up without Russia, its service to peace will depend on the skill and sincerity with which it is done. Emphasis should always be apparent on the desire to have Russia take part. It must be clear to Russia, and no less so to the nations comprising the organization, that no penalty is incurred or implied because a nation declines to join. If the Russians do not join at the outset, they must be sure of a welcome when they do decide to join. Those who create the organization must understand that they are building with the final objective of obtaining Russian adherence.

These are abstractions, and it is not easy to outline the specific lines a partial world government must follow to induce the Russians to join. But two conditions are clear to me: the new organization must have no military secrets; and the Russians must be free to have observers at every session of the organization, where its new laws are drafted, discussed, and adopted, and where its policies are decided. That would destroy the great factory of secrecy where so many of the world's suspicions are manufactured. . . .

Membership in a supranational security system should not, in my opinion, be based on any arbitrary democratic standards. The one requirement from all should be that the representatives to a supranational organization—assembly and council—must be elected by the people in each member country through a secret ballot. These representatives must represent the people rather than any government—which would enhance the pacific nature of the organization.

To require that other democratic criteria be met is, I believe, inadvisable. Democratic institutions and standards are the result of historic developments to an extent not always appreciated in the lands which enjoy them. Setting arbitrary standards sharpens the ideological differences between the Western and Soviet systems.

But it is not the ideological differences which now are pushing the world in the direction of war. Indeed, if all the Western nations were to adopt socialism, while maintaining their national sovereignty, it is quite likely that the conflict for power between East and West would continue. The passion expressed over the economic systems of the present seems to me quite irrational. Whether the economic life of America should be dominated by relatively few individuals, as it is, or these individuals should be controlled by the state, may be important, but it is not important enough to justify all the feelings that are stirred up over it. . . .

I do not hide from myself the great difficulties of establishing a world government, either a beginning without Russia or one with Russia. I am aware of the risks. Since I should not wish it to be permissible for any country that has joined the supranational organization to secede, one of these risks is a possible civil war. But I also believe that world government is certain to come in time, and that the question is how much it is to be permitted to cost. It will come, I believe, even if there is another world war, though after such a war, if it is won, it would be world government established by the victor, resting on the victor's military power, and thus to be maintained permanently only through the permanent militarization of the human race. . . .

25 THE POLICY OF CONTAINMENT

"X" (George F. Kennan [1904–   ])

No enunciation of American views on Russia has had a greater impact on the formulation of U.S. foreign policy than an article entitled "The Sources of Soviet Conduct," which appeared in the prestigious journal *Foreign Affairs* in July 1947. The author, identified only as "X," was subsequently discovered to be George F. Kennan, then Director of the Policy Planning Staff of the State Department and one of America's most renowned Kremlinologists. Born in Milwaukee, Wisconsin, and nephew of the famous expert on tsarist Russia, George Kennan, the younger Kennan graduated from Princeton University in 1925 and entered the Foreign Service of the State Department the following year. He was one of a group of young officers trained in the Russian language in anticipation of the establishment of diplomatic relations with Russia, and when the American Embassy was re-opened in Moscow in 1933 he was assigned as a member of Ambassador Bullitt's staff. In the years which followed, Kennan occupied many senior positions in the State Department, including that of Ambassador to the Soviet Union in 1952 and Ambassador to Yugoslavia from 1961 to 1963. The following excerpts from his article in *Foreign Affairs* describe the basis of the postwar American policy of "containment" of the Soviet Union.

THE POLITICAL PERSONALITY of Soviet power as we know it today is the product of ideology and circumstances: ideology inherited by the present Soviet leaders from the movement in which they had their political origin, and circumstances of the power which they now have exercised for nearly three decades in Russia. There can be few tasks of psychological analysis more difficult than to trace the interaction of these two forces and the relative rôle of each in the determination of official Soviet conduct. Yet the attempt must be made if that conduct is to be understood and effectively countered. . . .

The circumstances of the immediate post-revolution period— the existence in Russia of civil war and foreign intervention, together with the obvious fact that the Communists represented only a tiny minority of the Russian people—made the establishment of dictatorial power a necessity. The experiment with "war Communism" and the abrupt attempt to eliminate private production and trade had unfortunate economic consequences and caused further bitterness against the new revolutionary régime. . . .

Now it lies in the nature of the mental world of the Soviet leaders, as well as in the character of their ideology, that no opposition to them can be officially recognized as having any merit or justification whatsoever. Such opposition can flow, in theory, only from the hostile and incorrigible forces of dying capitalism. As long as remnants of capitalism were officially recognized as existing in Russia, it was possible to place on them, as an internal element, part of the blame for the maintenance of a dictatorial form of society. But as these remnants were liquidated, little by little, this justification fell away; and when it was indicated officially that they had been finally destroyed, it disappeared altogether. And this fact created one of the most basic of the compulsions which came to act upon the Soviet régime: since capitalism no longer existed in Russia and since it could not be admitted that there could be serious or widespread opposition to the Kremlin springing spontaneously from the liberated masses under its authority, it became necessary to justify the retention of the dictatorship by stressing the menace of capitalism abroad. . . .

Now the maintenance of this pattern of Soviet power, namely, the pursuit of unlimited authority domestically, accompanied by the cultivation of the semi-myth of implacable foreign hostility, has gone far to shape the actual machinery of Soviet power as we know it today. Internal organs of administration which did not serve this purpose withered on the vine. Organs which did serve this purpose became vastly swollen. The security of Soviet power came to rest on the iron discipline of the Party, on the severity and ubiquity of the secret police, and on the uncompromising economic monopolism of the state. The "organs of suppression," in which the Soviet leaders had sought security from rival forces, became in large measure the masters of those whom they were designed to serve. Today the major part of the structure of Soviet power is committed to the perfection of the dictatorship and to the maintenance of the concept of Russia as in a state of siege, with the enemy lowering beyond the walls. And the millions of human beings who form that part of the structure of power must defend at all costs this concept of Russia's position, for without it they are themselves superfluous.

As things stand today, the rulers can no longer dream of part-ing with these organs of suppression. The quest for absolute power, pursued now for nearly three decades with a ruthlessness unparalleled (in scope at least) in modern times, has again pro-duced internally, as it did externally, its own reaction. The ex-cesses of the police apparatus have fanned the potential opposi-tion to the régime into something far greater and more dangerous than it could have been before those excesses began. . . .

This means that we are going to continue for a long time to find the Russians difficult to deal with. It does not mean that they should be considered as embarked upon a do-or-die program to overthrow our society by a given date. The theory of the in-evitability of the eventual fall of capitalism has the fortunate connotation that there is no hurry about it. The forces of progress can take their time in preparing the final *coup de grâce*. Mean-while, what is vital is that the "Socialist fatherland"—that oasis of power which has been already won for Socialism in the person of the Soviet Union—should be cherished and defended by all good Communists at home and abroad, its fortunes pro-moted, its enemies badgered and confounded. The promotion of premature, "adventuristic" revolutionary projects abroad which might embarrass Soviet power in any way would be an inexcus-able, even a counter-revolutionary act. The cause of Socialism is the support and promotion of Soviet power, as defined in Moscow.

This brings us to the second of the concepts important to contemporary Soviet outlook. That is the infallibility of the Kremlin. The Soviet concept of power, which permits no focal points of organization outside the Party itself, requires that the Party leadership remain in theory the sole repository of truth. For if truth were to be found elsewhere, there would be justification for its expression in organized activity. But it is precisely that which the Kremlin cannot and will not permit.

The leadership of the Communist Party is therefore always right, and has been always right ever since in 1929 Stalin formalized his personal power by announcing that decisions of the Politburo were being taken unanimously.

On the principle of infallibility there rests the iron discipline of the Communist Party. In fact, the two concepts are mutually self-supporting. Perfect discipline requires recognition of infallibility. Infallibility requires the observance of discipline. And the two together go far to determine the behaviorism of the entire Soviet apparatus of power. But their effect cannot be understood unless a third factor be taken into account: namely, the fact that the leadership is at liberty to put forward for tactical purposes any particular thesis which it finds useful to the cause at any particular moment and to require the faithful and unquestioning acceptance of that thesis by the members of the movement as a whole. This means that truth is not a constant but is actually created, for all intents and purposes, by the Soviet leaders themselves. It may vary from week to week, from month to month. It is nothing absolute and immutable—nothing which flows from objective reality. It is only the most recent manifestation of the wisdom of those in which the ultimate wisdom is supposed to reside, because they represent the logic of history.

But we have seen that the Kremlin is under no ideological compulsion to accomplish its purposes in a hurry. Like the Church, it is dealing in ideological concepts which are of long-term validity, and it can afford to be patient. It has no right to risk the existing achievements of the revolution for the sake of vain baubles of the future. The very teachings of Lenin himself require great caution and flexibility in the pursuit of Communist purposes. Again, these precepts are fortified by the lessons of Russian history: of centuries of obscure battles between nomadic forces over the stretches of a vast unfortified plain. Here caution, circumspection, flexibility and deception are the valuable qualities; and their value finds natural appreciation in the Russian or the oriental mind. Thus the Kremlin has no compunction about retreating in the face of superior force. And being under the compulsion of no timetable, it does not get panicky under the necessity for such retreat. Its political action is a fluid stream which moves constantly, wherever it is permitted to move, toward a given goal. Its main concern is to make sure that it has filled every nook and cranny available to it in the basin of world power. But if it finds unassailable barriers in its path, it accepts these philosophically and accommodates itself to them. The main thing is that there should always be pressure, unceasing constant pressure, toward the desired goal. There is no trace of any feeling in Soviet psychology that that goal must be reached at any given time. . . .

In these circumstances it is clear that the main element of any United States policy toward the Soviet Union must be that of a long-term, patient but firm and vigilant containment of Russian expansive tendencies. It is important to note, however, that such a policy has nothing to do with outward histrionics: with threats or blustering or superfluous gestures of outward "toughness." While the Kremlin is basically flexible in its reaction to political realities, it is by no means unamenable to considerations of prestige. Like almost any other government, it can be placed by tactless and threatening gestures in a position where it cannot afford to yield even though this might be dictated by its sense of realism. The Russian leaders are keen judges of human psychology, and as such they are highly conscious that loss of temper and of self-control is never a source of strength in political affairs. They are quick to exploit such evidences of weakness. For these reasons, it is a *sine qua non* of successful dealing with Russia that the foreign government in question should remain at all times cool and collected and that its demands on Russian policy should be put forward in such a manner as to leave the way open for a compliance not too detrimental to Russian prestige.

In the light of the above, it will be clearly seen that the Soviet pressure against the free institutions of the western world is something that can be contained by the adroit and vigilant application of counter-force at a series of constantly shifting geographical and political points, corresponding to the shifts and manœuvres of Soviet policy, but which cannot be charmed or talked out of existence. The Russians look forward to a duel of infinite duration, and they see that already they have scored great successes. It must be borne in mind that there was a time when the Communist Party represented far more of a minority in the sphere of Russian national life than Soviet power today represents in the world community.

But if ideology convinces the rulers of Russia that truth is on their side and that they can therefore afford to wait, those of us on whom that ideology has no claim are free to examine objectively the validity of that premise. The Soviet thesis not only implies complete lack of control by the west over its own economic destiny, it likewise assumes Russian unity, discipline and patience over an infinite period. Let us bring this apocalyptic vision down to earth, and suppose that the western world finds the strength and resourcefulness to contain Soviet power over a period of ten to fifteen years. What does that spell for Russia itself?

The Soviet leaders, taking advantage of the contributions of modern technique to the arts of despotism, have solved the question of obedience within the confines of their power. Few challenge their authority; and even those who do are unable to make that challenge valid as against the organs of suppression of the state.

The Kremlin has also proved able to accomplish its purpose of building up in Russia, regardless of the interests of the inhabitants, an industrial foundation of heavy metallurgy, which is, to be sure, not yet complete but which is nevertheless continuing to grow and is approaching those of the other major industrial countries. All of this, however, both the maintenance of internal political security and the building of heavy industry, has been carried out at a terrible cost in human life and in human hopes and energies. It has necessitated the use of forced labor on a scale unprecedented in modern times under conditions of peace. It has involved the neglect or abuse of other phases of Soviet economic life, particularly agriculture, consumers' goods production, housing and transportation . . .

In these circumstances, there are limits to the physical and nervous strength of people themselves. These limits are absolute ones, and are binding even for the cruelest dictatorship, because beyond them people cannot be driven. The forced labor camps and the other agencies of constraint provide temporary means of compelling people to work longer hours than their own volition or mere economic pressure would dictate; but if people survive them at all they become old before their time and must be considered as human casualties to the demands of dictatorship. In either case their best powers are no longer available to society and can no longer be enlisted in the service of the state. . . .

Meanwhile, a great uncertainty hangs over the political life of the Soviet Union. That is the uncertainty involved in the transfer of power from one individual or group of individuals to others.

This is, of course, outstandingly the problem of the personal position of Stalin. We must remember that his succession to Lenin's pinnacle of preëminence in the Communist movement was the only such transfer of individual authority which the Soviet Union has experienced. That transfer took 12 years to consolidate. It cost the lives of millions of people and shook the state to its foundations. The attendant tremors were felt all through the international revolutionary movement, to the disadvantage of the Kremlin itself.

It is always possible that another transfer of preëminent power may take place quietly and inconspicuously, with no repercussions anywhere. But again, it is possible that the questions involved may unleash, to use some of Lenin's words, one of those "incredibly swift transitions" from "delicate deceit" to "wild violence" which characterize Russian history, and may shake Soviet power to its foundations.

But this is not only a question of Stalin himself. There has been, since 1938, a dangerous congealment of political life in the higher circles of Soviet power. The All-Union Congress of Soviets, in theory the supreme body of the Party, is supposed to meet not less often than once in three years. It will soon be eight full years since its last meeting. During this period membership in the Party has numerically doubled. Party mortality during the war was enormous; and today well over half of the Party members are persons who have entered since the last Party congress was held. Meanwhile, the same small group of men has carried on at the top through an amazing series of national vicissitudes. Surely there is some reason why the experiences of the war brought basic political changes to every one of the great governments of the west. Surely the causes of that phenomenon are basic enough to be present somewhere in the obscurity of Soviet political life, as well. And yet no recognition has been given to these causes in Russia.

It must be surmised from this that even within so highly disciplined an organization as the Communist Party there must be a growing divergence in age, outlook and interest between the great mass of Party members, only so recently recruited into the movement, and the little self-perpetuating clique of men at the top, whom most of these Party members have never met, with whom they have never conversed, and with whom they can have no *political* intimacy . . .

Thus the future of Soviet power may not be by any means as secure as Russian capacity for self-delusion would make it appear to the men in the Kremlin. That they can keep power themselves, they have demonstrated. That they can quietly and easily turn it over to others remains to be proved. Meanwhile, the hardships of their rule and the vicissitudes of international life have taken a heavy toll of the strength and hopes of the great people on whom their power rests. It is curious to note that the ideological power of Soviet authority is strongest today in areas beyond the frontiers of Russia, beyond the reach of its police power. This phenomenon brings to mind a comparison used by Thomas Mann in his great novel "Buddenbrooks." Observing that human institutions often show the greatest outward brilliance at a moment when inner decay is in reality farthest advanced, he compared the Buddenbrook family, in the days of its greatest glamour, to one of those stars whose light shines most brightly on this world when in reality it has long since ceased to exist. And who can say with assurance that the strong light still cast by the Kremlin on the dissatisfied peoples of the western world is not the powerful afterglow of a constellation which is in actuality on the wane? This cannot be proved. And it cannot be disproved. But the possibility remains (and in the opinion of this writer it is a strong one) that Soviet power, like the capitalist world of its conception, bears within it the seeds of its own decay, and that the sprouting of these seeds is well advanced.

It is clear that the United States cannot expect in the foreseeable future to enjoy political intimacy with the Soviet régime. It must continue to regard the Soviet Union as a rival, not a partner, in the political arena. It must continue to expect that Soviet policies will reflect no abstract love of peace and stability, no real faith in the possibility of a permanent happy coexistence of the Socialist and capitalist worlds, but rather a cautious, persistent pressure toward the disruption and weakening of all rival influence and rival power.

Balanced against this are the facts that Russia, as opposed to the western world in general, is still by far the weaker party, that Soviet policy is highly flexible, and that Soviet society may well contain deficiencies which will eventually weaken its own total potential. This would of itself warrant the United States entering with reasonable confidence upon a policy of firm containment, designed to confront the Russians with unalterable counter-force at every point where they show signs of encroaching upon the interests of a peaceful and stable world.

But in actuality the possibilities for American policy are by no means limited to holding the line and hoping for the best. It is entirely possible for the United States to influence by its actions the internal developments, both within Russia and throughout the international Communist movement, by which Russian policy is largely determined. This is not only a question of the modest measure of informational activity which this government can conduct in the Soviet Union and elsewhere, although that, too, is important. It is rather a question of the degree to which the United States can create among the peoples of the world generally the impression of a country which knows what it wants, which is coping successfully with the problems of its internal life and with the responsibilities of a World Power, and which has a spiritual vitality capable of holding its own among the major ideological currents of the time. To the extent that such an impression can be created and maintained, the aims of Russian Communism must appear sterile and quixotic, the hopes and enthusiasm of Moscow's supporters must wane, and added strain must be imposed on the Kremlin's foreign policies. For the palsied decrepitude of the capitalist world is the keystone of Communist philosophy. Even the failure of the United States to experience the early economic depression which the ravens of the Red Square have been predicting with such complacent confidence since hostilities ceased would have deep and important repercussions throughout the Communist world.

By the same token, exhibitions of indecision, disunity and internal disintegration within this country have an exhilarating effect on the whole Communist movement. At each evidence of these tendencies, a thrill of hope and excitement goes through the Communist world; a new jauntiness can be noted in the Moscow tread; new groups of foreign supporters climb on to what they can only view as the band wagon of international politics; and Russian pressure increases all along the line in international affairs.

It would be an exaggeration to say that American behavior unassisted and alone could exercise a power of life and death over the Communist movement and bring about the early fall of Soviet power in Russia. But the United States has it in its power to increase enormously the strains under which Soviet policy must operate, to force upon the Kremlin a far greater degree of moderation and circumspection than it has had to observe in recent years, and in this way to promote tendencies which must eventually find their outlet in either the break-up or the gradual mellowing of Soviet power. For no mystical, Messianic movement —and particularly not that of the Kremlin—can face frustration indefinitely without eventually adjusting itself in one way or another to the logic of that state of affairs.

Thus the decision will really fall in large measure in this country itself. The issue of Soviet-American relations is in essence a test of the over-all worth of the United States as a nation among nations. To avoid destruction the United States need only measure up to its own best traditions and prove itself worthy of preservation as a great nation.

26 SOVIET UNFRIENDLINESS

Henry L. Stimson (1867–1950)

After a long and illustrious career in government service spanning a third of a century, Henry Stimson was among those Americans who in the early postwar years alerted the country to the need to guard against Soviet expansionism. Born in New York City, Stimson graduated from Yale in 1888 and then attended Harvard Law School. He held a senior cabinet position in three different administrations: as Secretary of War in the Taft administration from 1911 to 1913, as Secretary of State for President Herbert C. Hoover from 1929 to 1933, and as Secretary of War under President Franklin D. Roosevelt from 1940 to 1945. The following excerpts come from an article entitled "The Challenge to Americans," published in *Foreign Affairs* in October 1947.

. . . IT HAS BEEN one of the more dangerous aspects of our internationalism in past years that too often it was accompanied by the curious assumption that the world would overnight become good and clean and peaceful everywhere if only America would lead the way. The most elementary experience of human affairs should show us all how naïve and dangerous a view that is.

The most conspicuous present examples of this sort of thinking are to be found among those who refuse to recognize the strong probability that one of our great and powerful neighbor nations is at present controlled by men who are convinced that the very course of history is set against democracy and freedom, as we understand those words. A very large part of what I believe to be the mistaken thinking done by my friend Henry Wallace about

198 · HENRY L. STIMSON

Soviet Russia results simply from a goodhearted insistence that nobody can dislike us if we try to like them.

We have been very patient with the Soviet Government, and very hopeful of its good intentions. I have been among those who shared in these hopes and counseled this patience. The magnificent and loyal war effort of the Russian people, and the great successful efforts at friendliness made during the war by President Roosevelt, gave us good reason for hope. I have believed—and I still believe—that we must show good faith in all our dealings with the Russians, and that only by so doing can we leave the door open for Russian good faith toward us. I cannot too strongly express my regret that since the early spring of 1945—even before the death of Mr. Roosevelt—the Soviet Government has steadily pursued an obstructive and unfriendly course. It has been our hope that the Russians would choose to be our friends; it was and is our conviction that such a choice would be to their advantage. But, for the time being, at least, those who determine Russian policy have chosen otherwise, and their choice has been slavishly followed by Communists everywhere.

No sensible American can now ignore this fact, and those who now choose to travel in company with American Communists are very clearly either knaves or fools. This is a judgment which I make reluctantly, but there is no help for it. I have often said that the surest way to make a man trustworthy is to trust him. But I must add that this does not always apply to a man who is determined to make you his dupe. Before we can make friends with the Russians, their leaders will have to be convinced that they have nothing to gain, and everything to lose, by acting on the assumption that our society is dying and that our principles are outworn. Americans who think they can make common cause with present-day Communism are living in a world that does not exist . . .

In dealing with the Russians, both uncritical trust and unmitigated belligerence are impossible. There is a middle course. We do not yet know surely in what proportion unreasonable fears and twisted hopes are at the root of the perverted policy now followed by the Kremlin. Assuming both to be involved, we must disarm the fears and disappoint the hopes. We must no longer let the tide of Soviet expansion cheaply roll into the empty places left by war, and yet we must make it perfectly clear that we are not ourselves expansionist. Our task is to help threatened peoples to help themselves.

This is not easy. It is quite possible, indeed, that the blind reaction of some anti-Communist governments may succeed to some extent in nullifying our labors. We must make every effort to prevent such a result. Success in this task depends so much on men and circumstances that I do not venture to prescribe a theoretical solution. It is an undertaking that demands a bold and active policy, combined with skilful and understanding execution. In such an undertaking, it is only the exceptionally well-informed who may properly give advice from the sidelines.

But our main answer to the Russians is not negative, nor is it in any sense anti-Russian. Our central task in dealing with the Kremlin is to demonstrate beyond the possibility of misunderstanding that freedom and prosperity, hand in hand, can be stably sustained in the western democratic world. This would be our greatest task even if no Soviet problem existed, and to the Soviet threat it is our best response.

Soviet intransigence is based in very large part on the hope and belief that all non-Communist systems are doomed. Soviet policy aims to help them die. We must hope that time and the success of freedom and democracy in the western world will convince both the Soviet leaders and the Russian people now behind them that our system is here to stay. This may not be possible; dictators do not easily change their hearts, and the modern armaments they possess may make it hard for their people to force such a change. Rather than be persuaded of their error, the Soviet leaders might in desperation resort to war, and against that possibility we have to guard by maintaining our present military advantages. We must never forget that while peace is a joint responsibility, the decision for war can be made by a single Power; our military strength must be maintained as a standing discouragement to aggression.

I do not, however, expect the Russians to make war. I do not share the gloomy fear of some that we are now engaged in the preliminaries of an inevitable conflict. Even the most repressive dictatorship is not perfectly unassailable from within, and the most frenzied fanaticism is never unopposed. Whatever the ideological bases of Soviet policy, it seems clear that some at least of the leaders of Russia are men who have a marked respect for facts. We must make it wholly evident that a nonaggressive Russia will have nothing to fear from us. We must make it clear, too, that the western non-Communist world is going to survive in growing economic and political stability. If we can do this, then slowly—but perhaps less slowly than we now believe—the Russian leaders may either change their minds or lose their jobs.

27 SLAVE LABOR

International Free Trade Union News

One of the obstacles faced by the Soviet Union in its drive to establish Communist regimes abroad has been an inability to win the support of American labor. Indeed, far from finding common ground with the Soviets, organized American labor has generally been in the forefront of criticism of the communist system. As early as January 1947 the *International Free Trade Union News* of the Free Trade Union Committee of the American Federation of Labor published the following strong attack on Soviet forced labor camps.

ABOUT A QUARTER OF A CENTURY AGO it seemed as if the complete extinction of the last remnants of slavery throughout the world might not be far off. Slavery had been outlawed by international conventions and its abolition in those backward countries where it still existed was, apparently, only a question of time.

However, the rise of totalitarianism brought about a complete reversal of this historical trend. During the last 20 years the world has witnessed the reintroduction of slavery on a gigantic scale. The widespread use of forced labor by the modern dictatorships and those under their influence is, indeed, nothing but a reappearance of slavery under a different name. This reversion to servitude—and that is what it is, in the literal sense of the word —is one of the principal characteristics of modern totalitarianism and totalitarian tendencies.

The process of creating huge forced labor armies began in Russia under the first Five-Year Plan. Since that time, slave labor has become a regular and integral factor of the Russian economy

201

as it has developed under subsequent Five-Year Plans. A net of so-called corrective labor camps has been gradually extended all over the Soviet Union. Various estimates of the number of the inmates of these camps have been made, but the figure of 10,000,000—not including prisoners of war and other deported non-Soviet citizens—seems to be not exaggerated.

When Hitler seized power in Germany, he immediately followed the Soviet example by creating concentration camps for political opponents and any other persons whom the Nazi regime considered harmful; and when the Nazis overran Europe they created an immense reservoir of forced labor by deporting millions of workers to Germany.

But the defeat and destruction of the Nazi dictatorship has failed to ring the knell for the system of modern slavery which had been introduced by totalitarianism. The situation in Russia remains unchanged. In spite of the high-sounding declarations of the Soviet Constitution, the Russian political police still retains the power, conferred upon it by a decree of 1934, to send anyone to a concentration camp without a trial. The provision of this decree that the political police may not impose terms in concentration camps for longer than five years is virtually meaningless, since the practice is to impose additional terms after the expiration of the first. There is no indication that the Soviet government has thought of rewarding the sufferings and sacrifices of the peoples of the Soviet Union during the war by abolishing or reducing the number of concentration camps, or by liberating any appreciable portion of their gigantic forced labor army. On the contrary, we have been informed that as a collective punishment for the collaborationism of some, several autonomous republics were abolished and their entire populations deported.

The new purges sweeping all sections of Soviet public *and* economic life indicate that the activities of the Soviet political police, aimed at assuring a constant supply of forced labor, are as ruthless as ever.

Not only has the forced labor situation failed to improve inside the borders of the Soviet Union, but the Soviet government has extended its methods far beyond its own frontiers. Reports from Yugoslavia, Bulgaria and Poland prove that the Russian system of concentration camps and forced labor has been fully adopted by the satellite states of the Soviet Union. In addition, the Soviet government has continued the practice which it inaugurated in 1939 and 1940 when, during its pact with Hitler, it occupied the Eastern provinces of Poland and the Baltic states and deported over 1,000,000 Poles and a considerable number of Lithuanians, Letts and Estonians to remote parts of the Soviet Union. Recently, the deportation of German workers from the Soviet zone of occupation was resumed on a large scale. The mass expulsions of the German population from their homes in the Sudeten districts of Czechoslovakia and in the Eastern provinces of Germany are intimately connected with the system of totalitarian slavery.

Such treatment of millions of people, driven from their homes after being stripped of all their possessions, is conceivable only in a political and moral climate saturated and infected by the totalitarian practice of slave-raiding—a practice in which, unfortunately, other powers have so far diplomatically acquiesced.

The question of German war prisoners must also be considered from this point of view. Eighteen months have passed since the cessation of hostilities in Europe, but there are still more than 3,000,000 German war prisoners in Russia (to say nothing of the still uncounted number of Japanese), about 600,000 in France and 360,000 in England. These are being used for forced labor. In this particular instance, it is done under the guise of collecting reparations. However, servitude is prejudicial to free labor and to human liberty in general, regardless of the pretext under which it is practiced. It is particularly deplorable that democratic nations should make use of the forced labor of war prisoners, and thereby help to fortify the totalitarian system of outright slavery as it exists in the Soviet Union.

Free labor has always opposed slave labor in any form or under any pretext. Slave labor anywhere in the world adversely affects the standards of free labor everywhere. Moreover, each highly centralized political system based on slavery engenders aggressive policies, since it tends to enslave new populations in order to satisfy its need for an additional supply of forced labor. Furthermore, such a system tends to resort to conquest as a means of acquiring sources of wealth which it cannot create fast enough because of the notoriously low productivity of slave labor.

There is really an "irrepressible conflict" between free labor and every system of forced labor. To those who excuse the Soviet methods on the ground that such practices serve the aims of socialism, the reply can only be that the founders of the socialist doctrine proclaimed it as a path for workers' liberation, and not their enslavement. In discussing the totalitarian system of slavery now represented by the Soviet Union, the problem of socialism, as such, does not enter. In this case the question is simply one of free labor versus slave labor.

The A. F. of L. has condemned all forms of forced labor and servitude. The A. F. of L., through its Bill of Rights, appeals to all forces of free labor throughout the world to support it in this crucial struggle.

28 A CONSPIRACY FROM WITHIN

Joseph R. McCarthy (1908–1957)

During his eleven years in the United States Senate from 1946 to 1957, Joseph R. McCarthy became one of the most controversial men ever to serve in that chamber. To his supporters he was the arch-foe of Communism, fearlessly exposing Communists and Soviet agents who had infiltrated the American government as a result of the connivance or stupidity of senior U.S. officials. His opponents charged that he was irresponsibly and recklessly accusing many individuals of membership in the Communist Party, including a large number of innocent people.

Born in Grand Chute, Wisconsin, Joseph McCarthy obtained a law degree from Marquette University in 1935. After serving as a judge in Wisconsin and as a Marine officer in World War II, he was elected to the Senate as a Republican in 1946. McCarthy first attracted national attention in February 1950, when he publicly charged that there were fifty-seven known Communists working in the State Department. Most of his allegations are now regarded as partially or totally false, and he died in relative obscurity after losing prestige in a nationally televised encounter with senior civilian and military officials of the Army. The views he espoused, however, are important as reflecting the widespread concern of many Americans that the Soviet Union could not have become such a threat to the United States without "something being wrong in Washington." The following excerpts come from Senator McCarthy's book *America's Retreat from Victory* (1951), in which he implied that General George C. Marshall, Army Chief of Staff in World War II and subsequently Secretary of State and then Secretary of Defense, was a Soviet agent.

DURING THE SUMMER OF 1945 America stood at what Churchill described as the "highest pinnacle of her power and fame." The President and the man who was to be his Secretary of Defense commanded the greatest military instrumentality on land, sea and in the air that the world had ever seen. Our forces had fought victoriously on every continent except the American—in Africa, in Europe, in Asia, and above, on and over the seven seas. The Soviet empire, which would have fallen before the Nazis but for our assistance, was nursing its wounds, but glowering, self-confident and on the march from its own weakness. Britain had declined into the incompetent, self-righteous and doctrinaire hands of its Labor Party. Britain was economically prostrated, its empire was dwindling and was to dwindle further.

Only the United States among the great powers found its economic strength undiminished, its Territories uninvaded and unswept by war, its full powers still unflexed. Everywhere America had friends, everywhere its power suggested friendship to others. In terms of the division of the world into spheres of interest, the United States, at the head of the coalition of the West, exercised friendly influence over nearly all the masses of the earth. The Soviet Union's own people and the few millions in the bordering satellites upon which it was already laying its hands constituted a small minority of the earth's peoples.

What do we find in the winter of 1951? The writs of Moscow run to lands which, with its own, number upward of 900 millions of people—a good forty per cent of all men living. The fear of Russia or the subservience that power inspires inclines many hundreds of other millions, as in India, toward Moscow. The fear of Russia, plus other reasons, the chief of which is the supine and treacherous folly of our own policies, places other hundreds of millions in a twilight zone between the great poles of Moscow and Washington.

The United States stands today virtually alone as it faces its greatest trials. Where have we loyal allies? In Britain? I would not stake a shilling on the reliability of a Government which, while enjoying billions in American munificence, rushed to the recognition of the Chinese Red regime, traded exorbitantly with the enemy through Hong Kong and has sought to frustrate

The early 1950s saw the addition to the language of a new word, McCarthyism. Here Senator Joseph R. McCarthy of Wisconsin addresses a dinner in his honor, against a backdrop of one of the questions he raised about Communist influence in the Army.

American interest in the Far East at every turn. Let us not blame our long-time friends, the British people. They have their Attlee and Morrison directing their foreign policy. We have our Marshall. We have our Acheson. Or perhaps I should say their Acheson. . . .

The will to resist Russia here at home is vitiated. Gone is the zeal with which we marched forth in 1941 to crush the dictatorships. The leftist-liberals who preached a holy war against Hitler and Tojo are today seeking accommodation with the senior totalitarianism of Moscow. Is this because we are today arrayed against, to recall the phrase of General Bradley, "the wrong enemy" in the "wrong war"? We were on Russia's side in the last war—our strategy after the first Quebec conference might as well have been dictated in the Kremlin and teletyped to the Pentagon—and is that why the Marshall who prosecuted World War II with bloodthirsty zeal, eager to storm fortified shores, sat this one out?

The administration preached a gospel of fear and Acheson and Marshall expounded a foreign policy in the Far East of craven appeasement. The President threatens the American people with Russian-made atomic bombs. What is the purpose of such actions and utterances? Is it to condition us to defeat in the Far East, to soften us up so that we shall accept a peace upon the Soviet empire's terms in Korea; a peace which would put the enemy one step nearer to Alaska? And how did Russia acquire the technical secrets, the blueprints, the know-how to make the bombs with which the administration seeks to terrify us? I have yet to hear a single administration spokesman raise his voice against the policy of suppression, deceit, and false witness with which this administration has protected the Soviet agents who have abstracted those secrets from us.

The people, I am convinced, recognize the weakness with which the administration has replaced what was so recently our great strength. They are troubled by it. And they do not think it accidental. They do not believe that the decline in our strength from 1945 to 1951 just happened. They are coming to believe that it was brought about, step by step, by will and intention. They are beginning to believe that the surrender of

China to Russia, the administration's indecently hasty desire to turn Formosa over to the enemy and arrive at a cease-fire in Korea instead of following the manly, American course prescribed by MacArthur, point to something more than ineptitude and folly. . . .

How can we account for our present situation unless we believe that men high in this Government are concerting to deliver us to disaster? This must be the product of a great conspiracy, a conspiracy on a scale so immense as to dwarf any previous such venture in the history of man.

Who constitutes the highest circles of this conspiracy? About that we cannot be sure. We are convinced that Dean Acheson, who steadfastly serves the interests of nations other than his own, who supported Alger Hiss in his hour of retribution, who contributed to his defense fund, must be high on the roster. The President? He is their captive. I have wondered, as have you, why he did not dispense with so great a liability as Acheson to his own and his party's interests. It is now clear to me. In the relationship of master and man, did you ever hear of man firing master? President Truman is a satisfactory front. He is only dimly aware of what is going on.

It is when we return to an examination of General Marshall's record since the spring of 1942 that we approach an explanation of the carefully planned retreat from victory. Let us again review the Marshall record, as I have disclosed it from the sources available. This grim and solitary man it was who, early in World War II, determined to put his impress upon our global strategy, political and military. . . .

It was Marshall who, after North Africa had been secured, took the strategic direction of the war out of Roosevelt's hands and who fought the British desire, shared by Mark Clark, to advance from Italy into the eastern plains of Europe ahead of the Russians.

It was a Marshall-sponsored memorandum, advising appeasement of Russia in Europe and the enticement of Russia into the Far Eastern war, circulated at Quebec, which foreshadowed our whole course at Teheran, at Yalta, and until now in the Far East. . . .

It was Marshall who enjoined his chief of military mission in Moscow under no circumstances to "irritate" the Russians by asking them questions about their forces, their weapons, and their plans, while at the same time opening our training schools, factories, and gradually our secrets to them. . . .

It was Marshall who sent Deane to Moscow to collaborate with Harriman in drafting the terms of the wholly unnecessary bribe paid to Stalin at Yalta. It was Marshall who ignored the contrary advice of his senior, Admiral Leahy, of MacArthur and Nimitz; manipulated intelligence reports, brushed aside the potentials of the A-bomb, and finally induced Roosevelt to reinstate Russia in its pre-1904, imperialistic position in Manchuria; an act which, in effect, signed the death warrant of the Republic of China.

It was Marshall, with Acheson and Vincent assisting, who created the China policy which, destroying China, robbed us of a great and friendly ally, a buffer against the Soviet imperialism with which we are at war. . . .

It was Marshall who, upon returning from a diplomatic defeat for the United States at Moscow, besought the reinstatement of forty millions in lend-lease for Russia. . . .

It was Marshall who fixed the dividing line for Korea along the thirty-eighth parallel, a line historically chosen by Russia to mark its sphere of interest of Korea. . . .

It was Marshall who, advocating timidity as a policy so as not to annoy the forces of Soviet imperialism in Asia, admittedly put a brake on the preparations to fight, rationalizing his reluctance on the ground that the people are fickle and, if war does not come, will hold him to account for excessive zeal. . . .

What is the objective of the conspiracy? I think it is clear from what has occurred and is now occurring: to diminish the United States in world affairs, to weaken us militarily, to confuse our spirit with talk of surrender in the Far East and to impair our will to resist evil. To what end? To the end that we shall be contained and frustrated and finally fall victim to Soviet intrigue from within and Russian military might from without. Is that far-fetched? There have been many examples in history of rich and powerful states which have been corrupted from within, enfee-bled and deceived until they were unable to resist aggression.

29 THE SOVIET THREAT

Dwight D. Eisenhower (1890–1969)

During the eight years of his presidency (1953 to 1961), Dwight D. Eisenhower was generally very popular with the American people. Born in Denison, Texas, he graduated from the U.S. Military Academy at West Point and had a long and successful army career, climaxed by his service as the Allied Supreme Commander in Europe during World War II and subsequently as the first commander of the North Atlantic Treaty Organization forces. Although in favor of American assistance to anticommunist groups around the world, he attempted to improve relations with Russia and played host to Soviet Premier Nikita Khrushchev during the latter's historic visit to America in 1959. Unfortunately, the progress toward improved relations following the visit came to a sharp halt when the U.S. U-2 reconnaissance aircraft piloted by Francis Gary Powers was shot down over Russia in May 1960, dismantling the Big Four Summit Conference scheduled for Paris later in the month. The following critical appraisal of Soviet intentions was given by Eisenhower at the Alfred E. Smith Memorial Foundation dinner at the Waldorf-Astoria Hotel in New York on October 16, 1952, during his campaign for the presidency and a few days after the closing of the Nineteenth Congress of the Soviet Communist Party in Moscow.

IN THESE VERY WEEKS, decisions and events of special moment and meaning have been shaping themselves at a distant point on our globe. So grave are they, I believe, that all thoughtful Americans of all parties and persuasions should pause to analyze these events, to discern if possible their significance for our safety, our freedom, our whole future.

I am speaking, of course, of the Communist Congress that convened just eleven days ago under the Kremlin's towers in Moscow and adjourned just forty-eight hours ago.

Some 1,500 delegates and representatives from the Soviet Union and from forty-four other countries met in the Great Hall of the Kremlin. This, the Nineteenth Congress of the Communist Party of the Soviet Union, was the first such assembly since 1939. It was the largest assembly of Communist leaders ever met together at any time, in any place. This is an event that the Free World cannot ignore. It is an event that sternly summons our most sober attention, our wisest understanding. . . .

The torrent of words has been formidable. Stalin anticipated the Congress a few days by publishing a 25,000-word essay bringing Soviet economic doctrine up to date. Malenkov read the Communist party report to the Congress, an oratorical endurance test lasting some five and a half hours. From Molotov and Beria came the familiar short, sharp thunderclaps of invective against the United States. . . .

The first fact whose outline we must clearly make out through this thick fog of rhetoric is the crucial matter of ultimate Soviet purpose. What is it? In the words of Stalin, it is the old and implacable chant: "In order to destroy the inevitability of wars, it is necessary to destroy imperialism." For this pronouncement no interpretation is necessary other than to note that the word "imperialism" is standard Soviet shorthand for democracy in general and for the United States in particular.

I stress this fact because out of all of Stalin's 25,000 words these few are likely to receive least attention for the simple reason that their sound is so familiar. The drums of Soviet hate are still rolling for the same old enemy. America is still marked with indelible invective as Communism's final and greatest victim-to-be. In the grim and candid prophecy of Lenin: "A series of frightful clashes between the Soviet Republic and the bourgeois states is inevitable . . . In the end . . . a funeral requiem will be sung either over the Soviet Republic or over world capitalism. . . ."

A second fact scarcely less important is that while the purpose of Soviet policy remains steadfastly the same, its plan for action is always undergoing revision. The consistency in Soviet behavior we have long known does not come from neat, precise adherence to a straight line. It comes from a meticulously measured zig-zagging back and forth to right and to left to achieve a result carefully calculated and balanced. This, again, is venerable Soviet practice, as Lenin described it bluntly in 1920, "We have to use any ruse, dodges, tricks, cunning, unlawful method, concealment, veiling of truth. . . ."

The last 200 years tell one simple, sensational story about Russia's relationship to Europe. Through all this time one of the commonest ways of measuring Russia's pressure upon the Continent has been in terms of the distance of the Russian frontier from Europe's center at Berlin. In 1750 that frontier was 1,200 miles from Berlin. In 1800 the distance was but 750 miles; in 1815 only 200 miles. Now, innumerable border changes later, the Russian frontier has moved westward until it includes Berlin within its limits. Thus, under Communist impulse, the old Russian vision of an empire spanning two continents, "from Aachen to Vladivostok," has come closer to fact than fantasy. . . .

The last twelve years tell a cruel story. It is the story of a growth in the Soviet Empire so fast and fabulous as to make all prior fears seem conservative. With the conquest of China on one continent and the Sovietization of Eastern Europe on the other, the number of people under effective Soviet rule has swelled in little more than a decade from some 190 million to 800 million. This great mass signifies the largest empire in the history of mankind. Never before in man's long pilgrimage from darkness toward light has tyranny dragged so many millions back into the night. . . .

Meanwhile, these same years have witnessed the rapid economic and military recovery of the Soviet Union itself from the blows and losses of World War II. This means, as but one important example, a steel production that today approaches double what it was when Hitler attacked Russia. It also means of course a continuing atomic development.

These, then, are the key historic facts that set the scene for the words of Stalin, Molotov, Malenkov and Beria in the last ten days. These facts define a Soviet diplomacy leading from growing strength. And they spell a formula for that diplomacy's conduct:

as the Communist world carefully marshalls its gigantic new sources of strength, the free world crowded back on its own defences may be led to fall into factions and prey upon itself. . . .

We might see in all this a kind of change in tempo in the cold war, even in the beginning of a kind of cold peace. But whatever language we use to describe this Soviet formula for action, we could I think make few blunders so serious as to doubt its menace to the free world's unity. Perhaps the only more serious blunder we could make would be to hold any deep doubt that if we are both wise and courageous we can beat back this challenge and the forces behind it. . . .

There is yet more solace and hope, I believe, to be found in some of the grave weaknesses of Soviet communism itself. It is one of the crude ironies of our times that this system, so charged with internal strife and tension, should preach such lengthy sermons on the "internal contradictions" of the free world.

The truth of course is that the "internal contradictions" of communism are constant and stupendous threats to the Soviet Union's own safety. There is the colossal "contradiction" of slave labor, both a mockery of the pretensions of the workers' paradise and a source of constant political and economic danger. It is indeed strange that a Government so loudly shouting that the free world is going to be destroyed by harsh, inescapable economic laws itself ignores the ancient historic law that no economy is so explosive as a slave economy.

There is the "contradiction" of nationalism itself, a risky weapon to be wielded by a government whose own empire presumes the denial of national identity and freedom.

And there is this most curious of all "contradictions," the fact that Soviet policy constantly becomes frightened by demons of its own invention. Thus its self-induced hysteria over fear of Western attack led it into a truculence which solidified the free world against it as nothing else could have done. Its neurotic fear of nonexistent Western alliances spurred it to actions, which have in effect brought those alliances into being. Rarely in history has a nation been so justly punished for its own wild and ugly imagination.

30 MOSCOW DIVIDES THE WORLD

Harry S Truman (1884–1972)

Elevated to the presidency by the death of Franklin D. Roosevelt in April 1945, Harry Truman confronted one of the most difficult problems of his administration—dealing with the Soviet Union, which quickly moved from the status of wartime ally of the United States to major cold war antagonist. At the Potsdam Conference with Stalin and Churchill in July–August 1945, the attitudes displayed by the Soviets led Truman to conclude that Moscow's expansionist aims represented a threat to America. The policies established by the Truman administration of bolstering friendly nations to resist communist pressures, later referred to as the Truman Doctrine, have continued until today to represent the overall thrust of American foreign policy.

Harry Truman was born in Lamar, Missouri, and worked on the family farm after graduating from public school in Independence, Missouri. After service as an army captain in World War I, he became a judge. Elected to the Senate as a Democrat in 1934, he was selected by President Roosevelt as his vice-presidential running mate in 1944. The following comments were made by President Truman in January 1953, in his last State of the Union Message to Congress.

THE SECOND WORLD WAR radically changed the power relationships of the world. Nations once great were left shattered and weak, channels of communication, routes of trade, political and economic ties of many kinds were ripped apart.

And in this changed, disrupted, chaotic situation, the United

216 · HARRY S TRUMAN

States and the Soviet Union emerged as the two strongest powers of the world. Each had tremendous human and natural resources, actual or potential, on a scale unmatched by any other nation.

Nothing could make plainer why the world is in its present state—and how that came to pass—than an understanding of the diametrically opposite principles and policies of these two great powers in a war-ruined world.

For our part, we in this Republic were—and are—free men, heirs of the American Revolution, dedicated to the truths of our Declaration of Independence:

". . . That all men are created equal, that they are endowed by their Creator with certain unalienable rights . . . That to secure these rights, governments are instituted among men, deriving their just powers from the consent of the governed."

Our post-war objective has been in keeping with this great idea. The United States has sought to use its pre-eminent position of power to help other nations recover from the damage and dislocation of the war. We held out a helping hand to enable them to restore their national lives and to regain their positions as independent, self-supporting members of the great family of nations. This help was given without any attempt on our part to dominate or control any nation. We did not want satellites but partners.

The Soviet Union, however, took exactly the opposite course.

Its rulers saw in the weakened condition of the world not an obligation to assist in the great work of reconstruction, but an opportunity to exploit misery and suffering for the extension of their power. Instead of help, they brought subjugation. They extinguished, blotted out, the national independence of the countries that the military operations of World War II had left within their grasp.

The difference stares at us from the map of Europe today. To the west of the line that tragically divides Europe we see nations continuing to act and live in the light of their own traditions and principles. On the other side, we see the dead uniformity of a tyrannical system imposed by the rulers of the Soviet Union. Nothing could point up more clearly what the global struggle between the free world and the communists is all about.

It is a struggle as old as recorded history; it is freedom versus tyranny.

For the dominant idea of the Soviet regime is the terrible conception that men do not have rights but live at the mercy of the state.

Inevitably this idea of theirs—and all the consequences flowing from it—collided with the efforts of free nations to build a just and powerful world. The "cold war" between the communists and the free world is nothing more or less than the Soviet attempt to checkmate and defeat our peaceful purposes, in furtherance of their own dread objective.

We did not seek this struggle, God forbid. We did our utmost to avoid it. In World War II, we and the Russians had fought side by side, each in our turn attacked and forced to combat by the aggressors. After the war, we hoped that our wartime collaboration could be maintained, that the frightful experience of Nazi invasion, of devastation in the heart of Russia, had turned the Soviet rulers away from their old proclaimed allegiance to world revolution and communist dominion. But instead, they violated, one by one, the solemn agreements they had made with us in wartime. They sought to use the rights and privileges they had obtained in the United Nations, to frustrate its purposes and cut down its powers as an effective agent of world progress and the keeper of the world's peace.

Despite this outcome, the efforts we made toward peaceful collaboration are a source of our present strength. They demonstrated that we believed what we proclaimed, that we actually sought honest agreements as the way to peace. Our whole moral position, our leadership in the free world today, is fortified by that fact.

The world is divided, not through our fault or failure, but by Soviet design. They, not we, began the cold war. And because the free world saw this happen—because men know we made the effort and the Soviet rulers spurned it—the free nations have accepted leadership from our Republic, in meeting and mastering the Soviet offensive.

It seems to me especially important that all of us be clear, in our own thinking, about the nature of the threat we have faced

—and will face for a long time to come. The measures we have devised to meet it take shape and pattern only as we understand what we were—and are—up against.

The Soviet Union occupies a territory of 8 million square miles. Beyond its borders, East and West, are the nearly five million square miles of the satellite states—virtually incorporated into the Soviet Union—and of China, now its close partner. This vast land mass contains an enormous store of natural resources sufficient to support an economic development comparable to our own.

That is the Stalinist world. It is a world of great natural diversity in geography and climate, in distribution of resources, in population, language, and living standards, in economic and cultural development. It is a world whose people are not all convinced communists by any means. It is a world where history and national traditions, particularly in its borderlands, tend more toward separation than unification, and run counter to the enforced combination that has been made of these areas today.

But it is also a world of great man-made uniformities, a world that bleeds its population white to build huge military forces; a world in which the police are everywhere and their authority unlimited; a world where terror and slavery are deliberately administered both as instruments of government and as means of production; a world where all effective social power is the state's monopoly—yet the state itself is the creature of the communist tyrants.

The Soviet Union, with its satellites, and China are held in the tight grip of communist party chieftains. The party dominates all social and political institutions. The party regulates and centrally directs the whole economy. In Moscow's sphere, and in Peiping's, all history, philosophy, morality and law are centrally established by rigid dogmas, incessantly drummed into the whole population and subject to interpretation—or to change—by none except the party's own inner circle.

And lest their people learn too much of other ways of life, the communists have walled off their world, deliberately and uniformly, from the rest of human society.

That is the communist base of operation in their cold war. In addition, they have at their command hundreds and thousands of dedicated foreign communists, people in nearly every free country who will serve Moscow's ends. Thus the masters of the Kremlin are provided with deluded followers all through the free world whom they can manipulate, cynically and quite ruthlessly, to serve the purposes of the Soviet state.

Given their vast internal base of operations, and their agents in foreign lands, what are the communist rulers trying to do?

Inside their homeland, the communists are trying to maintain and modernize huge military forces. And simultaneously, they are endeavoring to weld their whole vast area and population into a completely self-contained, advanced industrial society. They aim, some day, to equal or better the production levels of Western Europe and North America combined—thus shifting the balance of world economic power, and war potential, to their side.

They have a long way to go and they know it. But they are prepared to levy upon living generations any sacrifice that helps strengthen their armed power, or speed industrial development.

Externally, the communist rulers are trying to expand the boundaries of their world, whenever and wherever they can. This expansion they have pursued steadfastly since the close of World War II, using any means available to them.

Where the Soviet army was present, as in the countries of Eastern Europe, they have gradually squeezed free institutions to death.

Where post-war chaos existed in industrialized nations, as in Western Europe, the local Stalinists tried to gain power through political processes, politically-inspired strikes, and every available means for subverting free institutions to their evil ends.

Where conditions permitted, the Soviet rulers have stimulated and aided armed insurrection by communist-led revolutionary forces, as in Greece, Indo-China, the Philippines, and China, or outright aggression by one of their satellites, as in Korea.

Where the forces of nationalism, independence, and economic change were at work throughout the great sweep of Asia and Africa, the communists tried to identify themselves with the cause of progress, tried to picture themselves as the friends of freedom and advancement—surely one of the most cynical efforts of which history offers record.

Thus, everywhere in the free world, the communists seek to fish in troubled waters, to seize more countries, to enslave more millions of human souls. They were, and are, ready to ally themselves with any group, from the extreme left to the extreme right, that offers them an opportunity to advance their ends.

Geography gives them a central position. They are both a European and an Asian power, with borders touching many of the most sensitive and vital areas in the free world around them. So situated, they can use their armies and their economic power to set up simultaneously a whole series of threats—or inducements—to such widely dispersed places as Western Germany, Iran, and Japan. These pressures and attractions can be sustained at will, or quickly shifted from place to place.

Thus the communist rulers are moving, with implacable will, to create greater strength in their vast empire, and to create weakness and division in the free world, preparing for the time their false creed teaches them must come: the time when the whole world outside their sway will be so torn by strife and contradictions that it will be ripe for the communist plucking.

This is the heart of the distorted Marxist interpretation of history. This is the glass through which Moscow and Peiping look out upon the world, the glass through which they see the rest of us. They seem really to believe that history is on their side. And they are trying to boost "history" along, at every opportunity, in every way they can.

I have set forth here the nature of the communist menace confronting our Republic and the whole free world. This is the measure of the challenge we have faced since World War II— a challenge partly military and partly economic, partly moral and partly intellectual, confronting us at every level of human endeavor and all around the world.

It has been and must be the free world's purpose not only to organize defenses against aggression and subversion, not only to build a structure of resistance and salvation for the community of nations outside the iron curtain, but in addition to give expression and opportunity to the forces of growth and progress in the free world, to so organize and unify the cooperative community of free men that we will not crumble but grow stronger over the years, and the Soviet empire, not the free world, will eventually have to change its ways or fall. . .

We were prepared, and so were the other nations of the free world, to place our reliance on the machinery of the United Nations to safeguard peace. But before the United Nations could give full expression to the concept of international security embodied in the Charter, it was essential that the five permanent members of the Security Council honor their solemn pledge to cooperate to that end. This the Soviet Union has not done.

I do not need to outline here the dreary record of Soviet obstruction and veto and the unceasing efforts of the Soviet representatives to sabotage the United Nations. It is important, however, to distinguish clearly between the principle of collective security embodied in the Charter and the mechanisms of the United Nations to give that principle effect. We must frankly recognize that the Soviet Union has been able, in certain instances, to stall the machinery of collective security. Yet it has not been able to impair the principle of collective security. The free nations of the world have retained their allegiance to that idea. They have found the means to act despite the Soviet veto, both through the United Nations itself and through the application of this principle in regional and other security arrangements that are fully in harmony with the Charter and give expression to its purposes.

The free world refused to resign itself to collective suicide merely because of the technicality of a Soviet veto. . .

From 1945 to 1949, the United States was sole possessor of the atomic bomb. That was a great deterrent and protection in itself.

But when the Soviets produced an atomic explosion—as they were bound to do in time—we had to broaden the whole basis of our strength. We had to endeavor to keep our lead in atomic weapons. We had to strengthen our armed forces generally and to enlarge our productive capacity—our mobilization base. Historically, it was the Soviet atomic explosion in the fall of 1949, nine months before the aggression in Korea, which stimulated the planning for our program of defense mobilization. . .

Eight years ago, the Kremlin thought post-war collapse in

Western Europe and Japan—with economic dislocation in America—might give them the signal to advance. We demonstrated they were wrong. Now they wait with hope that the economic recovery of the free world has set the stage for violent and disastrous rivalry among the economically developed nations, struggling for each other's markets and a greater share of trade. Here is another test that we shall have to meet and master in the years immediately ahead. And it will take great ingenuity and effort—and much time—before we prove the Kremlin wrong again. But we can do it. It is true that economic recovery presents its problems, as does economic decline, but they are problems of another order. They are the problems of distributing abundance fairly, and they can be solved by the process of international cooperation that has already brought us so far.

These are the measures we must continue. This is the path we must follow. We must go on, working with our free associates, building an international structure for military defense, and for economic, social, and political progress. We must be prepared for war, because war may be thrust upon us. But the stakes in our search for peace are immensely higher than they have ever been before.

For now we have entered the atomic age, and war has undergone a technological change which makes it a very difficult thing from what it used to be. War today between the Soviet empire and the free nations might dig the grave not only of our Stalinist opponents, but of our own society, our world as well as theirs.

This transformation has been brought to pass in the seven years from Alamogordo to Eniwetok. It is only seven years, but the new force of atomic energy has turned the world into a very different kind of place.

Science and technology have worked so fast that war's new meaning may not yet be grasped by all the peoples who would be its victims; nor, perhaps, by the rulers in the Kremlin. But I have been President of the United States, these seven years, responsible for the decisions which have brought our science and our engineering to their present place. I know what this development means now. I know something of what it will come to mean in the future.

We in this Government realized, even before the first successful atomic explosion, that this new force spelled terrible danger for all mankind unless it were brought under international control. We promptly advanced proposals in the United Nations to take this new source of energy out of the arena of national rivalries, to make it impossible to use it as a weapon of war. These proposals, so pregnant with benefit for all humanity, were rebuffed by the rulers of the Soviet Union.

The language of science is universal, the movement of science is always forced into the unknown. We could not assume that the Soviet Union would not develop the same weapon, regardless of all our precautions, nor that there were not other and even more terrible means of destruction lying in the unexplored field of atomic energy.

We had no alternative, then, but to press on, to probe the secrets of atomic power to the uttermost of our capacity, to maintain, if we could, our initial superiority in the atomic field. At the same time, we sought persistently for some avenue, some formula, for reaching an agreement with the Soviet rulers that would place this new form of power under effective restraints— that would guarantee no nation would use it in war. I do not have to recount here the proposals we made, the steps taken in the United Nations, striving at least to open a way to ultimate agreement. I hope and believe that we will continue to make these efforts so long as there is the slightest possibility of progress. All civilized nations are agreed on the urgency of the problem, and have shown their willingness to agree on effective measures of control—all save the Soviet Union and its satellites. But they have rejected every reasonable proposal.

Meanwhile, the progress of scientific experiment has outrun our expectations. Atomic science is in the full tide of development; the unfolding of the innermost secrets of matter is uninterrupted and irresistible. Since Alamogordo we have developed atomic weapons with many times the explosive force of the early models, and we have produced them in substantial quantities. And recently, in the thermonuclear test at Eniwetok, we have entered another stage in the worldshaking development of atomic energy. From now on, man moves into a new era of destructive power, capable of creating explosions of a new order of magnitude, dwarfing the mushroom clouds of Hiroshima and Nagasaki.

We have no reason to think that the stage we have now reached in the release of atomic energy will be the last. Indeed, the speed of our scientific and technical progress over the last seven years shows no signs of abating. We are being hurried forward, in our mastery of the atom, from one discovery to another, toward yet unforeseeable peaks of destructive power.

Inevitably, until we can reach international agreement, this is the path we must follow. And we must realize that no advance we make is unattainable by others, that no advantage in this race can be more than temporary.

The war of the future would be one in which man could extinguish millions of lives at one blow, demolish the great cities of the world, wipe out the cultural achievements of the past— and destroy the very structure of a civilization that has been slowly and painfully built up through hundreds of generations.

Such a war is not a possible policy for rational men. We know this, but we dare not assume that others would not yield to the temptation science is now placing in their hands.

With that in mind, there is something I would say, to Stalin: You claim belief in Lenin's prophecy that one stage in the development of communist society would be war between your world and ours. But Lenin was a pre-atomic man, who viewed society and history with pre-atomic eyes. Something profound has happened since he wrote. War has changed its shape and its dimension. It cannot now be a "stage" in the development of anything save ruin for your regime and your homeland.

I do not know how much time may elapse before the communist rulers bring themselves to recognize this truth. But when they do, they will find us eager to reach understandings that will protect the world from the danger it faces today.

It is no wonder that some people wish that we had never succeeded in splitting the atom. But atomic power, like any other force of nature, is not evil in itself. Properly used, it is an instrumentality for human betterment. As a source of power, as a tool of scientific inquiry, it has untold possibilities. We are already making good progress in the constructive use of atomic power. We could do much more if we were free to concentrate on its peaceful uses exclusively.

Atomic power will be with us all the days of our lives. We cannot legislate it out of existence. We cannot ignore the dangers or the benefits it offers.

I believe that man can harness the forces of the atom to work for the improvement of the lot of human beings everywhere. That is our goal. As a nation, as a people, we must understand this problem, we must handle this new force wisely through our democratic processes. Above all, we must strive, in all earnestness and good faith, to bring it under effective international control. To do this will require much wisdom and patience and firmness. The awe-inspiring responsibility in this field now falls on a new administration and a new Congress. I will give them my support, as I am sure all our citizens will, in whatever constructive steps they may take to make this newest of man's discoveries a source of good and not of ultimate destruction.

We cannot tell when or whether the attitude of the Soviet rulers may change. We do not know how long it may be before they show a willingness to negotiate effective control of atomic energy and honorable settlements of other world problems. We cannot measure how deep-rooted are the Kremlin's illusions about us. We can be sure, however, that the rulers of the communist world will not change their basic objectives lightly or soon.

The communist rulers have a sense of time about these things wholly unlike our own. We tend to divide our future into short spans, like the two-year life of this Congress, or the four years of the next Presidential term. They seem to think and plan in terms of generations. And there is, therefore, no easy, short-run way to make them see that their plans cannot prevail.

This means there is ahead of us a long hard test of strength and stamina, between the free world and the communist domain —our politics and our economy, our science and technology against the best they can do—our liberty against their slavery—

our voluntary concert of free nations against their forced amalgam of "people's republics"—our strategy against their strategy —our nerve against their nerve.

Above all, this is a test of the will and the steadiness of the people of the United States.

31 RUSSIA IS BEING MADE A SCAPEGOAT

Corliss Lamont (1902–   )

Both before and after World War II, Corliss Lamont was one of the Americans most sympathetic in his views of the Soviet Union. A long time expert and writer on developments in Russia, Lamont was born in Englewood, New Jersey. After graduating from Harvard College in 1924, he received his Ph.D. from Columbia University eight years later. From 1943 to 1946 he was Chairman of the National Council for American-Soviet Friendship and he ran unsuccessfully for a seat in the U.S. Senate from New York in 1952 as the candidate of the American Labor Party. Lamont's comments on the Soviet Union come from his book *Soviet Civilization* (1955).

THE CURIOUS NOTION HAS TAKEN HOLD in the United States that only those who are basically anti-Soviet are qualified to write and speak objectively about the U.S.S.R. This is an absurd idea. In learning about the Civil War we do not depend primarily on the memoirs of southern slave-owners who favored secession; nor in evaluating the principles of democracy do we rely principally on the opinions of the fascists or others who despise the democratic way. A deep-seated and overpowering emotion of hate is not conducive to an objective treatment of any country. And it is to be recalled that the classic study of democracy in the U.S.A. was made in *The American Commonwealth* by James Bryce, who had an attitude of critical sympathy toward American institutions.

Thus an attitude of critical sympathy toward the Soviet Union does not disqualify anyone as an objective observer concerning Soviet affairs, so long as he retains a hearty respect for the facts. Actually, the temptation that beckons most persistently for American writers on the U.S.S.R. is to take an *unsympathetic* attitude toward that country and to conform to the prevailing hostility against it. . .

This kind of attitude tends to blame all evil in the sphere of international affairs on Moscow. In this manner the Russia-haters turn the U.S.S.R. into a convenient scapegoat for the collective sins of mankind; and in effect assign to it the role of the old-time devil. Professor Phillip Marshall Brown, formerly of Princeton University provided a good example of what I mean in his letter to *The New York Times* on February 2, 1949, in which he attributed to Soviet Russia not only the troubles among the Jews, the Arabs and the British in Palestine, but also the violence and unrest in Indonesia resulting in armed hostilities between the Netherlands Government and the Indonesian Republic. Anyone with a mite of information knows that seething cauldrons of local tensions had long existed in both Palestine and Indonesia and required no Communist intrigue to make them boil over. . . .

In examining the status of democracy in the Soviet Union, we likewise need to consider future prospects. In the first place, the lack of democratic institutions and the low cultural level in the old Tsarist autocracy did not provide an auspicious starting point for the development of democracy under the Soviets. It was obvious from the beginning that the evolution of the Soviet people into modern democracy in the best sense of that term would take decades to accomplish. As America's greatest philosopher, the late John Dewey, repeatedly pointed out, the intelligent and efficient functioning of political democracy requires a fairly high development of popular education. But as we have seen, the population of Russia was only about 30 percent literate in 1917; most of them, therefore, did not possess the elementary cultural prerequisites for proper participation in the complicated processes of democratic government. They did not even know what a ballot was or how to mark it.

In the second place, the Soviet Communists have frankly put into effect the Marxist theory that a temporary dictatorship of the proletariat is necessary during the transition from capitalism to socialism, with that dictatorship having strong elements of democracy within it. Again in line with Marxist doctrine, the Communists claim that the dictatorship will sink into the past entirely as the need for it passes with the disappearance of pressing dangers both internal and external. They insist, above all, that the enduring *economic* foundations of democracy must be securely established in the new socialist system; and that democratic institutions in capitalist countries remain weak, unstable and in danger of complete overthrow by fascist movements precisely because capitalist economies are constantly floundering about in the quicksand of financial crisis, economic depression and mass unemployment.

To *explain* is not always to excuse. The Soviet Government has from time to time used unnecessarily harsh measures to maintain itself. Yet we should not lose sight of the ultimate democratic aims of the Soviet Republic. In my opinion the Soviet people and their leaders have never relinquished those objectives. In the nature of the case, however, since the Communists both in theory and in practice give priority to the economic base of their socialist society, and believe that democracy can grow and expand only if this fundamental substructure is sound, it is not surprising that the full flourishing of democratic institutions in the Soviet Union should come gradually and late. . .

Many people in the Western democracies thought that the famous Moscow Trials of 1936–38, in which a number of prominent Communist leaders were convicted of treason, were a ghastly travesty on due process of law and were complete frame-ups. I myself, after reading carefully the voluminous verbatim testimony in the three big trials—something which few critics of Soviet justice have bothered to do—became convinced that the defendants' sweeping confessions were genuine and that they were indeed guilty of conspiring with Leon Trotsky and outright fascist agents to overthrow the Soviet Government. Since Trotsky, Zinoviev, Bukharin and the others firmly believed that Stalin

had betrayed socialism both at home and abroad, they felt justified as revolutionaries in adopting any methods whatever to get
rid of his regime. . .

Especially since the end of World War II reckless charges have
been made that the Soviet Union is a horrible slave state keeping
from ten to twenty million people at forced labor in concentration camps situated in Siberia and other places. While there is
no question that the Soviet authorities have isolated political
prisoners and ordinary criminals in special work camps, the
numbers involved have steadily declined in recent years and
have at no time reached the huge totals conjured up in the lurid
imaginations of anti-Soviet propagandists. . .

Soviet socialism as a whole, together with the physical characteristics of the country, definitely makes for the elimination of
the chief economic roots of war-making and war-mongering in
the U.S.S.R. The Soviet Union, from east to west twice the width
of the United States and stretching all the way from the Baltic
Sea to the Pacific Ocean, possesses within its continental domains
practically all the raw materials necessary for its economy. It
needs no new territories to provide it with natural resources,
although it is glad to supplement its own basic wealth through
doing business with other nations. The huge size of Soviet Russia,
together with its material riches and accelerating economic development, means that it has plenty of room for and can readily
support its expanding population. Over-population, which has
often been a spur to military conquest, is not a problem in the
U.S.S.R.

Today a majority of Americans tend to reject almost automatically any idea, in the controversial realms of economics,
politics and international relations, which originated in Soviet
Russia or is generally approved there. In fact, this trend has gone
so far that the relatively few dissenters who do express agreement with some Soviet doctrines may be indicted or jailed as
foreign agents on the grounds of "parallelism" between their
views and those of the Soviet Government. Yet if Americans for
one reason or another feel unable ever to agree with Soviet
opinions, then the Soviets are actually controlling them in reverse
by forcing them always to support contrary conclusions. The

truly independent mind cannot permit itself to be placed in such a senseless position. . .

The artificially created anti-Soviet atmosphere in the United States so stifles objective thinking that there is a tendency here among many leaders in government, business and public opinion automatically to discard as bad any move that would be good for the Soviet Union or the other Communist countries. Now indubitably international peace, disarmament and a normal exchange of goods on the world market would be beneficial for the Communist nations. But to reject these aims on this account is to negate the processes of reason. For plainly the fulfilment of such goals would also be immensely beneficial to America and the rest of the non-Communist world. *Mutual self-interest is the key to ending the present American-Soviet impasse. . .*

War and violence have always been the worst ways to deal with problems between countries. There is a far better method for the solution of current dilemmas—for nations, for peoples, for governments, for capitalists, for Communists, for conservatives, for radicals, for politicians, for businessmen, for this alliance and that bloc, for East and West. That is the method of reason, understanding, negotiation and compromise. I believe that this method now demands that the American Government give more serious and reasonable consideration to the major Soviet peace proposals; and that it should accept the invitation of the Soviet Government to have highest ranking officials from each side sit down and talk things over calmly, with the aim of settling the chief issues in dispute on terms advantageous to both. . .

Do the evils existent during the first thirty-five years of the Communist regime, especially in the realm of means, outweigh the total good achieved or reasonably to be anticipated for the near future? My answer is "No"; in a complete and true balance sheet, the Soviet good greatly outweighs the bad. . .

And while the American people have attained the highest material standard of living on record, that considerable advantage functions as a disadvantage in their judgment of other nations. For it tends to make Americans forget or neglect the abysmally low living standards of the majority of the human race, whose struggle to maintain a bare existence necessarily comes first and often to the neglect of democratic and cultural values which more advanced peoples take for granted. . .

Malnutrition or famine, debilitating disease, exhausting overwork or heart-breaking unemployment, inadequate clothing and pitiful housing afflict at least one-half of the earth's population, possessors of an annual per capita income of less than $100.

Those same evils, for ages past the lot of the masses of mankind, prevailed to a large extent in the old Russia. To eliminate them was the primary aim in the domestic program of the Soviet Communists; they have gone far in achieving this goal. What they have not achieved are the democratic patterns of living which they believe can be permanently established only on the basis of economic security and with the assurance of international peace. Accordingly, the need for more time is of the essence, considering the pressing initial problems—such as counter-revolution, foreign intervention and fascist aggression—with which the Soviet regime has had to cope.

Westerners who today dismiss Soviet socialism as a horrible failure and an international menace disregard the lesson of history that it is reckless to make hasty adverse judgments on far-reaching revolutionary movements before those tradition-shattering upsurges of peoples and nations have had an opportunity to work themselves out, to correct their cruelties and crudities, to fulfill the generous ideals of their founders. I could be wrong; but in my opinion the objective verdict of coming generations will be that the Soviet Russians, during their first thirty-five years, laid the foundations of a great new civilization of enduring achievement and high promise, ranking in world historical significance with the outstanding civilizations of the past.

32 VIOLENCE IN SOVIET COMMUNISM

John Foster Dulles (1888–1959)

When the new Republican administration took office in 1953, President Eisenhower selected John Foster Dulles to be Secretary of State. From then on until his illness in 1956, Dulles dominated American foreign policy. Born in Washington, D.C., into a family closely associated with foreign affairs, he grew up to be a lawyer deeply involved in international finance. Prior to his appointment to the Cabinet, Dulles served as United States Senator from New York and, under President Truman, as special representative responsible for negotiating a peace treaty with Japan. Dulles was usually characterized as a "cold warrior" who negotiated American military alliances with nations around the world.

The following speech, delivered by Dulles to a meeting of the Kiwanis International at San Francisco, California, on June 21, 1956, echoed his deep distrust of Soviet intentions.

THE FORCES OF DESPOTISM are more highly organized than ever before. Already they control one third of the entire human race, and they openly proclaim their ambition to extend their system throughout the world.

So far, their gains have come through the use of violence, or the threat of violence. During the Stalin era, fifteen nations, in whole or in large part, were forcibly subjected to Soviet Communist dominion. But the free nations became aroused to the danger. They built up their deterrent power and joined in measures of collective defense. It was no longer possible for Soviet communism to pick up nations one by one.

So the Soviet rulers now say that they will renounce the use of violence. But they say that they still expect their system to win its way in the world because, they say, it is so good that all will want it.

We welcome and shall encourage these developments. But it would be foolhardy to assume that danger is past and that we can abandon the mutual-security policies which have frustrated the old Soviet tactics. The Soviet rulers retain capabilities which enable them quickly to revert to their old policies of violence and attempted coercion, and they would surely be tempted to do so if ever the free nations abandoned their policy of standing together. For violence is the classic and natural tactic of Soviet communism as taught not merely by Stalin but by Lenin.

Soviet industries are working at top speed to develop ever more potent atomic and nuclear weapons. Their nuclear experiments are being multiplied. They work unceasingly to increase the means for the delivery of new weapons by means of bombers, intercontinental rockets, and submarines.

They are also developing new techniques of indirect aggression. They are, for example, striving to introduce their agents into other countries—persons who are technicians but also part of the political apparatus of international communism. And they try to ensnare needy countries with economic lures. Thus they prepare the possibility of subverting other governments, irrespective of the will, or even knowledge, of the peoples concerned.

It is therefore vital that the free nations should maintain their guard and their peace insurance policies, including in our case the mutual security now pending in Congress. . .

Are not the free peoples entitled to presume that there is something basically wrong about a system that has never been accepted voluntarily by any people and that the Soviet rulers are unwilling to submit to the verdict of the peoples who know it best?

Let us, however, not reason solely on the basis of this presumption, however reasonable. Let us look more closely at the Soviet system.

Of course, dictatorship seems to offer some short-range advantages. It permits of opportunism. It makes possible a flexibility of action which is denied to democratically based governments. Despots can go in one direction one day and then in another direction the next day without need to explain or to justify their zigs and zags. They are not bound by parliamentary directives or budgets. They can channel the education of their people in accordance with the dictates of expediency, and they can compel persons of their choice to perform governmental tasks at home and abroad. Also, Communist dictatorships, being atheistic and materialistic, can and do treat human labor as a commodity to be used for the glorification of the State.

Through such powers dictators can do some things that cannot be done by governments which derive their powers from the consent of the governed.

Many of the despotic societies of the past have created notable monuments—pyramids, coliseums, palaces, and temples—built by slave labor to glorify kings and potentates who personified the State. The Soviet State has comparable achievements to its credit. By the ruthless use of forced labor, the dictators have created modern monuments in the form of industrial plants, power developments, and the like. They have subjected their economy to a forced and unbalanced growth and, with the help of natural resources and a temperate climate, attained a rapid rate of industrialization and a rapid increase of technical training.

All of this is featured in the Soviet Communist propaganda.

However, there is another side of the picture.

I shall not attempt here to catalog all of the many evils of Soviet Communist despotism. I do wish, however, to call attention to the revelations recently made by Mr. Khrushchev, the present head of the Soviet Communist party, in his initially secret speech before the twentieth party congress of the Soviet Communist party. It is the most damning indictment of despotism ever made by a despot. It should of itself be sufficient to make all free peoples shun that type of despotism as they would shun a plague. . .

What did Mr. Khrushchev say? He said that the man who for many years headed the Soviet Communist party and Soviet state, who was portrayed as a demigod and whose writings were treated as authoritative by international communism the world over, was, as regards doctrine, a "deviationist"; was, as head of state, so blind to the dangers to his nation as to be almost a traitor; and was, as a human being, so brutal and sadistic in character as to rival one of the most evil of the Roman emperors, Caligula. Furthermore—and this the main point—Mr. Khrushchev exposes the inability of the Soviet Communist system to liquidate its own evil leadership, because it was the evil leader who had the supreme power to liquidate others. . .

He alleges that Stalin, to satisfy his sadistic lusts, constantly invoked torture to procure false confessions, which were then made the basis of judicial murder. He directed "long tortures" and habitually himself "called the investigative judge, gave him instructions, advised him on which investigative methods should be used; these methods were simple—beat, beat and, once again, beat." Mr. Khrushchev recites incident after incident of the application of these tortures.

Mr. Khrushchev's speech portrays a loathsome scene. The speech cannot be read without horror and revulsion. But we must not stop at that instinctive emotional reaction. We must go on to ask the basic question: Why was not this situation unmasked during Stalin's life, or indeed not until three years after Stalin died?

In short, the Soviet Communist system provides no safeguards against even such extreme abuses as those that Mr. Khrushchev recounts. There are no checks and balances. The system is, as even Lenin said, one of "unlimited power, based on force and not on law." It operates in the dark. It provides no dependable method of changing the ruler. When there is misrule, only death or violence can assure the end of that misrule, and even that is not assurance, for Beria, whom Mr. Khrushchev calls even worse than Stalin, would probably have succeeded Stalin had not Beria been violently liquidated in the post-Stalin contest for power.

It is not often that despotism can be publicly unmasked, as by the publication of Mr. Khrushchev's speech. To overcome this ability of despotism to mask itself, the free societies must make clear, so that none can doubt, their own constant dedication to liberal principles of peaceful change.

It is not enough to prove that despotism is bad. It is equally necessary to go on—and on—proving that freedom is good.

Unless the free peoples do that, despotism will [succeed] again, if only because peoples in need, such as those of the newly developing countries, can readily be tempted by what seems a prospect of rapid economic change, which is the specialty of the Soviet rulers.

That is the great mission to which the free nations are dedicated. If we can continue to show freedom as a dynamic liberalizing force, then we need not fear the results of the peaceful competition which the Soviet rulers profess to offer. More than that, we can hope that the forces now at work within the Soviet Union and within the captive countries will require that those who rule shall increasingly conform to principles of freedom. This means that they shall increasingly recognize the dignity of the human individual, shall increasingly satisfy the aspirations of the people, and shall increasingly be themselves subject to peaceful change by the will of the governed. Thus will come about the beginning of a world-wide era of true liberalism.

That possibility is now clearly visible for the first time in many years. That possibility should spur us on to increased effort. For now we can be confident that it may be possible for our generation to share in building the kind of a world which we will be proud to bequeath to our children.

33 I SHOULD DIE IF I HAD TO LIVE THERE

Eleanor Roosevelt (1884–1962)

Although well-known as a liberal and supporter of humanitarian causes, Eleanor Roosevelt felt that the totalitarian aspects of the Soviet system overshadowed its strengths insofar as it undertook to advance the welfare of the Russian people. The wife of Franklin D. Roosevelt, Eleanor Roosevelt was famous in her own right as a leader in educational and welfare affairs. Born in New York City, she was educated in private schools and married Franklin D. Roosevelt in 1905. Following the death of her husband, she served from 1949 to 1952 as American representative to the United General Assembly. In 1957 she visited the Soviet Union; her impressions are recorded in *The Autobiography of Eleanor Roosevelt* (1961).

I HAVE WRITTEN FREQUENTLY about my enjoyment from visiting many delightful places around the world, including the police-run state of Yugoslavia. I would not want to live in Yugoslavia, nor would anyone who values personal freedom. But I think I should die if I had to live in Soviet Russia. I traveled there extensively for almost a month in 1957. When I went to Moscow, the Stalinist dictatorship had been replaced by the less fearful—in theory, at least—dictatorship of Nikita S. Khrushchev, but the people still existed under a system of surveillance that must cause anxiety and the power over them still seemed to me a hand of steel.

My trip to the Soviet Union was one of the most important, the most interesting and the most informative that I have ever made. I tried to understand what was happening in Russia by looking at the country through Russian eyes, and unless all of us in the free world approach the Soviet Union from that point of view we are going to deceive ourselves in a catastrophic manner. I remembered that only forty years ago this great mass of people was largely made up of peasants living in houses with mud floors and, perhaps, with a farm animal or two in the kitchen in wintry months. They were illiterate. They were oppressed. They were frightened of conquest by the Germans, and for many years they were bound together by a readiness to defend their home-land no matter how hard their lives might be.

We must never forget these things when we look at what Russia is today. I looked and was frightened. My fear was not of the Communist power or philosophy, not of awesome missiles or hydrogen bombs. What I feared was that we would not under-stand the nature of the Russian Revolution that is still going on, and what it means to the world. If we fail to understand, then we shall fail to protect world democracy no matter what missiles or earth satellites or atomic warships we produce. So I want to explain carefully why I am frightened. . . .

For three weeks in the Soviet Union I had felt more than at any time in my life that I was cut off from all the outside world. For three weeks I do not believe I had heard anyone really laugh on the streets or in a crowd. I had been among hospitable people but they were people who worked hard, who lived under con-siderable strain, and who were tired. It was only after I had landed at Copenhagen and heard laughter and gay talk and saw faces that were unafraid that I realized how different were our two worlds. Suddenly I could breathe again!

But I was frightened too, and after I reached home my nagging fear continued. I was—I still am—afraid that Americans and the peoples of the rest of the free world will not understand the nature of the struggle against Communism as exemplified by the Soviet Union. It is urgently important for the sake of our country and people that we get rid of some of our great misunderstand-ings and that we see clearly the things that must be done.

We are in a great struggle between two vastly different ways of life. While we must have guns, atomic weapons and missiles for retaliation against aggression, they are not going to win this struggle or prevent a catastrophic world war. Nor is belief in the idea of democracy likely to have great effect in areas where democratic institutions are not established. To overemphasize the importance of military power or to propagate merely the abstract idea of democracy is to miss the point. There is much, much more to be done if Western leadership is to be accepted by the masses of the world's underdeveloped countries, if our way of life and our hard-won freedoms are to survive in the atomic age—and flourish. We must provide leadership for free peoples, but we must never forget that in many countries, particularly in Asia and Africa, the freedom that is uppermost in the minds of the people is freedom to eat.

I think it is time for us Americans to take a good look at ourselves and our shortcomings. We should remember how we achieved the aims of freedom and democracy. We should look back in an effort to gauge how we can best influence the peoples of the world. Perhaps we made the greatest impression on underdeveloped countries in the 1930s when we ourselves were making a tremendous effort to fight our way out of a great economic depression. In that period we united behind bold ideas and vigorous programs, and, as they watched us, many people in far countries of the world began to realize that a government could be intensely interested in the welfare of the individual. They saw what was happening and it gave them hope that it could happen to them too. That was a generation ago, but again today it seems to me that it is essential for us to examine carefully our actions as a nation and try to develop a program for the welfare of the individual.

In this connection I was sometimes astonished during my visit to Russia to see what the Soviet government had brought about during four decades of Communist dictatorship. Illiteracy, which was once 90 per cent, has been reduced until it is now probably less than 10 per cent. The people have been educated in every field—crafts, arts, professions, sciences—and the government has used the educational system for political purposes, to shape the people to the will of the leadership.

Eleanor Roosevelt goes to see for herself. In 1957, during a tour of the Soviet Union, she stops to inspect a textile mill in Tashkent.

Educators are sent where they are most important for the purposes of the government. Doctors are sent where they can be most useful. Workers are sent to distant areas of Asia because new fields must be plowed and crops planted. This is dictatorship and it is hateful; but the results achieved by the Soviet regime are obvious to anyone visiting Russia. The water is pure; the milk is clean; the food supply is increasing; industry has made mighty strides. The people are not free, but they are better off materially every year. They know little of other countries and they are willing to accept a hard life because of the insidious Communist propaganda that unites them in fear of aggression by the United States. Most of them are sustained by a belief in communistic aims.

The Russians recognize that there are vast masses of people in Asia, Africa and parts of Latin America who are closer to the economic conditions that existed forty years ago in Russia than they are to conditions that have existed for many years in the United States. The leaders of the Soviets can say to them: "We know your conditions. Our people were once hungry, too; not only for food but for health and education, for knowledge and for hope for the future. Look at what we have done in forty years! Take heart. We can help you."

This is a challenge to democracy. This is the real challenge, and it cannot be met by mere words. We have to show the world by our actions that we live up to the ideals we profess and demonstrate that we can provide all the people in this country with the basic decencies of life, spiritually as well as materially. In the United States we are the showcase for the possibilities inherent in a free world, in democracy. If the lives of our people are not better in terms of basic satisfactions as well as in material ways than the lives of people anywhere in the world, then the uncommitted peoples we need on our side will look elsewhere for leadership.

We have spent a great deal in grants to our friends abroad but there is more than that to the struggle for the minds of men. For example, we have taken no trouble to invite delegations from other parts of the world to look at our system and see what we are doing under government auspices. If we are to be leaders we must offer needy countries technical know-how to help them achieve the freedom to eat, and practical help in developing, step by step, a democratic way of life. It is not enough to say that we do not like the Communist idea. We have to prove that our own idea is better and can accomplish more.

We.*can* accomplish more. There is no reason for us to be frightened by the scientific achievements under direction of the Soviet government, which has concentrated money and manpower on sputniks and rockets for obvious propaganda reasons. We have been complacent and given as little money and as few men as possible for work that we should have pressed vigorously. We were more interested in our comforts, in making money, and in having all the luxuries possible in this comfortable world of ours. We have to change and we *will* change that approach. If we are to lead the free world we must become a mature people—or we may one day wake up to find that fear and laziness have reduced us from a strong, vital nation to a people unable to lead other nations in the only way to win the struggle against Communism, the way of the mind and the heart.

I can think of nothing more foolish than looking at the Russian scientific achievements and saying that we must rush to catch up with them by resorting to their methods. We have always said that our objectives were those that could be achieved only by a free people. Why should a free people slavishly follow a Communist lead? We must develop all our own way. We want our people to decide whether their children shall go to school, whether they shall be scientists or playwrights or mechanics. We don't want to be told what to do. What the world wants today is leadership in the true sense, and we had better decide what we want to achieve and then go ahead and do it as leaders and not as imitators.

The only thing that frightened me in Russia was that we might be apathetic and complacent in the face of this challenge. I can well understand why the Russian people welcome the good that has come to them. But I cannot understand or believe that anything that has to be preserved by fear will stand permanently against a system which offers love and trust among peoples and removes fear so that all feel free to think and express their ideas.

It seems to me that we must have the courage to face ourselves in this crisis. We must regain a vision of ourselves as leaders of the world. We must join in an effort to use all knowledge for the good of all human beings.

When we do that we shall have nothing to fear.

34 SOVIET IMPERIALISM

George Meany (1894–   )

American labor leader George Meany has been consistently warning Americans of the danger of Soviet expansionism. He was born in New York City and became an apprentice plumber in 1910. Rising through the ranks of the Plumbers Union, he became president of the New York State Federation of Labor in 1934 and served as secretary treasurer of the American Federation of Labor from 1940 to 1952. Upon the death of William Green he was elected president of the American Federation of Labor in 1952 and became president of the combined American Federation of Labor–Congress of Industrial Organizations when the two organizations merged in 1955. On June 11, 1957, Meany made the following comments in a radio broadcast as a rebuttal to statements made earlier by Soviet leader Nikita Khrushchev.

RECENTLY, Nikita Khrushchev, the Soviet Communist Party boss, appeared on an American television program. He skillfully used this occasion to promote the interests of Soviet imperialism and the aims of the world-wide Communist movement. He performed amiably and adroitly in combining persuasion, boasts and outright lies to advance the current Soviet "peace offensive."

Khrushchev painted a glowing picture of Soviet economy, especially agriculture. He did not say a word about the low standards of life, the intense exploitation of labor, the denial of all democratic rights, and forced labor which plague the Soviet peoples. He was completely silent about the discontent among the peoples behind the Iron Curtain, as evidenced by student unrest, criticism voiced by writers, and the continued forced transfer of many thousands from their homes and jobs within the USSR.

Khrushchev declared that there had been and would be, no other party in the Soviet Union than the Communist Party which, he stated, "reflects the desires and wishes of the people so much." This Khrushchev boast reminds one of the boast by Hitler that the Nazi Party regime would last for at least a thousand years in Germany. Actually, the Soviet people have been denied the chance to express through free elections their real desires and wishes. The last time the Russian people had an election, which was at all free, was more than 39 years ago.

In his television performance, Khrushchev admitted that the Kremlin was jamming the Voice of America broadcasts to the Soviet Union. He admitted that his government was denying the Soviet peoples the right to listen to America. He tried to explain it away, or excuse it, by saying that Russia "is a very musical country." He went on to say that whether the Voice of America is jammed or not, therefore, depends on whether "it is a good voice" or "it's a voice which cuts on the ear." And, of course, it is Khrushchev and his ruling clique who decide what is a good voice and what is not a good voice for the Russian people to hear.

Khrushchev went even further when he said: "If the Voice of America does really become the Voice of America . . . it will not be jammed in our country." How nice of Mr. Khrushchev, he not only insists on deciding what the Soviet peoples shall hear or not hear. He also insists on determining what is and what should be the *real* voice of the American people and what shall be their national policies. To Khrushchev, a real Voice of America would be the voice of an America dominated by a Communist puppet government controlled and manipulated by Moscow.

Such are the Communist blessings that Khrushchev would extend to the other nations, including the American people. In this spirit, he boldly announced that the grandchildren of present-day Americans will live under what he calls "socialism"—that is, Communist totalitarianism. He expressed the belief that Communism would eventually triumph "because it is a younger system, the most healthy system". Mr. Khrushchev forgot that the young system of Fascism had to yield to the much "older" system of democracy. Actually, the "young" system of Communism is the oldest existing system—namely, slavery. In regard to Khrushchev's claim that Communism is the "most healthy" system, that might be so for the bosses who profit from it—but that is certainly not true for the millions of people who have perished under it or who are now being exploited and oppressed by it.

Khrushchev's grandfather tale was told in order to hide the Communist tyranny of *today* by talking about the grandchildren who are to live under some so-called benign socialism in the future.

I submit, the Soviet rulers are notoriously poor prophets. Foreseeing the victory of Hitler, the Soviets relied on him and signed the Nazi-Soviet Pact which was the signal for World War II. After World II, Khrushchev joined other Kremlin leaders in prophesying that American economy would collapse. In the nearly forty years of their dictatorship, they have continually, but falsely, *predicted* and *promised* better conditions of life and labor for the Soviet people.

These grandfather tales and all their silly prophecies should not fool anyone. And, judging by the way the youth behind the Iron Curtain has been reacting, there is increasing reason to believe that the Soviet parents and their grandchildren will likewise take Khrushchev's bragging with a very big grain of salt.

Khrushchev hastened to assure us that Communism in America will be the result of an ideological struggle between capitalism and "socialism" and not through a war. We were told that Moscow does not want to impose Communism on anyone. Clearly, the Soviet dictator has only contempt for our memory. Less than eighteen months ago, at the Twentieth Soviet Communist Congress, Khrushchev himself scornfully rejected the idea that Communism could be achieved without a revolution. He then branded the idea of a peaceful transition to "socialism" as "reformism" and a betrayal of Leninist doctrine. In the Soviet Domain, this is treason and punishable by death.

Shrewdly attempting to exploit the abhorrence of war by the American people, Khrushchev posed as a man deeply devoted to the cause of peace. While accusing the United States of planning a war against the USSR, he made himself the advocate of the "people of the world" who "want peace and want a normal life." But all the world knows that it is aggressionist Soviet imperialism which has prevented mankind from enjoying peace and leading a normal life.

Khrushchev could not hide the ugly truth that the Kremlin is interested in peace, *only* to the extent that it advances Moscow's policies at home and abroad. He stated frankly that under cover of its "peace" program and propaganda, the Soviet government seeks the lifting of all Western trade restrictions and the resumption of so-called cultural exchange programs. His plea for cultural exchanges is dishonest. At the Conference of the Big Four Foreign Ministers in November 1955, America, Britain and France proposed a seventeen point program for breaking down the barriers between the people under Communist domination and the free world. Molotov then denounced this program as a blueprint for espionage. Later on, President Eisenhower again offered this program to the Kremlin rulers and was once more turned down.

Moscow is interested in trade agreements in order to obtain from the highly industrialized countries badly needed goods. Moscow wants "cultural exchanges" in order to acquire the scientific and technical "know-how" of the "capitalist" countries which it despises and seeks to destroy. Khrushchev realizes the vital contributions which the Western World can make *and has already made* to the upbuilding of the Soviet economic system. Moscow wants the free world, through trade, credits and availability of its superior technique—to help bail the Communist rulers out of the difficulties into which the follies of Communist economy and intense militarization have led them.

Khrushchev's entire cultural exchange program is completely one-sided. America would derive no benefits from such contacts. These would *not* be contacts with the Russian people but only with individuals hand-picked by the Kremlin and its police system. Khrushchev made that perfectly clear when he hedged even in regard to unconditional abolition of the existing travel restrictions for United States diplomats in Russia.

The current Soviet "co-existence" campaign is particularly designed to serve the expansionist aims of Soviet imperialism. What "co-existence" means to the present Kremlin rulers was demonstrated with painful clarity last November in Hungary. The Hungarian people and their democratic government offered to live in peace with Russia. They offered friendship to and trade and cultural relations with the Soviet government, with all neighbors of Hungary and all the nations of the world. What was the answer of the Kremlin to this Hungarian plea for co-existence? It rushed hundreds of thousands of troops and thousands of tanks and jets into Hungary to crush and kill defenseless men, women and children. And what was the crime of this brave people? All they sought was national independence and democracy and the right to co-exist peacefully alongside of Soviet Russia and other countries.

In recent years, Soviet expansion has been blocked through the collective defense system of the West and through American superiority in the thermo-nuclear field. The primary purpose of Soviet foreign policy is to destroy these safeguards of world peace. This is the motivating force for the so-called positive participation by Moscow in the current London disarmament talks. Khrushchev stressed the advantages of disarmament from his domestic point of view. He even dangled, before an American public yearning for a tax cut, the possibility of reducing the armament burden.

But, in repeating the Soviet position for banning atomic and hydrogen weapons and further test explosions, he made sure not to commit himself to a comprehensive system of international control of disarmament measures. He even belittled the proposals for announcing and registering all future nuclear tests. Certainly, he knows better than to believe that there can be any guarantee that a disarmament agreement will be carried out unless its enforcement is assured through the establishment of a foolproof system of international inspection and control.

The Communist boss also tried to give the impression that only the Soviet Union had taken constructive measures in the disarmament field. He cited the reduction of Soviet armed forces by 1,800,000—but he refused to cast any light on the well-kept secret—the present military strength of the Red Army. He pretended not to have the exact figures at hand! But, even after this Kremlin-reported decrease of its armed forces—the truth of which no outsider has even been permitted to check—Soviet Russia still has the strongest military machine in the world. Nor did Khrushchev mention that this was the first decrease reported by the USSR since 1945. In contrast, the democratic powers had carried out almost total demobilization after the war. The Free World started to rearm only after it was forced to do so in the face of continued Soviet military aggression, especially in the Korean War.

The most sensational part of the Khrushchev interview was his offer to pull back Soviet troops from Eastern Germany and the satellites in exchange for a withdrawal of American armed forces from Europe. In making this proposal, Khrushchev was fully aware of the fact that the American troops in Europe are the backbone of NATO and that their return to the United States would mean the breakup of the Western collective defense system. When one of his American interviewers argued that this proposal would mean an American withdrawal over a distance of more than 3,000 miles in the face of a Russian pull back of only two hours away, he dismissed that argument by resorting to a rather shoddy trick. He compared the distance between New York and Western Europe with the distance between Vladivostok and Eastern Europe. He then concluded that "the distances are about the same." But the decisive point is not which is the farthest but what is the nearest distance between the United States and Western Europe and between Russia and Western Europe.

In spite of the obvious dangers involved, some people in Germany and in the satellites, being very anxious to get rid of Russian military occupation, might have some illusions about the Khrushchev proposal. When the American correspondents drew Khrushchev's attention to the possibility that the withdrawal of Soviet troops from Eastern Europe might mean the end of Communist rule in the satellites, he haughtily denied it. He waxed demagogic to the point of asserting that even the Kadar regime could continue to exist in Hungary without the presence of the Red Army. He boldly exclaimed: "Let's have a test."

But Hungary has already furnished just such a test. In October, 1956, the Hungarian people revolted not only against Soviet domination, but against their own Communist bosses. For this, they were crushed by Soviet might. After what happened in Hungary last fall, however, there can no longer be any illusions about the iron determination of the Kremlin to maintain its stranglehold of the captive nations. Khrushchev's proposal for a mutual troop withdrawal was not made to bring about the liberation of the enslaved people. It was made solely for the purpose of propagandizing and promoting the withdrawal of America's armed forces from European soil. Such a withdrawal could only make final the enslavement of the captive peoples. In order to thwart this dangerous Soviet maneuver, the West should demand that Moscow should, at least, implement the Yalta accord on free elections in the satellites and should accept German reunification in freedom.

In his appearance, Khrushchev used the word "peace" rather freely and loosely. However, he did not speak of freedom in his entire television performance. Yet, we know that, without freedom, there can be no real world peace today. The history of the turbulent post-war period, with its massive Soviet aggression and annexations, confirms the validity of this axiom. That is why the free world must stress and strengthen the link between peace and freedom—especially in view of the renewed hypocritical Soviet "peace" offensive.

The American people know what Communism has done to the Russian people. We know the plight of the captive peoples in Europe and the Chinese mainland. We should never forget what Khrushchev, after he succeeded Stalin, did to the freedom-loving Hungarian people. None of us should have any doubts of what Moscow is up to in its newest campaign for so-called peaceful co-existence. For the sake of our children and their children who come after us, we should always be fully conscious of the basic objective of Communism for complete world domination. And then let us always remember—that this basic objective can be attained only by the complete destruction of our free American way of life.

35 THE GROWTH OF SOVIET POWER

Dean Acheson (1893–1971)

As Secretary of State from 1949 to 1953 in the Truman administration, Dean Acheson played a pivotal role in the development
of postwar American policy toward Russia. Ironically, he was
criticized both by conservative Republicans as being "soft on
Communism" and by liberal Democrats as being too harsh
toward Moscow. Born in Middletown, Connecticut, Acheson
graduated from Yale College in 1915 and received his law degree
from Harvard three years later. Prior to his term as Secretary,
Acheson served as Assistant Secretary in 1941 and as Under
Secretary from 1945 to 1947. The following comments, which
reveal his distrust of Soviet motives, were made in October 1957
as part of the Clayton lectures at The Fletcher School of Law
and Diplomacy, Tufts University.

BEFORE THE PRESENT century was two decades old, the system
which had provided an international order since Waterloo was
mortally stricken. Twenty years later, it had disappeared altogether. . . .

The First World War ended the Austro-Hungarian, German,
and Ottoman Empires and the Czarist regime in Russia, unloosed
nationalism in Eastern Europe, and gravely weakened the French
and British Empires. The Second World War eliminated the
empires of Japan and Italy, and the military power of Germany.
France, defeated and occupied, lost her position in the Near East
and Far East, and only with increasing difficulty maintains herself in Africa, at the expense of power in Europe. Great Britain,

economically exhausted and, save for the African colonies, politically and militarily reduced to her island resources, has by her recent budget decision made clear that the security of the United Kingdom lies in association with other states, and by concentrating military effort in the nuclear field has sought a means of influencing the decision of the United States to fight should Britain's survival be at stake. . . .

The disappearance of a world system and of the power which sustained it, together with the growth of Soviet power and ambitions, means that the nations which wish to preserve independent national identity can do so only if the material strength and the political and economic leadership of the United States are enlisted in the effort. However much all of us may dislike this thought, the requisite power does not reside anywhere else.

Europe, however, remains of great importance. Its population is still the largest aggregation of skilled workers in the world, its resources are many and varied. Its industry is second only to our own, though closely pressed in many fields by the Russians. Its traditions of civilization go back through two and a half millennia. If Europe should, by evil chance, become subject to Soviet domination, the problems of the remainder of the non-communist world would become unmanageable. The agreement and support of Western European nations are necessary for any successful foreign policy and defense arrangement on our part. One must not discount the importance of Europe. But the fact remains that Europe without American strength and leadership can neither preserve its own independence nor foster an international system in which anyone's independence will survive.

In the other alignment, Russian power, which has for two centuries been great, appears to be towering now. In part this is so because it stands out like a great tree in a forest where all around it have been felled; in part, because it has fed on the surrounding decay, and grown. In the past Russian strength lay in its vast area and its large and disciplined manpower. The Soviet regime has added to these assets industrial productive power, which is today the indispensable basis of military power, economic penetration, and political attraction. The Soviet regime gives first importance to its own perpetuation. A strong second effort goes to keeping confusion and unrest as widespread as possible outside the communist area, and to frustrating all attempts to build an international system other than a communist one. All this paves the way for the inevitable—so the regime believes—collapse of capitalistic governments and systems, and for the hegemony of the Soviet Union in a communist world. The regime's efforts gain immense vigor, subtlety, and—for the West —deep deceptiveness from the fact that the Soviet is a revolutionary society, repudiating the most fundamental postulates of the established order, and is in the grip of an ideology which imbues it with unquestioning confidence in its superiority and its destined progression to triumph and dominion.

No matter how plainly the Russians talk and act, we simply refuse to believe what they say and to understand the meaning of what they do. President Eisenhower and Secretary Dulles keep insisting that the test must be deeds, not words. Floods of deeds follow, amply explained by torrents of words. Yet our leaders and, indeed, our people cannot believe what they see and hear.

As I write, President Eisenhower tells us that relations between the United States and the Soviet Union might be improved by a visit from Marshal Zhukov. The President recalls that he and the Marshal "had a most satisfactory acquaintanceship and friendship," and remembers having had "a very tough time trying to defend our position" against the Marshal's contention "that their system appealed to the idealistic, and we completely to the materialistic." The President seems to forget that the same satisfactory friend and persuasive debater insisted upon and carried out the bloody liquidation of the Hungarian revolt. The friendliness which underlies American life makes it impossible to believe that congeniality can accompany the most profound hostility to ourselves and all we believe. As Justice Holmes correctly observed, candor is the best form of deception. . . .

The object of competition Khrushchev points out, is the triumph of the Soviet system. He does not "*need*" a war to ensure this victory; but he would quite clearly not reject force if the risks were low, or if, as in Hungary, he felt that the deepest interests of the regime were at stake. Despite all this, we go on seeing in each new move of the Kremlin to divide and weaken us signs that the Russians may at last be "sincere." The very word shows our lack of understanding. The Russians are and have been wholly sincere in what they believe and are pursuing. But their moves and proposals in dealing with other states are coldly and carefully calculated to advance their own purposes, not any common purpose with the West. In this context "sincerity" is a silly and, indeed, a very dangerous word.

Russian industrial production has been growing at a rate as fast as that of any society of which we have record, and greater than most. The technical competence and quality of their heavy industry is no less impressive. For a decade after the Bolshevik revolution in 1917, the period of the consolidation of power, Soviet industry did not equal production under the Czarist regime. This was achieved in 1926; and pre-war production was surpassed in 1928. In the ten years from 1938 to 1948 industrial growth was suspended by the Second World War, preparing for it and recovering from it—a period in which United States production increased enormously; steel production, for instance, by a third. So the Russian achievement has taken place during twenty productive years. . . .

Well, we may say, suppose that Soviet production does become equal to ours, what of it? How does it hurt us economically? From the military point of view, will there be any more wars determined by great industrial potential converted to the production of overwhelming quantities of war material? Won't nuclear attacks destroy industrial capacity, so that the wars of the future will be won or lost by the forces in being at the beginning of the war? Or won't they be limited in area and in the size and nature of forces involved and the type of strategy employed?

We shall see later that there is much sense in these questions. It seems also likely that eventually Russian productive power will approximate ours. Nevertheless, should it do so before a workable and working non-communist world system has been established and has enlisted the loyalty of great sections of the world, a most fundamental shift of power would most certainly occur. The Russians understand the necessity for production in their communist area system, and are making great efforts to provide it. They are quite sure that the competition of "peaceful coexistence," if nothing else, will, as Mr. Khrushchev expressed it, "ensure the victory of socialism." The odds would be overwhelmingly against them if under the leadership of the United States, industrial productive power in the non-communist world were also increased to meet unprecedented calls upon it. These calls will be to furnish a military establishment and weapons system more extensive and varied than now exists; to satisfy expanding internal needs; and, in a magnitude not yet understood, to provide foreign investment for those undeveloped areas which are ready and pressing for capital. To many countries this capital would furnish the only alternative to forced saving in the authoritarian style and to dependence for equipment on Soviet industry.

The growth of Soviet power requires the growth of counter-power among those nations which are not willing to concede Soviet hegemony. With this counter-power the future can be faced with hope and confidence, as well as with a sober appreciation of its dangers. Growth of counter-power is needed in our own country, in other industrially developed nations, and in countries only at the beginning of industrial development. There may be a different reason moving each country which objects to Soviet domination. That is unimportant. There will be great differences in their capacity for industrialization. This is important. For help to industrialize (though not subsidy) should be centered in those areas not willing to accept the hegemony of the Sino-Soviet axis and now capable of industrial advance.

36 THE SOVIET WAR AGAINST RUSSIANS

Eugene Lyons (1898–   )

His experiences in Russia as a United Press correspondent between 1928 and 1934 turned Eugene Lyons from a communist sympathizer into an opponent of the Soviet regime. Born in Russia, Lyons emigrated to the United States in 1907, and grew up in New York City. A socialist, he served as editor of the Soviet propaganda magazine "Soviet Russia Pictorial" in New York in 1922. Although he never joined the Communist Party, he worked for the official Soviet news agency TASS until 1927. After leaving Russia in 1934 Lyons, now very much an anti-communist, edited *American Mercury* magazine and was roving editor and then senior editor of *Readers Digest* from 1946 to 1968. He has published many books on Russia and frequently lectures on the Soviet Union. The following comments were made on May 20, 1958, in a talk to the advertising Club of Springfield, Massachusetts.

TRADITIONALLY, IN RUSSIA, it has been the so-called intelligentsia that has given voice to what the suffering and inarticulate masses felt. In Tsarist times, the most daring critics of social evils, the most effective crusaders for change, were novelists and playwrights and poets. The centers of idealistic protest, the seed-beds of revolution, were the colleges and the universities.

That pattern has held true in the Soviet period. If this has not often been apparent to the naked eye, it is only because oppression and censorship have been a hundred times more brutal under the Soviets than in the worst Tsarist years. The opportunities for overt protest have been meager, the penalties swift and terrible.

Despite this, the ratio of political arrests has always been higher on the Soviet campus than in the population as a whole. Writers and artists, historians and scientists, professors and students have provided a larger share of the inmates of Soviet prisons and concentration camps, percentage wise, than any other groups.

With few exceptions, the Russian intelligentsia today is Soviet born and Soviet bred. Yet we have had striking proof in recent years that it is, from the Kremlin's viewpoint, deeply subversive.

After the death of Stalin, his successors cautiously relaxed some of the police terror and thought controls—not because they are any more humane than their dead master but because they had reason to dread the wrath of their subjects. The first and most startling effect of this minor moderation was a burst of books and plays, articles and poems critical of Soviet conditions that sent a chill down the spine of the Kremlin bosses.

The short-lived period of reduced pressure has come to be called "The Thaw," from the title of a novel dealing, for the first time in many years, with the personal interests and the private emotions of real people, rather than the stock emotions of stock characters of official propaganda.

But it was another novel, "Not By Bread Alone," by a young writer named Dudintsev, which became the symbol and storm center of the muted revolt. Considered as literature, it was hardly of first rank. But it told a story that dramatized the struggle between an individual and the state bureaucracy. Millions of Soviet people, most of whom hadn't even read the novel, therefore saw in it an assertion of their dignity as human beings as against the faceless and soulless state.

In the universities especially the Dudintsev book became a kind of banner of protest. Literary discussions overran their bounds into the dangerous area of political debate. At one session, in Moscow University, the author was present. Scared by the Pandora's box his book had opened, Dudintsev tried to minimize its political implications. But the students turned on him, accused him of showing less courage than the hero of his story.

At one point the Writers Union in Moscow called a conference to appraise the novel. What followed was more like a riot. The police had to be called to control the crowds trying to get in. The same kind of thing happened all over the country. And the book was merely typical of a rash of outspoken and sometimes angry writings.

This was only part of the intellectual revolt to which I referred. Its significance was that it reflected, as in a mirror, the feelings of a large part of the population—how large we can only guess.

It was with good reason, therefore, that the men in the Kremlin were thoroughly alarmed. They saw the immensity of the resentments and despairs under the seemingly calm surface of their monolithic dictatorship. To add to their fright, they saw how, across the frontiers in Poland and Hungary, what started with the same sort of literary mutiny was exploding into nationwide popular mutinies.

So they cracked down hard on the new literary freedom. The thaw was over. A new freeze set in. Outwardly today intellectual life in Soviet Russia is again almost as wintry and barren as in the toughest Stalin years. No more truth-telling books can be published. Most of the angry authors have been forced publicly to recant their "sins."

Thousands of students have been purged from Soviet universities, many of them being hustled off to the slave camps. Last year, in the University of Leningrad alone, according to one report, 4000—about half the entire student body—were expelled for political reasons.

But we now know as a certainty that under the new layer of ice, Soviet writers and artists and students are thinking their own thoughts. We have no reason to doubt that at the first opportunity they will again break through the crust. And in the end, I for one am convinced, the autocrats will find it impossible to suppress them.

Of all the big communist lies, the biggest and most cynical

is their claim that the Soviet regime is loved and cherished by those who live under it. The claim has been so continually repeated, and echoed by gullible non-communists, that millions in the free world accept it as a fact.

The myth, for this is what it is, has been reinforced by simple-minded tourists to the communist Mecca. They take a quick look, note that there are no barricades or riots, and return home with the glad tidings that the people enthusiastically support the regime.

Since another travel season is in the offing, I might say in passing that I have very little respect for tourist testimony, and that includes U. S. Senators and one-shot journalistic visitors to Russia. If I sound a bit emphatic on the subject, it's because I watched them close-up during the six years when I lived in Moscow and have followed their accounts ever since.

In other places these travelers seem content to take in the sights and sample the night life. No sooner, however, do they cross the Soviet frontier than they turn into combination sociologists, economists and historians. Almost invariably they report that conditions have "improved" a lot—though they haven't the faintest notion what conditions used to be. If one tenth part of the improvement vouched for by tourists through the years were true, Soviet Russia by this time would have been a full-fledged paradise.

Then these two-week or six-week experts report, as I said, that the people support the regime. As one prominent journalist put it in a *Saturday Evening Post* article not too long ago, they have "learned to love their chains."

Fortunately that's a libel, a cruel libel, on the Russians.

Why, if the people loved their chains, would the Kremlin have needed, through all these decades, a secret-police establishment and concentration camps on a scale without precedent in all human history?

The Russian Tsars, though openly menaced by organized revolutionary movements, got by with a political police force—the Okhrana—of four or five thousand officials and operatives. Their political prisoners and Siberian exiles, in the most repressive periods, never numbered more than 20 or 30 thousand.

The *Soviet* Tsars, by contrast, have a political police machine —the Cheka, the G. P. U., the N. K. V. D. and now the M. V. D., but just as ruthless under the changing names—of close to two million men, including a special army for purely internal operations. Their political prisoners numbered 15 million at the peak and must still be counted by the million. Their political executions have run into the hundreds of thousands.

Never before, not even in a world that still included Hitler's Germany and Mussolini's Italy, has a state spawned such gigantic organs of surveillance and terror, censorship and intimidation.

Why, if the people were already sold on the Soviet way of life, would the Kremlin need hundreds of thousands of agitator-propagandists giving their full time to "selling" the regime to its subjects? Soviet Russia is the only nation on record which maintains a vast network of special schools training these agitators; and propaganda is a daily and standard part of every school curriculum, every office and factory routine, every newspaper and radio program.

Let us have one common-sense fact clear in mind. Even the most sadistic police state doesn't murder its citizens wholesale or confine millions of them in pestiferous slave camps just for the fun of it. It does not without some good reason impose the death penalty for so-called crimes which in normal countries are unknown or treated as misdemeanors.

No government assigns a major part of its energies and manpower and resources to internal security unless it feels itself terribly insecure. These are measures of self-protection by the regime against actual or potential resistance.

Even under the abominated Nazis, it was comparatively easy for Germans to leave the country. But in Russia legal emigration is prohibited, and trying to leave the country illegally is punishable by death. Strange, is it not, that a dictatorship which boasts every hour on the hour of the enthusiastic loyalty of its "happy" people should take such extreme measures to keep them from escaping their Garden of Eden.

No less strange, under the circumstances, are the extremes to which the Kremlin crowd goes to shield the minds of its devoted subjects from the contamination of competing ideas. It maintains an absolute embargo against infidel newspapers, magazines and books from the non-Soviet world, except for purely technical and scientific publications. It has spent literally billions of rubles to jam foreign radio programs.

It happens that I had a hand myself in founding the American Committee for Liberation—a private group that finances Radio Liberation, a radio station in Germany over which former Soviet citizens broadcast to their countrymen. Moscow has paid us the unpleasant compliment of murdering two of the emigres on our staff and has been trying to intimidate others. We have calculated that the Soviets invest at least ten times more to jam our programs than we invest in broadcasting them.

Surely this gigantic and costly effort to isolate the Soviet people from outside influences would be unnecessary if the Kremlin rulers were really confident of the loyalty of those whom they rule.

The communists have fairly well succeeded in convincing the world that the peoples of Russia bent their necks meekly to the yoke of communism. But this is sheer bluff. Contrary to the general belief, both the Italian and German people submitted to their respective totalitarian afflictions more quickly, more fully, with less violent resistance, than the Russians.

The first four years of Soviet power saw a bloody civil war. Because the people were divided among themselves and without effective leaders, they were defeated. But they never really surrendered. They continued the struggle by other means—by means that were called non-cooperation when they were used in India. Never doubt that there has been plenty of fire under the smoke of the Kremlin's hysterical outcries against counter-revolutionaries, saboteurs and other enemies within.

The one constant in the muffled turbulence of Soviet history, from 1917 to date, has been the struggle between the regime and the people. There have been periods of reduced hostilities, like the one under Stalin in the middle 1930's and the one under Khrushchev now. But there has never been a true armistice, let alone a reconciliation.

It is useful to recall that in the middle 1930's, too, the terror was relaxed, a new fine-sounding Constitution was promulgated and a smiling Stalin was having himself photographed kissing babies and prize-winning milkmaids. Abroad the prevailing view, then, was that the worst was over—the dictatorship was mellowing or evolving in the direction of moderation. Soon enough that wishful thinking fantasy collapsed in the bloodiest purges in history. I'm not suggesting that history will necessarily repeat itself, but I wouldn't bet to the contrary.

What the world has witnessed in Russia without understanding it is *a permanent civil war*. In the early years it was active and military; since then it has been passive but no less bloody. Once you grasp this concept of a continuing internal conflict, much about Soviet Russia that seems baffling begins to make sense.

The many millions who have perished at the regime's hands, whether finished off in police dungeons or starved in punitive man-made famine, are the casualties of that war. The hordes of inmates of slave camps are its prisoners-of-war. The perennial purges and liquidations are battles in that war. The incessant thunder of propaganda is the psychological offensive that has become an essential element in modern warfare.

Yes, permanent civil war—that is the reality under all the pretenses, the key to an understanding of the dictatorship. Russia has been and remains a nation occupied from within. Its communist masters are in essence an occupation force.

The fairy tale of unity between regime and people does not jibe with the terrible compulsion the regime has been obliged to apply; with the vast slave-labor population; with the chronic Kremlin alarums over sabotage and espionage and the ubiquitous enemy within.

The great historic test of the claim of popular acceptance of the regime, of course, came in 1941, when the Germans suddenly invaded Soviet Russia. Consider the facts:

For nearly a quarter of a century the Soviet dictators had been forcibly remolding the older generation, killing off those who would not lend themselves to the process, and rearing a new generation in its own ugly image. Toward this end it had applied its monopoly of force—the physical force that breaks bodies and the propaganda force that maims mind and spirit. Presumably a new "Soviet man" had taken the place of the historic Russian. This presumption was widely credited abroad; some solemn books were written describing this triumph of what Moscow called "human engineering."

Then, on the morning of June 22, 1941, came the first concrete test of this handiwork, and it turned out to be a silly figment of propaganda.

One would suppose that as the Nazi hordes poured into the land, the Kremlin, as a matter of course, would summon its engineered Soviet men to a holy crusade in defense of the new Soviet society, of the communized farms and the socialized industry. One expected Stalin and his minions to invoke the hallowed names of Marx and Lenin.

But they did nothing of the sort. The celebrated "Soviet man" might never have been. Instead, the dictators appealed to the Russian past and its maligned leaders. They invoked the names of Peter the Great and Ivan the Terrible and General Suvorov. They exhorted the people to review the spirit that defeated Napoleon's Grand Army more than a century before.

Communist slogans were dropped and the word "socialism" was hardly mentioned. Even the outlawed Church was restored and church-bells were rung on the Soviet radio. Why? Because Stalin knew, because every Soviet person knew, what their foreign admirers didn't—that the masses might be moved to defend their native soil but would not lift a finger to defend the regime that had exploited and terrorized them. To this day that conflict figures in the Soviet history textbooks not as a communist war but as the Fatherland War or the Great Patriotic War.

Stalin himself repeatedly told American visitors in the war years that the people were not fighting for him or for communism but for their native land. And he was right. In the first stages of the war, the desperate Russian people, cut off from the rest of Europe and knowing little of what had happened in Germany, looked upon their invaders as liberators from the communist yoke.

In the initial six months the Germans gathered in more than three million prisoners, which would have been impossible had the Red forces really put up a fight. Entire Soviet regiments and whole armies gave up without offering real resistance. And everywhere—Belorussia, in the Ukraine, in all-Russian areas like Smolensk, Vyazma and Bryansk—the civilian population met the Germans joyously and thousands offered their services to the conquerors.

Had the invaders been free men, in truth bringing liberation instead of a new form of slavery, it would have been curtains for the Soviet regime. But Hitler at that point saved Stalin. His black and brown legions unleashed their own brands of terror, made worse by the arrogance of their master-race pretensions. Quickly enough the people realized that they had only a grim choice between their native tyranny and an imported tyranny, and gradually they made the inevitable choice, rallying around the hated Kremlin against the Germans.

Even at that, close to a million Soviet soldiers donned German uniforms—the only massive quisling army the Nazis were able to raise among conquered peoples—in the naive hope of using the Germans to defeat the Soviets. And vast numbers took to the woods and hills and swamps to fight against both the Red and the German armies—remnants of those forces were holding out in the Carpathian mountains and other areas ten years after the end of the war. . . .

The rest of the world has forgotten that amazing piece of fairly recent history. But the men in the Kremlin, we may be sure, never forget it. They must reckon that in any future conflict there is at least the possibility that they would again have to fight against their own people.

Since the end of the war the Soviets have had 13 years more for their job of human engineering. But they still cannot count, like normal governments, on the automatic allegiance of their subjects. They have not yet achieved what the political scientists call "legitimacy"—the natural, unquestioning loyalty of the citizens to their rulers.

Their government does not rest on free consent of the governed, as under a traditional monarchy or a democracy. It continues to rest on the world's largest police establishment, on unlimited agitation and indoctrination, on hysterical propaganda about enemies within and threats from without.

For all its unlimited power—because of this absence of limits—the regime is perpetually on the defensive in relation to its citizenry, boasting, promising and above all, threatening. The identity between rulers and the ruled that other regimes take for granted, this one is continually proclaiming. In truth it is thus proclaiming its feeling of uncertainty about its own status and tenure.

Provided we recognize it and make use of it, this tension between the Kremlin and its people may prove more decisive than the Sputniks and ballistic missiles.

It would be suicidal folly to underestimate the threat of Soviet scientific achievements and growing military might. They leave us no alternative, in terms of sheer survival, but to maintain industrial and military leadership, regardless of sacrifices involved. We have no margins for complacency.

This does not mean, however, that we should paralyze ourselves with panic fear of the Soviets. Never forget that Soviet Russia made its greatest territorial conquests, enslaving nation after nation, in the very years when the United States had a monopoly of atomic power. Stalin did not allow himself to be overawed by our indubitable military *superiority*. Why need the free world allow itself today to be overawed by what is at worst *equality*?

It seems to me, ladies and gentlemen, that the defeatist attitudes spreading in the free world are a far greater menace than intercontinental missiles. If we sink into a mood of appeasement and surrender, the communists will take over the world without war, by intimidating one country after another into submission.

After all, the Kremlin leaders have as much reason to dread war as we have. Only if we convince them—as some spokesmen in the free world seem eager to convince them—that we have suffered a loss of nerve, that we no longer have the will to fight and die if necessary, will they be tempted to start a war. Now, as always in the past, every appeasement of a dynamic expansionist power brings the world closer to the ultimate catastrophe.

Ever since the Pharaohs built the Pyramids, tyrants, contemptuous of the needs and sufferings of their people, have been able to make dramatic achievements in limited areas. The Sputniks have been paid for out of the bellies and off the backs of a helpless population. They have been made possible by the ruthless sweating and exploitation of 200 million people. The same regime which orbits artificial moons is still unable to provide its masses with decent homes, clothes and food. Incredibly primitive living conditions and political tyranny are the price the people pay for the spectacular gains in the might of the state.

Without doubt the ordinary Russian takes pride in the technological progress, but he does not fail to see the irony of the contrast between Sputniks in his skies and wretchedness on his earth.

Even in the nuclear age, a nation's fundamental industry is agriculture. But Soviet agriculture is so backward that 52 million farmers—half of the country's total work force—can't raise enough food for an adequate diet. In the United States, by contrast, some eight million farmers, only an eighth of the work force, produce such abundance that their serious problem is surplus food.

As measured in over-all industrial production, Soviet Russia stands today approximately where the United States stood in 1900. In its 21 basic industries, the Russian lag behind our country in per capita output is greater today than it was before the 1917 revolution.

With half its laboring force on the farms, the manpower left for industrial purposes is actually smaller than ours, despite its larger population. And this bottleneck is made worse by the fact it takes two or three workers in the Soviet Union to produce what one worker does in the United States. At the same time Moscow's hope of exploiting its empire in Eastern Europe has been dissipated. Communism has so depleted the economic vitality of the satellite countries that they are now a drain on Russia.

I have no intention, I repeat, of underestimating the Soviet industrial-military potential. But the Russians are not ten feet tall. If they have temporarily outstripped us in a few selected items, it is only because we have been remiss in making the most of our clear superiority. Ours has been primarily a failure in vigilance that can and will be remedied.

Meanwhile, we should not yield an inch in our detestation of Soviet depotism, our compassion for its first and worst victims—the peoples of Russia—and our resolve that human decency shall prevail upon this earth. No matter how many Sputniks it hurls into the stratosphere, Soviet Russia remains a cruel police state, rooted in terror, feared and detested by its own people.

37 UNDECLARED WAR AGAINST THE WEST

Sidney Hook (1902–   )

Sidney Hook, writer, educator, and philosopher, was pointing out the threat posed to human freedom by Soviet communism as early as the 1920s, when he was still a graduate student. Born in New York City, he graduated from the City College of New York in 1923. Often regarded as John Dewey's disciple, Hook studied under him at Columbia University, earning his doctorate in 1927. For over forty years he was a member of the faculty of New York University, retiring as a professor in 1969. His many volumes include *Political Power and Personal Freedom* (1959), which reflects his views as a liberal critic of the Soviet form of government. The following excerpts are taken from that book.

By ALL ODDS the central political fact of our time is the existence of Soviet Communism, and its implications for the survival of free institutions everywhere. If one has any doubts about this, the headlines of the world's press would confirm it. The speeches and memoranda of statesmen concern themselves with it. One cannot intelligently discuss many domestic issues without reference to it—whether it be our policy with respect to atomic energy, or our programs of trade, taxation, and education.

Unfortunately our discussions of communism as an international movement are not infrequently unintelligent. Worse, they are not even informed. And worst of all, they sometimes reflect narrow partisan bias that converts the issue of communism

269

into a political football, kicked around for some fancied party advantage, actually profiting no one but the Communists. . . .

Contemporary communism is not Marxism as much as it is Bolshevik-Leninism. Its ideology is authentically presented in the writings, teachings, and practices of Lenin and Stalin—two of the most event-making men of all times, whose activity, we may note in passing, is difficult to explain in terms of their professed philosophy of history. Although since his death Stalin is no longer coupled with Lenin in every breath drawn by his successors, none of his major political ideas has been repudiated. Only the fury of the internal terror has been somewhat abated. . . .

The fact that we are dealing with political thoughtways foreign to the secular political mind of the West should not make us incredulous about their existence. Nor should we imagine that the Communist leaders are unaware of the fantastic discrepancies between their professed ideal and the sad realities of Communism in practice. For them these are the transitional costs of progress, to be redeemed by the felicities of the higher stage of communism in the future.

Marx once observed that no ruling class ever voluntarily surrenders its power. We might apply that maxim to the Communist ruling class, and maintain that unconsciously it seeks a justification in historic necessity for the social privileges it enjoys through political tyranny. Nonetheless, it is important to realize that we are dealing with neither frightened nor unintelligent men but rather with determined men, fortified by an absolute assurance in their program and its messianic significance for the entire world. So much so that they cannot even conceive that anyone who understands their program could reject it except on the three grounds of (a) self-interest, among the bourgeoisie the destruction of whose power and social position is threatened by the state monopoly of production; (b) ignorance or stupidity, among workers who remain insensitive to the Communist message; and (c) dishonesty, among all intellectuals who are critical of Communism, and who are dubbed "the lackeys of Capitalism."

Whether we are dealing here with a fanaticism of virtue or vice is again not so important as to recognize it for what it is, *a fanaticism of program* which subordinates everything to a pre-determined end. This end justifies the use of any means in the struggle for power—literally *any* means—and explains why Communist practice is marked by the extremest kind of opportunism and deceit in its slogans, strategy, and tactics. No communist feels bound by any code of honor or principles of morality. . . .

There is a myth currently prevalent that, after Lenin's death, Stalin espoused socialism in one country, and turned his back on international revolutionary communism which Trotsky had sought to continue as part of Lenin's legacy. The truth is that for all their differences, which were largely tactical and personal, both Stalin and Trotsky were out of the same Leninist mold. When Western Europe failed to imitate Russia, Lenin's problem was to build as much socialism as possible in Russia while encouraging revolutionary activities against capitalism in other countries. Stalin emphasized building up the socialist economy but did not neglect revolutionary activity abroad; Trotsky emphasized revolutionary action abroad but also called for the industrialization of the Soviet Union.

What Stalin meant by "socialism in one country" was that *if* the Soviet Union were left alone to work out her own destiny she would achieve socialism out of her own resources. But he never made any bones of the fact that the Soviet Union would not and could not be left alone, and that the final victory of socialism in one country can only be assured when the communist revolution had triumphed in the main countries of the world. . . .

There are several reasons why Communist ideologists are convinced that the Soviet Union cannot survive alone in a world of capitalist states, but the chief reason is the nature of the capitalist system. According to their analysis every capitalist system must expand or die, and before it dies it must make an attempt to expand by war unless it is overthrown from within. So fundamental is the belief that capitalism of every variety leads ultimately to economic breakdown and war that even during World War II, when some capitalist countries were helping the Soviet Union resist an invasion by another capitalist country, instead of making common cause with the invader, as Communist analysis would have led us to expect, this belief was still being fostered in official Communist text books although absent from government proclamations. To admit that any economy but a completely state-owned economy could possibly stabilize itself under conditions of modern technology, and provide full employment and general prosperity, would pull one of the chief props from under the argument for the Soviet system itself. The Soviet leaders cannot sincerely abandon this belief without having the whole structure of Communist ideology crash to the ground.

Given the dogma, however, that all countries not in the Soviet sphere are impelled to war by the very processes of their economic life, then with characteristic Bolshevik realism the consequences are logically drawn. Until the final conflict is won, the Communist economy must be a war economy and all measures, domestic or in regard to foreign policy, must enhance its military potential as well as its military geographical position. Since the final *dénouement* can be avoided only if Communist regimes are established in other countries, Communist Parties in those countries must function as fifth columns, disorganizing them by propaganda, infiltration, intensification of class struggles, espionage, and striking for power if a favorable revolutionary situation develops. At the very least, once hostilities break out they must sabotage to the death the cause of their own country for the sake of the worker's true fatherland, the Soviet Union.

Unpalatable as it may be to us, the sobering truth is that from the very founding of the Communist International, whose organization was called for by communist ideology even *before* the October Revolution, the Soviet regime has been in a state of undeclared war against the West. This war was launched on the basis of strictly ideological considerations, long before the foolish and fruitless efforts of some Western states to overthrow the Soviet Union by invasion in its early years. . . .

[The] basic issue, it cannot be repeated too often, is whether human beings are to be entrusted with freedom of choice to determine their own governments, their own cultural outlook, and their own economic system, or whether it is to be chosen *for* them. Despite their campaigns of semantic corruption with such terms as "democracy" and "freedom," the partisans of communist ideology have resolutely denied genuine liberty of choice to the people, first by the methods by which they seize power and even more by the methods by which they keep it. One can openly admit a multitude of evils, some of them shameful, in any existing democratic state, but so long as the processes of criticism, opposition, and education are not monopolized by a minority political party and supervised by a secret police, which is the case in every Communist state in the world, those evils are remediable. It is for this reason that according to the democratic ideology, *political* democracy is at the basis of all other forms of democracy no matter what the sphere of life.

Communism as an ideology cannot sincerely compete under the rules of the game of political democracy without giving up the ghost—but there is no reason to think it will oblige us by competing openly and sincerely. Within a national perspective the problems of coping with communism as a conspiratorial movement are difficult enough. But they are soluble in part by the techniques advocated by the President's Committee on Civil Rights—pitiless exposure and never-ceasing watchfulness, and in part by more effective measures which bar access to strategic posts in government and society to conspirators while taking care to uphold the individual liberties and dissenters.

Within the international perspective the problem is insoluble by these methods, short of the establishment of a democratic world sovereignty—a remote contingency. Until then, the undeclared cold war will go on between the U.S.S.R. and its satellite states and the Western world. To prevent this cold war whose temperature is daily rising from becoming an open war is the difficult task of Western statesmanship—an extremely difficult task when we reflect that it takes two to keep the peace but only one to violate it. Says a Chinese proverb: "No one can have more peace than his neighbors will allow him."

The danger, I submit, is not equal from both directions. For the existence of representative institutions and a free opinion in a democratic country acts as a brake upon the power of the executive arm to plunge the nation into war. Under totalitarian regimes, as history has amply evidenced, there is no comparable brake. It requires only the word of the dictator to send armies over the border and give the command for a Pearl Harbor. The problem then reduces itself to this: how can a country like the U.S.S.R., whose regime is fanatically devoted to the communist ideology, be prevented from overrunning, by direct or indirect aggression, one nation after another under the pretext of defensive action against encirclement?

No matter how fanatical the ideology, there is one force which can tame it: fear of failure. The fact that the Communist movement is free of traditional supernaturalism, and is more like a secular Mohammedanism than a Christian heresy (Mr. Toynbee to the contrary) works to a possible advantage if we are realistic enough. This history of the Bolshevik regime shows strategic retreats only when the policy of foreign adventure threatened to provoke a counter-action that might be too strong to withstand. Appeasement of the Soviet regime must fail even if it takes the most generous-hearted form, because according to Communist theory such appeasement always flows from weakness, not strength. So much are the Communist leaders prisoners of their own ideology that they cannot interpret any proposal to them, no matter how magnificent and magnanimous (even the Acheson-Lilienthal plan for the international control of atomic energy) except as maneuvers in the class war, a world civil war. The only remaining alternative, therefore, is the pooling of power by a union of democracies to a point where any major act of aggression by the Soviet regime would be considered too risky to be undertaken.

In this connection, we are sometimes told that it is impossible to prevent the spread of ideas or an ideology by force, or money, or other economic aid, and that the chief defense of the democratic ideology is the construction of a welfare economy with a functioning Bill of Rights. Put this way, two distinct sets of issues are confused which must be kept clear. Before a democratic people can build a better and freer society it must be safeguarded from interference by totalitarian powers. Social reforms in England and France by themselves would no more be sufficient to bring Soviet expansion to a halt than they would have sufficed to prevent Nazi expansion. It was not because Czechoslovakia suffered from economic distress or lack of civil freedom that she lost her democracy in 1948 or that Norway, Holland, and Finland came under the heel of dictatorship in 1941. It is not Soviet ideas that the democratic ideology needs fear, but Soviet paratroopers and illegally operating Communist Action Committees and fifth columnists. A better society by all means, but an iron-clad defense must go with it whenever any powerful nation refuses to submit all issues in dispute to the arbitrament of the democratic process. The adoption of economic measures to remove the whiplash of hunger and want throughout the non-Communist world must go hand in hand with reasonable measures of defence.

The democratic ideology should not fear the competition of communist ideology, it should welcome it. The shoe is really on the other foot: no communist regime will permit its subjects to read the literature of democracy or to hear the broadcasts of the free world. The peoples of totalitarian states are insulated completely from the truth about living and cultural conditions in the West. Because of the absolute monopoly such regimes exercise over all instruments of publication, it is well-nigh impossible to breach this intellectual quarantine. So complete is the control over news and facts about the West that the Russian soldiers who looted the apartment houses in the working-class sections of Vienna and Berlin believed that they were actually the homes of the bourgeoisie. In an official order of the day, the Red Army was even warned against being corrupted by the standard of living observable in—of all countries—Rumania! Far from fearing free and open competition between the democratic and communist ideologies in the market place of world opinion, we should encourage interchanges of ideas and personnel not only in technical fields, which the Soviets are eager to exploit in order to profit from Western technology, but in the fields of economics, and political and social philosophy.

38 THE MISTAKEN IMPRESSIONS OF TOURISTS

Charles Nutter (1902–   )

A good part of the American image of Russia is based on impressions by visitors from the United States who spend only a brief time in the Soviet Union. The great disparity between the conclusions they arrive at about the apparent state of affairs in Russia and the existing reality was pointed out by Charles Nutter—a business executive, foreign correspondent, and newspaper publisher—in a talk to the Export Managers Club of New Orleans in June 1960. Born in Falls City, Nebraska, Nutter graduated from the University of Missouri in 1923 before becoming a reporter. From 1927 to 1942 he served as a journalist with the Associated Press and was its Moscow correspondent in 1936–37.

THE ASSOCIATED PRESS, in its wisdom, recently distributed a story saying that around 15,000 Americans will crack the Iron Curtain and visit the Soviet Union this year. This number may be even greater if hotels and travel agencies can handle the influx. What Khrushchev and Eisenhower think of each other has not blighted the tourist crop to Russia this year.

These visitors will spend a week, a month or two hitting the tourist spots in Russia and will come home with a curious confusion of impressions which they will pass along from amateur lecture platforms all over America for the next year or so.

Get ready to hear these scarcely new facts about the Soviet Union: There are some churches open but not many; anti-religious museums are hard to enter; posted prices on food-stuffs

276

and clothing are skyhigh; there are very few automobiles and many pedestrians; lots of new housing is being built; Russian kids like gum and know a little English; women work at everything including day labor; hotels are adequate, but not luxurious; photographic restrictions seem to have disappeared.

Now and then some traveler will regale his listeners with an exciting story, mostly imaginary, of difficulty with the police, losing his passport, or another spicy account of hidden dangers he faced and mastered there beyond Minsk.

These bits of chit-chat will be passed along to Americans who have not seen Russia. They would be harmless enough if the visitors' accounts stopped there, or if they dug deeper into the real meaning of the Soviet Union and Communist International which you don't see or read from a hotel window or taxicab.

But unfortunately there will be many otherwise astute observers who will return with a belief that, because of its frontier appearance, high prices and scarcities and lack of many comforts and luxuries, this is a backward nation and is no economic threat to the United States because it has several generations to go before it catches up with capitalism.

International House of New Orleans recently conducted its Fortieth Trade and Travel Mission abroad in fifteen years and this time we took 85 persons to Russia, Czechoslovakia and Poland, being behind the Iron Curtain for two weeks and in Red Square in Moscow on May Day at the very time that the U-2 incident occurred.

I conducted this trip on behalf of International House and I am as convinced that few trade contacts or opportunities were uncovered as I am that very few of our traveling members grasped or understood the economic facts and threat of Communism as we glimpsed it in our brief mission.

The Soviet experiment, now 43 years old, is so vast, so different, so thought provoking and so startlingly successful at last that the Kremlin feels no fear in letting in large numbers of Americans to see their country and openly boasts of its economic plans for us all in the full belief that we cannot comprehend the facts and the danger.

A year or so ago Nikita Khrushchev told us over television

that our grandchildren would live under socialism (a sugar coated word for Communism which is used frequently so as not to alarm people too much), and he further declared that "we declare war upon you in the peaceful field of trade. We declare war and we will win over the United States. The threat to the United States is not the ICBM, but in the field of peaceful production. We are relentless in this and it will prove the superiority of our system."

Adolf Hitler in his celebrated book *Mein Kampf* never was more specific in the plans he had for the world than the Communists are and constantly have been for about a century since Karl Marx dreamed in the British Museum in London. So long as these plans were just dreams we could afford to pay little attention; now they are dreams backed by a billion captive people who have become, against their will or approval, economic serfs under an industrial empire which would engulf the world.

The recent trip to the Soviet Union was my second visit there. In 1936–1937, at the height of the great purges, I was a foreign correspondent there and saw Russia beginning to emerge from agricultural serfdom into an industrial state. Today, despite a great and disastrous war, the transition is far advanced, and the industrial power of Russia is beginning to roll and menace the world.

This visit to Russia left me with the very definite belief that the real Soviet threat is economic, not military. The Communists, by dint of clever planning, hard work and virtual slave or forced labor of their entire populace, have created an industrial power second only to the United States. In full view of the world but without its realization or alarm, the Kremlin has adapted outlawed and outdated malpractices of capitalism to establish a supreme state monopoly under state capitalism. It is called Communism.

The fruits of a labor force which is larger than the United States and which is surprisingly efficient in many areas and fields doesn't go to improve or help the people; it goes into a gigantic fund for use of the Kremlin, ample financing indeed for world revolution.

Communism in Russia is not communism at all, and probably never was. Today the Soviet Union is one gigantic trust in which the people are and have been exploited beyond the wildest dreams of capitalism in this or any other country. Everything and everybody belongs to the state and move and operate at the whim of the state. The state owns every job and every means of making a living, and it owns every living area, every bit of production, all land and factories, and resources, developed and unexploited.

The state controls all wages and salaries and it also controls the cost of living or rather it fixes both. It can raise or lower either overnight, closing or widening the gap without consultation or law, for some 210,000,000 people. It does so, of course, by holding wages down and raising living costs, particularly clothing or food, so that a whole family, including the wife and mother, has to work to make ends meet.

It looked to me as if the Soviet system, communism or so-called socialism in Russia today, economically speaking is a colossal distortion of the Company, the Company town, and the Company store, all monopolies, as we used to know them in the United States, but which have disappeared. The profits of this great all-embracing monopoly, which is nationwide, do not reach the people; they are used instead by the state for political purposes, national and international; ample financing indeed for the worldwide conquest plans which Communism espouses.

It is necessary to know and remember that profits and the profit motive didn't disappear in Russia; the government just took them over and gave them new names that are deceptive and misleading as always.

Profit is a dirty capitalistic word in Russia, something reserved for blasting the capitalistic world. Capitalism also is a dirty word, reserved for enemies of the Soviet Union. Yet there are profits beyond the wildest dream of anyone in the Soviet Union today, and a degree of capitalism that surpasses anything in the free world.

The difference is that under state capitalism, Kremlin style, profits are not distributed to many private owners, the profits

go to the sole owner of everything—the state. And this is by
no means the workers paradise, for the worker has nothing whatever to say about what goes on.

The high prices which we saw quoted in good stores in Moscow and Leningrad are not necessary or realistic. They are,
instead, a subtle form of taxation to drain off any surplus a
worker might accumulate. In a monopolistic economic state,
prices have no relationship to costs necessarily; prices are not
geared to cost but are fixed by political decisions taken in the
Kremlin. Shoes need not cost several weeks' salary, for they
could be sold for a day's salary or issued free, if desired. But this
might leave the individual with cash in hand which the state
dislikes. Private accumulation is the first step toward private
capitalism.

The worker is left drained dry at all times. He must exert his
maximum effort to make ends meet, and this work effort, multiplied by a hundred million souls, goes to enrich the parent cor-
poration, which uses the labor force's productivity for capital
expenditures and goods, for propaganda, for sabotage, espionage,
and subversion, for education, for military preparation and ad-
ventures, for sputnik and lunik, for training of communists to
work in other countries all over the world, and for any other
purpose it sees fit.

Better housing, food and clothing for the proletariat comes
into this scale at whatever level the leader decides. Usually it
is near the tail end. It is correct to say though that food and
living conditions are improving and are vastly better than they
were in the thirties.

The important thing also to remember about Soviet economics
is that despite ten million slogans and claims to the contrary, the
workers or proletariat have nothing whatever to say about what
goes on; they are as voiceless actually as slaves because there is
no way they can make their voices felt or heard.

The proletariat does not control, they comply. There are no
real unions, no strikes, no sitdowns, slowdowns, complaints;
nothing but obedience or disaster. The world's greatest private
corporations never approached this system in power or in numbers of workers. The Soviet Union has complete and absolute

mastery over a work force of more than 100,000,000 workers. The proletariat hasn't one thing to say about what jobs they hold, their wages, their rents or food costs, or any like factor. Russia has a dictatorship of state capitalism, big business beyond the wildest dreams of the hated trusts which the Soviet press and leaders are always denouncing.

Behind the curtain and always ready for action against a sullen or unresponsive worker, or a troublesome one, is compulsion. He might lose his work card, or his assigned room to live in, or he might be ordered to a new job thousands of miles distant. Finally there is the secret police and terror. The Soviets have killed more people for economic reasons in trying to uproot humanity and change its habits than they lost in World War II.

Under Secretary of State Dillon, wise to the ways of the Soviets, recently said that "in the thirties the Communists procured foreign capital equipment by exporting grain at prices below an already depressed world market—despite the fact that millions of Russians and Ukrainian peasants were dying of starvation." The graves of tens of millions of workers in the so-called workers paradise are the foundation for present industrial successes, and more will suffer and die as necessary to build this success higher.

This is the face of the enemy and the economic war in which we find ourselves. No day passes in Russia, or presumably in China, without millions of printed words exhorting greater production, greater efforts, greater sacrifices so that capitalism and particularly the United States may be surpassed, and then destroyed.

Big Business as above-explained now is working well in Russia after more than forty years, and is moving along rapidly. The people who make it possible, albeit perhaps reluctantly, are not unhappy actually for they are better off than they have been before and feel that their lot and living conditions have improved. This is the important thing always to remember about Russia; not that the people are not as well off as we are, but that they are better off than at any time previously. Things are improving for them and they are satisfied with this.

They really do not know of better things in the world. Ninety per cent of the present population grew up under so-called Socialism or Bolshevism, know little of the outside world, and are victims and believe in the Soviet's clever, well planned, monopolistic and universal propaganda.

No longer is it useful to dream that in educating the people the Kremlin will create a frankenstein to rise and destroy the master. The Soviets have sold the people on the system, and the alleged danger and threat from the outside, particularly the United States. It is safe to say that the Russian people, naturally friendly and broadminded, have been taught to fear and distrust the United States. They believe that the United States is a grave peace threat to the world, and that it would destroy Russia if possible.

Absurd as this may seem to Americans, it loses its absurdity and becomes a menacing fact when it is realized that this is a genuine fear held deeply in the hearts of people who lost twenty million dead and saw a third of their country laid waste only a generation ago.

Summarizing a little on this phase the sad fact for us is that the average Russian may not be very well off by our standards, but he doesn't know it and he thinks he is doing better by his standards. And he has actually been taught to believe that America endangers Russia's frontiers and he must work and sacrifice to prevent this.

The average Russian also has no idea of the extent of subversion and meddling in world affairs engaged in by the Kremlin, nor of the seriousness of the Communist International plans for world conquest. He is, in other words, providing the sinews and the financing for world conquest without knowing that this is the master plan of communist planners.

Russia has always been imperialistic to a certain extent but the Russians themselves are not conquest minded. This, though, makes no difference because they have not nor will they be asked their views; here again they are the foils of communism, and they obey.

Meanwhile we are confronted with an inexorable desire by the heads of the Communist International for taking over the world. The important aspect of Soviet foreign economic policies which must never be forgotten is their determination and powerful drive to penetrate and eventually capture the newly-developing countries of Asia, Africa and Latin America through trade and aid techniques. Economic warfare was developed and is thoroughly understood by the Soviet Union; to us it is largely a nuisance well remembered from World War II of which we'd like no more.

Khrushchev has told us openly and repeatedly that the Communists shall fill the needs of backward peoples better than the Americans and consequently shall win their minds, control of their lands, their resources and themselves. We do not seem to understand such language. We understood Pearl Harbor and we finally understood Hitler's Nazi Germany; but we do not seem to gather any alarm from a more determined, more resourceful, better financed and better planned threat from Communism.

Under Secretary Dillon once said that "in their offensive economic weapons have been cleverly blended with military assistance, propaganda and diplomatic moves, to inflame local passions and to create and aggravate situations of crisis. The long range aim is to create climates and attitudes in the newly-emerging areas conducive to eventual Communist take-over."

If Soviet penetration, economic subversion or trade succeeds in extending Communist rule in Asia, Africa, the Near East and Latin America the cost to the Kremlin is nothing compared to the results. Police power will be used to hold the people in line, and to hold control over immense wealth in the world's vital minerals.

Americans have been reluctant to grasp the awful significance of Soviet totalitarian plans, design and action. We'd rather relax and enjoy an economy that could be toppled by Soviet plans. We cannot or rather we have not understood that human beings can think, act and work from a set of motives and reasons completely the reverse of our own.

Last year President Eisenhower told the Congress in his State of the Nation speech that "we have learned the bitter lesson that international agreements, historically considered by us as sacred, are disregarded in Communist doctrine and in practice as mere scraps of paper . . . the demonstrated disregard for the Communists of their own pledges is one of the greatest obstacles to success in substituting the rule of law for rule by force."

There can be no doubt that the Communists live by the law of the jungle; stealing, lying, killing and destroying are virtues when done for the state. They dishonor their own word, their firmest commitments are meaningless. And this is the movement that teaches that Russia keeps its pledges but the United States does not; that Russia wants peace and we want war; that all powers are warmongers except the Communist powers.

For almost forty years the Soviets have been training nationals of every country in the world in revolutionary tactics; how to destroy and create chaos, how to inflame and arouse peoples against their rulers and leaders. They also have been dumping trade goods into desired areas of the world at giveaway or at extremely low prices. They know how to attack America's export market by dumping of their own goods. And they have the will to do this when they see fit. They also have the financial ability, thanks to very long and successful planning.

The industrial output of the Soviet Union today is very impressive, and is very menacing. Factories still are not as neat, well built and imposing as American factories but in many cases they are as productive; the Soviet workman has become a skilled workman. His productivity can and does rise as high as the American workman. Need is sparked by fear to drive him ever forward.

When we were in Europe Premier Khrushchev announced Russian abolition of income taxes over a five year period, starting next year. He made much of the fact that Russia could abolish income taxes while the United States very largely lived on such high taxes. Here is distortion and misrepresentation that takes keen analysis. The Kremlin can in fact abolish all income taxes without losing a single ruble of revenue; it shifts the emphasis to higher priced consumer goods or rents and collects just as much as ever. But in the remote areas of the world they can brag to an unsophisticated people that they alone can live without income taxes; bane of the capitalist world (their language).

The Soviet Premier said: "The abolition of taxes on workers and employes in our country is an impressive social gain for the peoples. One cannot speak of it without pride and emotion. This is an enormous gain, dear friends!

"Look at what is happening in the capitalist countries, where taxes are perpetually rising, unemployment reigns and prices are spiraling upwards. The insecurity of the working people lies like a heavy weight on the masses. . . .

"When people all over the world see that the living standard in the Soviet Union is regularly improving, that wages and pension benefits are rising, that taxation is being abolished and that the network of free medical, cultural and welfare facilities is expanding, they come to the clear realization that socialism is solving the most urgent problems and is showing the right way to get rid of exploitation, unemployment and poverty."

This kind of talk is for the export trade, not for home consumption since Khrushchev doesn't really care a fig for public opinion at home—that is already captive. He is trying to influence public opinion in the non-committed countries.

This is "black is white, white is black" at its pinnacle. But this is not the picture the American tourist will bring home. This is the reason that it is dangerous to accept at face value the impressions of tourists traveling in the Soviet Union and the reason that permitting 15,000 or more Americans to travel there this year is in reality part of the master plan to confuse and confound the world. Facts are not always facts in Russia and what you see with your own eyes or hear with your own ears may mean something wholly different than you think.

Travelers going to Russia therefore won't necessarily bring home the truth about that country, and often are dangerously misleading in their reports.

Russia has been called a puzzle, enigma and a riddle but it is none of these. Its purposes and plans are well advertised. It is of course difficult to understand how human beings can become so dedicated to a cruel, inhuman system which feeds on destruction—even of its own architects—but we must recognize there are several million such dedicated Communists in Russia and China.

Our job is to take the economic offensive and prove that the capitalistic system is a superior one to theirs.

39 SOVIET COMMUNISM: IDEOLOGY AND PRAXIS

Reinhold Niebuhr (1892–1971)

One of America's leading theologians, Reinhold Niebuhr demonstrated in his writings the philosophical inconsistencies between the theory and practice of Soviet communism. A native of Wright City, Missouri, he graduated from the Yale Divinity School in 1914 and became a minister of the Evangelical Synod of North America in 1915. He served as a minister in Detroit from 1915 to 1928, later becoming a professor at the Union Theological Seminary, where he won fame as a scholar and author. During the 1930s, Niebuhr was also active in the American Socialist Party. His comments on the Soviet Union are taken from the book *Reinhold Niebuhr on Politics* (1960).

———

COMMUNISM IS A RELIGION which has corrupted the Christian version of a Kingdom of God upon earth. It separated the part of the Christian faith contained in the prayer, "Thy Kingdom come upon earth," from that part of the Christian faith in which the taint of sin on all historic achievements is recognized. It sought for a kingdom of perfect justice, a classless and universal society. It vulgarized this dream even more than did bourgeois secularism. For it thought that the abolition of the institution of property would assure a harmonious society and ultimately a sinless human nature. Thus is promised a Kingdom of God without repentance.

Communism, in its pure form, is a secularized religious apocalyptic creed. The triumph of communism in Russia transferred the religious emotions associated with this apocalyptic hope to a particular locus. The hope that the Kingdom of God would come on earth was related to the assertion that it *had* come on earth and that Russia was the historical embodiment of it.

It may be questioned whether the Russian oligarchy which now controls the destinies of a nation committed to the achievement of such an ideal never-never land, is animated by these utopian dreams. The possession of power is sweet and the corruptions of power are great. We may assume therefore that those who exercise this power do not concern themselves too much with the dreams which originally endowed their power with moral legitimacy. But it is important to recognize that in the eyes of the faithful the power which this oligarchy exercises is still in a completely different category from the power of Nazi oligarchs. Furthermore, the capacity of the human soul for self-deception is so great that some of these Russian oligarchs may, for all we know, feel themselves completely justified by the original dream.

But speculation about the mixture of motives in the soul of the oligarch is comparatively irrelevant. For the end result remains a meretricious compound of Russian nationalism with communist dreams of world dominion; and the creation of a tyrannical oligarchy devoid of either internal or external checks upon its power. Hell knows no fury like the fanaticism of the prophets of a secular religion who have become the priest-kings of an utopian state.

In fact, the history of mankind does not record another instance of this type of enemy. For no previous center of power in human history ever had the advantage of a political religion, scattered beyond its borders, the tenets of which could persuade gullible men to regard even its most tortuous and cynical power politics as proofs of its virtues and good intentions. . . .

Let us recall how this tyranny developed. The Marxist dogma provided for a "dictatorship of the proletariat." According to the dogma, this dictatorship was necessary because the messianic class (the workers) was bound to be insecure until its class enemies were "liquidated." The theory was that the workers would exercise a dictatorship to eliminate their class enemies, but that among themselves they would enjoy a perfect brotherhood. They would not need courts and policemen because they would put down any anti-social behavior by spontaneous action.

It is well to note the utopian touch in the vision of a democracy within a dictatorship, because it is the first clue to the question why the Marxist utopia turned into a hell. The visionaries did not consider the ordinary problems of a community, the competition of interests, the arbitration of rights, the adjudication of conflict. The only cause for conflict, namely property, was abolished. But meanwhile, the community on the other side of the revolution needed to be organized. It could not rely on spontaneous action. The embryo of the organization lay in the party. The dogma had assumed that, while the workers were the messianic class, they needed the party to inform them of the logic of history and what good things it intended for them. The workers had an existential righteousness, but evidently no wisdom. Lenin declared that, left to themselves, they could not rise above a "trade union psychology." How right he was. The Marxist dogma would always outrage the common sense of common men. It could be believed only by the ideologues. These were the secular prophets who became the priest-kings of the utopian state.

So we proceed from the dictatorship of the workers to the dictatorship of the party. But the party must also be organized. Everywhere the need for government, which the dogma had defined as merely an instrument of oppression, made itself felt. Without integration, the masses were merely a mob. The party must have a "central committee." But the committee was, and is, too large for executive action. The ruling group within the committee was first a mere class war improvisation. But naturally, its powers grew rather than diminished. The real oligarchs emerged. They had the power. This was the "democratic centralism" of Lenin. It must be observed, however, that Lenin, while more subtle than Stalin, was potentially a dictator. He did not allow "factions." He was the charismatic leader who knew the logic of history better than his colleagues. Had he not prophesied correctly?

But without real freedom, either within the party or in the community, there was nothing to prevent a shrewd manipulator, Stalin, from bringing all the organs of power into his own hands, from liquidating even the oldest prophets who did not agree with him, and from terrorizing a whole generation of newer oligarchs—many of whom owed their positions to his favor and had helped him to eliminate his foes. It is this absolute monopoly of power which proved to be so vicious and which is now defined by Khrushchev's euphemism, "the cult of personality. . . ."

The Russian achievements in rocketry and space exploration have illuminated mistaken assumptions that we might not have made had we not been so fat and complacent. These include the following:

(1) Russia is not a "backward" country, except in living standards and political organization. Even the political tyranny is not backward; it is a novel form of harnessing utopian dreams to despotism. We forgot that it required Japan less than a half century to transmute its economy from an agrarian to an industrial and technical pattern. We were wrong to assume that a technical culture, requiring so many centuries to germinate in the West, could not be transplanted in much shorter time. Russia has been even a little quicker than Japan and probably for a reason which illustrates our second mistake.

(2) We were wrong in assuming that despotism excluded democracy in education, at least the democracy of freedom of opportunity. We should have known that the Russian young people had a passion for education and that the communist scholarship program, which recruits the bright sons and daughters of peasants for the most advanced scientific training, is better than our system of free education. We give everyone the right to acquire an education if the family budget and the resourcefulness of the youth are able to cope with our ever higher educational costs. That is "Jacksonian" democracy in practice. The Russian system is "Jeffersonian" in insisting on an aristocracy of excellence.

We can, of course, console ourselves with the comforting and true reflection that this is the only despotism in history which requires efficiency for its survival; and technical efficiency requires brains which may prove themselves ultimately—but only very ultimately—incompatible with tyranny.

(3) We were led astray by the fantastic Lysenko official biology of the Stalin era and imagined that science could not prosper in a dictatorship. The humanities and the arts in general feel the restraining power of the rulers who demand conformity to their standards of "social realism," for this means painting this false utopia according to the illusions of the oligarchs. But the pure scientists are apolitical, and have always been—whether here, or in Russia, or in Nazi Germany.

The technical advances in Russia are the more inevitable because bright young people, anxious to be co-opted as junior partners of the oligarchy which controls Russia, will go into pure science rather than into the humanities where they are bound to bow their knee to the Baal of dictatorship. In pure science and in technology the ambitions of the scientists and the ambitions of the oligarchs for international prestige coincide.

(4) We were probably most grievously in error in the complacency with which we equated all kinds of freedom: the freedom of science, of conscience, of religion, of enterprise and the freedom to buy a new model automobile every year. In short, our indiscriminate freedom and our tremendous productivity have made our culture soft and vulgar, equating joy with happiness and happiness with comfort.

We have in fact become so self-indulgent that one may raise the question whether our position vis-a-vis the Russians is not the old historic situation: the "barbarians," hardy and disciplined, are ready to defeat a civilization in which the very achievements of its technology have made for soft and indulgent living. . . .

If no other problem confronted the post-Stalin oligarchy its triumph in competition with the "free world" might be possible particularly since the launching of the earth satellites has given Russia the prestige of superior achievements in advanced technology. But the great problem of the post-Stalin era, which was assumed to be solved by Khrushchev's reconciliation with Tito, remains. The fact that it remains is attested by the subsequent hardening of the Russian line of authority over the satellites and the exclusion of Tito. Why was not the original revision of the dogma that "there are many roads to socialism" maintained? Why was it revised into a new Stalinism after Stalin has been discredited? Why was Hungary suppressed so brutally and Nagy murdered a year after the Hungarian revolt? Why was Poland's semi-autonomous status called in question? What prevented the devolution of the monolithic structure of the empire of Russia, particularly after the first steps to that end were taken after Stalin's death?

The answers to these questions are not simple because no question of dogma is involved. The idea of the dictatorship of the party was derived from the original dogma of the dictatorship of the class. But the dictatorship of Russia itself is not based on any dogma. It has simply been added by the contingencies of history which have made the first nation to have a revolution also the most powerful nation, and by the added fact that Stalin's enforced industrialization and the subsequent technical successes of a once backward nation have added to the Russian prestige in her empire. But the original necessity of exploiting her "colonies" has disappeared. Russia is exporting both capital and techniques to help the satellite nations to a rapid industrialization at a tempo which the creed demands but which is probably too rapid for the good of the satellites. There is no pressing economic reason for the tightened control. There is of course a strategic reason, for Tito has proved no longer a safe ally and if Titoism were to spread the strategic hazards would be multiplied.

But we must find the real reason for the return to Stalinist control of the empire by Russia in the realm of the ideological system from which the prestige of Russia as a ruling nation has drawn. That ideological system, as we have noted repeatedly, was based on utopianism and fanaticism. Russia was not designed to rule the Kingdom of God on Earth according to the Marxist creed. But it was forced to undertake the hegemony of the cohorts of socialism in achieving the victory of the righteous over the unrighteous imperialists. This fanatic and absolute distinction between the righteous and the unrighteous, between the "imperialist" nations and those who were "anti-imperialists by definition," was in conflict with the empirical facts, which anyone could see who was not bound by the dogma. The necessity of a tighter control arose from the dogmatic presuppositions of the communist system. If Russia were not to have this control what was to prevent Tito's policy from providing that the imperialists would not exploit Yugoslavia as the creed asserted? And what was to prevent both Tito and Gomulka from adopting a more melioristic policy toward the peasants than the dogma permitted? It is, of course, still difficult to see why this empirical policy was not permitted, particularly since the Russian oligarchy after Stalin made all kinds of empirical adjustments to the realities, including, for instance, the abolition of the "tractor stations" as a source of power over the collective farms.

But in an empire based upon a creed it is one thing to make slight adjustments to reality at the source of authority, and another to allow "different roads" to develop to such a degree that the original distinction between the socialists and the capitalist world disappears.

In any event the re-Stalinization of the Russian empire proves that an ideological system so glaringly at variance with the historic realities must not only have a fixed dogma, but also only one source of interpretation of the dogma. The dogma did not provide for Russia to be the authoritative source of interpretation any more than early Christian dogma made Rome the source of authority. In each case history supplied the seat of authority but the dogma supplied the necessity for a single authority.

40 A WARNING TO THE SOVIET UNION

John F. Kennedy (1917–1963)

In his "thousand days" as president, John F. Kennedy initiated a program of progress at home and support for democratic institutions abroad. The first president from the generation that fought in World War II, Kennedy was born in Brookline, Massachusetts and graduated from Harvard University in 1940. During his residence in Great Britain, where his father was U.S. Ambassador, Kennedy was deeply concerned with the failure of the policy of appeasement pursued by the world's democracies toward Hitler. Probably as a result of this experience, he gave high priority, upon entering the White House, to supporting nations around the world that were determined to resist communist expansion.

The finest hours of Kennedy's presidency are generally considered to have encompassed the days of the Cuban missile crisis in October 1962. In the following speech to the nation on October 22, 1962, he imposed an embargo on the shipment of offensive military weapons to that island and warned that use of the Cuban missiles could result in a U.S. attack on the Soviet Union.

THIS GOVERNMENT AS PROMISED has maintained the closest surveillance of the Soviet military build-up on the island of Cuba.

Within the past week unmistakable evidence has established the fact that a series of offensive missile sites is now in preparation on that imprisoned island.

293

The purpose of these bases can be none other than to provide a nuclear strike capability against the Western Hemisphere. . . .

Each of these missiles, in short, is capable of striking Washington, D.C., the Panama Canal, Cape Canaveral, Mexico City, or any other city in the southeastern part of the United States, in Central America or in the Caribbean area. . . .

Neither the United States of America nor the world community of nations can tolerate deliberate deception and offensive threats on the part of any nation, large or small. We no longer live in a world where only the actual firing of weapons represents a sufficient challenge to a nation's security to constitute maximum peril.

Nuclear weapons are so destructive and ballistic missiles are so swift that any substantially increased possibility of their use or any sudden change in their deployment may well be regarded as a definite threat to peace.

For many years both the Soviet Union and the United States, recognizing this fact, have deployed strategic nuclear weapons with great care, never upsetting the precarious status quo which insured that these weapons would not be used in the absence of some vital challenge. . . .

Our own strategic missiles have never been transferred to the territory of any other nation under a cloak of secrecy and deception and our history, unlike that of the Soviets since the end of World War II, demonstrates that we have no desire to dominate or conquer any other nation or impose our system upon its people.

Nevertheless, American citizens have become adjusted to living daily on the bull's-eye of Soviet missiles located inside the U.S.S.R. or in submarines. . . .

But this secret, swift, extraordinary build-up of Communist missiles in an area known to have a special and historical relationship to the United States and the nations of the Western Hemisphere, in violation of Soviet assurances and in defiance of American and hemispheric policy—this sudden, clandestine decision to station strategic weapons for the first time outside of Soviet soil—is a deliberately provocative and unjustified change in the status quo which cannot be accepted by this country if

**THE PURPOSE OF THE MEETING
IS TO TAKE MEASUREMENTS**

*President John F. Kennedy and Soviet leader Nikita
Khrushchev size each other up at their summit meeting in
Vienna, 1961.* Courtesy the Chicago *Tribune*

our courage and our commitments are ever to be trusted again by either friend or foe.

The nineteen thirties taught us a clear lesson. Aggressive conduct, if allowed to go unchecked and unchallenged, ultimately leads to war.

This nation is opposed to war. We are also true to our word.

Our unswerving objective, therefore, must be to prevent the use of these missiles against this or any other country; and to secure their withdrawal or elimination from the Western Hemisphere.

Our policy has been one of patience and restraint, as befits a peaceful and powerful nation which leads a world-wide alliance.

We have been determined not to be diverted from our central concerns by mere irritants, and fanatics. But now further action is required. And it is under way. And these actions may only be the beginning.

We will not prematurely or unnecessarily risk the course of worldwide nuclear war in which even the fruits of victory would be ashes in our mouth, but neither will we shrink from that risk at any time it must be faced.

Acting, therefore, in the defense of our own security and of the entire Western Hemisphere and under the authority entrusted to me by the Constitution as endorsed by the resolution of the Congress, I have directed that the following initial steps be taken immediately:

First, to halt this offensive build-up a strict quarantine on all offensive military equipment under shipment to Cuba is being initiated. All ships of any kind bound for Cuba from whatever nation or port will, where they are found to contain cargoes of offensive weapons, be turned back. This quarantine will be extended if needed to other types of cargo and carriers.

We are not at this time, however, denying the necessities of life as the Soviets attempted to do in their Berlin Blockade of 1948.

Second, I have directed the continued and increased close surveillance of Cuba and its military build-up. . . .

Third, it shall be the policy of this nation to regard any nuclear missile launched from Cuba against any nation in the Western Hemisphere as an attack by the Soviet Union on the United States requiring a full retaliatory response upon the Soviet Union. . .

. . . finally, I call upon Chairman Khrushchev to halt and eliminate this clandestine, reckless and provocative threat to world peace and to stable relations between our two nations.

I call upon him further to abandon this course of world domination and to join in an historic effort to end the perilous arms race and to transform the history of man.

He has an opportunity now to move the world back from the abyss of destruction by returning to his Government's own words that it had no need to station missiles outside its own territory and withdrawing these weapons from Cuba; by refraining from any action which will widen or deepen the present crisis, and then by participating in a search for peaceful and permanent solutions. . . .

We have no wish to war with the Soviet Union, for we are a peaceful people who desire to live in peace with all other peoples.

But it is difficult to settle or even discuss these problems in an atmosphere of intimidation.

That is why this latest Soviet threat or any other threat which is made either independently or in response to our actions this week must and will be met with determination.

Any hostile move anywhere in the world against the safety and freedom of peoples to whom we are committed including in particular the brave people of West Berlin will be met by whatever action is needed. . . .

My fellow citizens, let no one doubt that this is a difficult and dangerous effort on which we have set out. No one can foresee precisely what course it will take, or what course or casualties will be incurred.

Many months of sacrifice and self-discipline lie ahead, months in which both our patience and our will will be tested. Months in which many threats and denunciations will keep us aware of our dangers. But the greatest danger of all would be to do nothing.

The path we have chosen for the present is full of hazards as all paths are. But it is the one most consistent with our character and courage as a nation and our commitments around the world.

The cost of freedom is always high, but Americans have always paid it.

And one path we shall never choose, and that is the path of surrender, or submission.

Our goal is not the victory of might, but the vindication of right; not peace at the expense of freedom, but both peace and freedom here in this hemisphere and, we hope around the world.

God willing, that goal will be achieved.

41 THE CLOSED NATURE OF SOVIET SOCIETY

Adlai A. Stevenson (1900–1965)

Although he was twice defeated in running for the presidency by Dwight D. Eisenhower in 1952 and 1956, Adlai Stevenson was loved and respected by millions of Americans for his humanity, intelligence, and wit. Born in Los Angeles, California, Stevenson graduated from Princeton in 1922 and attended Harvard Law School. After visiting Russia as a reporter in 1926, he took up the practice of law in Illinois. During World War II he served as Special Assistant to the Secretary of the Navy from 1941 to 1944 and as Special Assistant to the Secretary of State in 1945. Stevenson was Governor of Illinois from 1949 to 1953 and after unsuccessful bids for the presidency served as American Representative to the United Nations from 1960 to 1965. These comments on the closed nature of the Soviet society were made in a commencement address at Boston University in June 1962.

MANY YEARS AGO, in the early days of the revolution, I spent some time in the Soviet Union. Four years ago I travelled there again and very extensively. I talked with Mr. Khrushchev and many senior officials in Western Russia, in Central Asia, in Eastern Siberia; and although we disagreed a good deal nobody lost his temper and I was most hospitably received. It is a wonderful, puzzling, frustrating country. The people are warm-hearted and hospitable, and filled with devotion and pride in their country. Having known so much suffering in war, they are deeply anxious for peace. Pleased with the improvements in their material lives since Stalin, they were hungry for more.

Wherever I went I was literally overwhelmed by the people's friendliness and curiosity about the United States. Yet, alas, enmity, mistrust and misunderstanding have been the official policy for decades, and the question is how to get through that enmity to establish a real peace?

We know that the only *short* road, by way of nuclear war, is suicidal and is thus closed to both sides. All the other roads are long and arduous. The diplomacy of safeguarded disarmament is one. Germany is another. Peaceful trade is another. Creative cooperation in the United Nations, in aid to emerging nations, in peaceful use of outer space—these roads all lead toward peace.

But our troubles with the Soviet Union far transcend the traditional realm of diplomacy, and it may well be outside that realm —or in a new kind of diplomacy, at any rate—that the best road to their solution will be found. The road I have in mind is one which our diplomacy has only recently begun to reconnoitre: namely, direct relations between the *people* of the Soviet Union and the *peoples* of the outside world—from whom, even today, they remain almost entirely cut off.

This is the road to an Open World. Possibly it will prove the longest road of all; but if we dare to travel it, as I think we must, we may find that the longest way round is the shortest way home.

No small part of the ills of today's world stem from the closed society of the Soviet Union. This closedness—the exclusion of the outer world, the suppression of dissent, the control of personal movements, the secrecy and suspicion—all this goes far back into Czarist Russian history. In the last few years, happily, it has been receding—but so far only a little.

Today that closed society is not only an anachronism; it is a danger to peace when all the peoples of the world, in their rapidly increasing numbers, are being pushed into ever-closer contact by the triumphs of science: global communications, modern air transportation, television by satellite, and all the rest. At the same time science has also placed in the hands of the strongest nations, for the first time in history, an almost limitless power of destruction.

And it is at this fateful moment that one of those strongest nations, the Soviet Union, whose people have so much to contribute to the community of mankind, keeps itself sealed off behind an iron curtain; requires its ill-informed citizens to live in daily fear of imaginary enemies; and proclaims that those imaginary enemies will continue to threaten its existence—until the whole world has been remade in the Soviet image. And, of course, by its attempts to remake the world it has made real enemies where none had been before.

Such are the tragic works of closed minds. Russia has no monopoly of them, of course. Every society, I suppose—including ours—has individuals who hunger for conflict, who seem to get a positive joy out of having an enemy to hate and destroy and will doubtless miss the cold war when it finally ends. Indeed, it is a rare individual who has in him none whatever of this warrior urge! But a closed society goes one fatal step further. It elevates the closed mind into an official requirement; it ordains struggle and conflict as the highest and permanent duty of the citizen; and it brands all those whom it cannot control as actual or potential foes.

It is quite a job to keep a closed society closed. Consider the radio jamming system which the Soviet Government uses to drown out the Russian-language programs of the B.B.C., the Voice of America, the Vatican radio and so on. This apparatus includes some 2,500 shortwave transmitters, all of them broadcasting nothing but noise. It costs about $100 million a year to run. Soviet authorities say it is worth it to protect the people from all those "lies," but for that price at least 20,000 Soviet families could travel through the United States or other non-communist countries, and find out for themselves whether the broadcasts are lies or not!

In Siberia in 1958 my party carried a shortwave radio and heard the jamming wherever we went. The United Nations General Assembly was then meeting in emergency session on the Lebanese crisis, and among the programs of the Voice of America which could not be heard because of Soviet jamming was the main speech in the Assembly of—the Soviet Foreign Minister!

Then there are other devices. One is *Glavlit*, a state agency whose permission is required for the publication in the Soviet Union of any book, pamphlet, newspaper, magazine, movie or television program—whether imported or domestic.

Then finally there is the control over the movement of people. It exists both within the Soviet Union and across its borders. When I went to Eastern Siberia and Kazakstan, I was, by courtesy of the Soviet Government, in a huge area, perhaps 25 per cent of the Soviet territory, which is normally closed not only to foreigners but even to Soviet travellers.

As for travel abroad, that is quite beyond the hopes of ordinary people in the Soviet Union. I shall always remember an eager group of young Russians who drew me into friendly conversation on a summer evening in Leningrad; and when it was time to say good night I said, almost as second nature, "Well, come and see us in America."

And one of them, standing there in the northern twilight, answered for all the rest with a single, poignant, memorable word: "How?"

By all these devices the Soviet rulers have made their country into a darkened theater, from which daylight and all the events of the outer world are shut out, and all the play of light and music and action on stage and among the audience is controlled by the director.

And just what is the myth which is enacted so dramatically every day in this enormous theater—before 200,000,000 Soviet spectators? It is the mighty struggle of the Soviet people and their communist allies to build a society throughout the world under the infallible leadership of the Communist party; and the stubborn resistance of a greedy, ruthless enemy called "capitalist imperialism," a shadowy conspiracy which rules the United States, which plots to destroy communism by war and to enslave the world—but which the common people, led by the communists, are destined at last to crush.

Facts which support the plot are published in an endless stream. Facts which contradict it are suppressed. It is taught to school children in their text books; to the millions of young men and women in the young Communist organization; to the soldiers and officers of the huge and powerful Soviet armed forces

—and in fact to all the Soviet people by every available means, year in and year out.

Now, fortunately, most of the plain people of the Soviet Union don't seem to believe all they had been told for 45 years. If they did, Americans would not be welcomed so eagerly, even in the midst of official hate campaigns.

But I fear many Russians do tend to accept the image of an America ruled by warlike imperialists. And, accepting this false premise, they justify under the heading of self-defense all the dangers and sacrifices imposed by an aggressive Soviet foreign policy.

If this is in fact the popular attitude in the Soviet Union— and I have found it so in talks with a good many Soviet citizens —we have little reason to be surprised. The people have a deep patriotism and a yearning for peace which makes them respond with their emotions to these stories. They have no free press, no freedom to travel, no independent way to check up.

Besides, it is hard for a Russian who has spent all his life under communism even to begin to comprehend America. He has no experience of an open society like ours, built to tolerate conflicting values—containing countless small, independent centers of influence—making decisions by majority rule but jealous of minority rights. Instead, like his rulers, he tends to picture America as a mirror image of his own system—a dictatorship of an economic class (in our case the rich businessmen) bent on world domination.

Mr. Khrushchev himself spoke for that view of America when he wrote in 1959, in an article published here, that probably many of his American readers "think that the idea of capitalism will ultimately triumph." He cannot seem to believe that for us Americans capitalism is not a total system of life, or a secular religion with which we seek to evangelize the world. We don't even *have* a "system" in the totalitarian sense, because we believe that the human personality requires a margin of freedom to make its own choices, which no total system can ever provide.

Such a view of life is evidently foreign to Mr. Khrushchev and, to a great extent, to the Russian people too.

Yet I believe they will come to it. History, even Russian history, moves on. The violent, fearful Bolshevik revolution, with all the dark weight of Russian history on its back, obviously felt the need of external foes to frighten the people into action. I believe that the modern Soviet Union will one day feel able to do without that dangerous stimulus. Its people are enjoying more and more security and the good things of life. Its leaders now openly proclaim that no enemy dares attack them. Surely it will do no harm now for the people of the Soviet Union to learn at last that nations can disagree, even about fundamentals, without hoping and working for each other's downfall; that we in the United States do *not* desire their destruction; that we do *not* want to dominate the world; that we *do* want a Russia that is strong and prosperous and at peace with its neighbors, and a wholehearted member of the community of nations.

The Russians have gained much in competence, and in self-confidence, in recent years. Along with this comes a new tendency to look abroad not so much with suspicion and fear as with frank curiosity. I met this curiosity everywhere, and particularly among the students who before very long will be the nation's leaders. There can be no doubt of their eagerness for contact with the outside world.

Of course there has already been progress in this direction in recent years. Soviet cultural and technical relations with non-communist countries, including the United States, have grown since Mr. Khrushchev came to power to a point which would have been unthinkable in the last years of Stalin's rule. The United States and the Soviet Union negotiated an exchange agreement in 1958 which was renewed in 1960 and again this year. There have been many useful exchanges, especially both in academic and technical fields and in the performing arts. Other Western countries have done the same.

Under these agreements, for instance, Van Cliburn was cheered to the rafters in the cities of Russia, and the Moiseyev and Ukrainian Dancers have been cheered to the rafters in the cities of America. A Soviet exhibition drew big crowds in New York and an American exhibition drew huge crowds in Moscow. American professors have lectured this past year, in Moscow and Leningrad, on American civilization—our literature, our history and our law.

And the full text of an interview with President Kennedy was read in *Izvestia* by millions of Russians.

The mood of the young people in Moscow was shown this spring in an article by Igor Moiseyev, the head of the famous dance troupe. He condemned what he called the "disgusting dynamism of rock-and-roll and the twist"—neither of which, of course, took long to reach Moscow. But then he laughed at the communist puritans who tried to suppress these new dances; and said: "The slogan of modern youth is, 'I want to know everything.' It aspires to independence of thought and opinion."

What a revolutionary trend such a statement suggests. And the visit of Benny Goodman to Russia this spring isn't likely to slow it down much, either.

There is a thaw too in the exchange of scientific information. In the past few years, Russians have presented important papers at world meetings on atomic science and many other subjects. Now, after a diplomatic launching at the United Nations, there are plans for a permanent "world weather watch"—space satellites managed jointly by the United States and the USSR, circling the globe and giving every country instantaneous knowledge of the world's weather. It would seem that the spirit of openness is going to break some altitude records; and one day I think President Kennedy's plea will be answered: "Together let us explore the stars."

The question is—what should be done now?

The least we can do, with the future of the world in the balance, is to encourage this delicate growth in every way we know.

—We should redouble our exchange programs and make them fully reciprocal.

—We should end forever such an obsolete practice as the closing off of forbidden zones to foreign travel.

—We should hold more exhibitions on each other's territory —not just in Moscow and New York but in cities from Minsk to Vladivostok, and from Portland, Maine to Portland, Oregon. And, if I may insert a personal note, I am still waiting and hoping to see the incomparable puppet theaters of the Soviet Union perform in the United States!

—We should adopt a world-wide rule that anybody, anywhere, has a right to read any document issued by the United Nations, and that member governments have a positive duty to facilitate the United Nations information program.

—We should agree that every nation will welcome to the newsstands of its major cities the serious newspapers and magazines of other nations, regardless of politics.

—We should continue to urge the joint TV appearances of President Kennedy and Chairman Khrushchev, about which Mr. Salinger has been negotiating.

—We should extend the free importation of books, without political censorship and without custom duty, to every nation.

—We should multiply international student exchanges.

—We should see that what school children study about each other's countries is balanced and free from politically inspired hatred and distortion.

—We should let the ordinary citizens of every country, by the thousands and tens of thousands, travel abroad for business or pleasure—and see that there are good hosts to receive them and to help them learn, and to learn from them.

And, I believe, we should do all we can to promote mutually profitable trade in those things which improve and adorn the life of the people.

Examples like these can be multiplied. They apply with special relevance to the Soviet Union and the United States, but ultimately they must apply to all countries. And there is not a country in the world which cannot improve in this field. . . .

And surely, at some point along the way, it will be necessary for each and all of us—Russians, Americans, Europeans and Latin Americans, Asians and Africans—not only to disarm our armies of dreadful weapons, but to disarm our minds of dreadful fears; to open our frontiers, our schools and our homes to the clean winds of fact and of free and friendly dialogues; and to have done with those exclusive fanatical dogmas which can make whole peoples live in terror of imaginary foes.

Not in order to save one people or one empire or one system, but to save Man himself, we must act on the truth which our experience makes inescapable: that the road to peace in this fearful generation—a generation of which you here are soon to be the custodians—is the road to an open world.

42 THE EFFECTS OF DESTALINIZATION

Hans J. Morgenthau (1904–   )

The German-born political scientist Hans Morgenthau is widely respected in the United States for his authoritative and realistic appraisals of international developments. Arriving in the United States in 1937, Morgenthau became a naturalized citizen in 1943 and served as professor of political science at the University of Chicago from 1943 to 1968. Included in his extensive list of publications is the following article, entitled "The Myth of Soviet Politics," which analyzes former Premier Nikita Khrushchev's 1956 speech denouncing Stalin and the effect this ultimately had in Khrushchev being ousted from power himself in 1964.

———————

EVEN IF ONE WERE TO ASSUME that he was retired from supreme power for reasons of ill health—an assumption obviously rendered untenable by the humiliating circumstances of his retirement —Nikita Khrushchev would go down in history both as the liberalizer of Communist totalitarianism and as the victim of that liberalization. That is to say, he will go down in history as a truly tragic figure.

Yet Khrushchev's personal tragedy is but a reflection of the contradictions which in the course of the 20th century have shattered one after another of the foundation stones of Communist philosophy. And it has been the ex-Premier's historic mission to push that process of destruction a mighty step forward while trying to arrest it. Here is indeed the element of tragedy in classic terms as well as in terms of Hegelian-Marxian irony: The hero trying to master fate only hastens its consummation, the political leader seeking to arrest the historic process on behalf of the interests of a particular class or nation only pushes the historic process forward toward the destruction of those interests.

Marxism as a living political philosophy, that is, a rational guide to political action, has been undermined by two sets of contradictions: contradictions with historic reality and contradictions within itself. The former prove Marxism to be untrue in one or the other respect; the latter prove Marxism to be absurd altogether. Marxists could take the former in their stride even though their cumulative effect could not fail to put into question the credibility of Marxism per se. But Marxism as a living political philosophy could not survive the revelation of its inner contradictions, and it has been Khrushchev's historic mission to reveal two of them.

Reality has inflicted upon Marxism in this century four major contradictions. The first occurred in August 1914, when the proletarians of the world started to kill each other on behalf of their respective nations, thereby disproving the Marxist dogma of the international solidarity of the proletariat. Yet Lenin could plausibly defend the integrity of Marxist teaching by branding the leaders of the European proletariat as "social-patriotic" traitors.

A second disavowal of Marxism by reality occurred at the end and in the immediate aftermath of World War I, when the Russian October Revolution was not followed by proletarian revolution in the most advanced capitalistic countries. Yet Lenin could explain the isolated character of the Bolshevist Revolution, incompatible with the Marxist concept of world revolution, as a kind of temporary interlude due to the remaining strength of reactionary forces and of a treasonous proletarian leadership. It was then left to Stalin to extend that interlude *ad infinitum* by proclaiming "Socialism in One Country."

The Communists of the '30s identified fascism with the last stage of a decaying capitalism which would of necessity be followed by Communism. They therefore first helped fascism destroy liberal democracy and then opposed it as a necessary evil. The shock to the Communist faith which the staying power

---

of fascism and, more particularly, the Communist alliance with it in the form of the Molotov-Ribbentrop Pact of 1939 constituted, was mitigated and in good measure obliterated by the transformation of World War II in June 1941 from an imperialist struggle into the "Great Patriotic War."

Finally, the persistent inability of Communist economics to solve the problem of agricultural production and to produce consumer goods in sufficient quantity and quality does not need to be laid at the door of Communism as a system of economic management, any more than the American economic system needs to be blamed for its persistent failure to solve the problem of agricultural over-production. The accidents of economic backwardness, mismanagement, sabotage, and war have taken the blame for economic failure in the Soviet Union.

The two great contradictions which have shattered Communism since 1956, and of which Khrushchev has been both the instrument and the victim, differ fundamentally from those discussed thus far. They do not only put into question the correctness of one or the other of the Marxist dogmas, they deny the truth of Marxism itself as a scientific system of political thought. Both of these contradictions stem from Khrushchev's revelation of Stalin's crimes in 1956: the polycentric replacement of Moscow's leadership of the world Communist movement and the internal challenge to Communist totalitarianism.

To appreciate fully the enormous and lasting destructive impact of Khrushchev's revelation of Stalin's crimes, one must remember that Marxism claims to be a body of scientific truths, the only science of society worthy of the name. Those who rule in the name of Marxism do so by virtue of their monopolistic possession of the Marxist truth. The Marxist rulers have risen to their position by a process of selection which has tested their understanding of Marxism against the practical tasks at hand.

Lenin is venerated as the authentic disciple of Marx who developed and applied the master's teaching, thereby becoming a master himself and earning the right to supreme rule. Similarly, Stalin was praised in the Soviet Union until 1956—and still is praised to a certain extent in China—as the incomparable genius who followed in the footsteps of Lenin and, hence, had the right to rule supreme. Thus the legitimacy of Communist rule derives from the monopolistic relationship between the ruler and the Marxist truth.

What Khrushchev did when he denounced Stalin in 1956 was not only to destroy the legitimacy of Stalin's rule but to cast doubt upon Marxist legitimacy as such. If a blood-stained tyrant could rule supreme for 20 years in the guise of Marxist legitimacy, how trustworthy was the test by which the successors of Marx and Lenin were chosen?

That question was raised implicitly in 1956 by the revolts in Poland and Hungary with regard to the legitimacy of their regimes and explicitly by Khrushchev with regard to Stalin— but it was bound to be raised with regard to Khrushchev as well. And it was raised in 1957 by a majority of the Presidium of the Central Committee, although Khrushchev managed through the plenum of the Central Committee to give a success-ful answer. He was less lucky in October 1964. The question, however, is bound to be raised again with regard to his successors and it will be answered with less and less confidence. If Marxist selection could produce a Stalin and Khrushchev in succession, why should we trust it to produce a good ruler for a change, and how shall we know whether or not the ruler is good?

In the realm of practical politics, two sets of consequences have ensued from the erosion of Marxist legitimacy, set in motion by Khrushchev: the polycentric disintegration of the Soviet camp, and the relaxation of totalitarian rule within the Soviet Union and elsewhere.

The monolithic character of the Communist camp under Stalin rested upon the moral foundation of the Marxist infallibility of the Soviet Union as incarnated by Stalin. Since the Soviet Union was the "Fatherland of Socialism," the most advanced Communist nation guided by the genius of Stalin, the duty of Communists everywhere to put the interests of the Soviet Union ahead of their respective nations was clear. The testimony of the members of the Communist spy ring operating in Canada and the United States during World War II as reported by the Canadian Royal Commission on the Gouzenko case conveys a vivid impression of the strength with which that duty was felt.

When Khrushchev stripped Stalin of his Marxist infallibility, he also deprived the Soviet Union of its moral claim to lead the Communist camp. It was only after the destruction of this claim that the diverse interests of different Communist nations and parties could assert themselves.

Polycentrism manifests itself in two different ways: as independence from the Soviet Union pure and simple, and as rivalry with the Soviet Union for leadership of the world Communist movement. The former manifestation is typically represented by Rumania and the Italian Communist party; the latter, by China. China, by denying Khrushchev's claim to Marxist legitimacy, has invoked the authority of Marx, Lenin, and even Stalin. How could Khrushchev meet that Chinese challenge? Here was one of Khrushchev's dilemmas.

He could reassert Lenin's and Stalin's claim that Moscow was in monopolistic possession of the Marxist truth. But that claim had lost its plausibility. This was not only because the exposure of Stalin had drastically weakened Marxist legitimacy, but also for two additional reasons stemming from that weakening.

The claim of Soviet infallibility and, hence, supremacy could no longer be enforced against recalcitrant Communist governments and parties. The restoration of Soviet rule in Hungary in 1956 in the face of the threat of complete disintegration could not be repeated elsewhere in the face of much more gradual and insidious threats. And it is characteristic of the ineluctable character of that process of disintegration that it is taking place even in Hungary, where less than 10 years ago Soviet supremacy had most drastically been restored.

Thus Khrushchev was reduced to arguing with Communist governments and parties and, more particularly, with the Chinese, but he could no longer command. Only if his arguments carried conviction and, more particularly, if his conclusions coincided with the interests of other Communist governments and parties could the Soviet position prevail. Otherwise, he had to swallow the intransigence of the Rumanians and accept in silence the challenge of Togliatti's political testament. As for the Chinese, whose interests are irretrievably at odds with those of the Soviet Union, he was reduced to vituperation.

Nevertheless, all the while Khrushchev had to maintain the claim that Moscow was the sole repository of Marxist truth. This inevitable contrast between claim and reality constituted one of the ironies of Khrushchev's position. It made him a comic figure in the tragic sense.

In the process of trying to reconcile claim and reality, Khrushchev had to weaken the substance of the claim itself. He had to relax the totalitarian rule he had inherited from Stalin. This, too, was a result of the erosion of Marxist legitimacy.

The dethronement of Stalin prompted within the Soviet Union and the other Communist countries and parties the same doubts and questions about the legitimacy of Marxist rule we have encountered in the relations between the Soviet Union and other Communist nations and parties. The dilemma with which Khrushchev had to cope here is different from that posed by the challenge of China and the assertion of independence on the part of the other Communist governments and parties. In the second instance, Khrushchev really had no choice.

When the Chinese challenged the supremacy of Moscow, he could rant against them as heretics, and when the Rumanians went their own independent way, he could do nothing at all; for he had no effective power to restore Moscow's supremacy. Within the Soviet Union, however, he had a choice; for here he had effective power. He could make concessions to the doubters and questioners or he could refuse to make them or, once made, he could take them back completely or in part.

But the outer limits to the concessions Khrushchev could afford to make were prescribed by the need of his own rule to survive. This is another way of saying that these limits were bound to be narrowly circumscribed and that they were unsatisfactory to the doubters and questioners. For the latter had raised, always implicitly and sometimes explicitly, the very legitimacy of Khrushchev's rule, which Khrushchev could not afford to have questioned.

As a result, Khrushchev was forced by the very logic of his position to take the stand of a modified and moderate, yet uncertain Stalinism. He could not answer the question he was asked without putting in jeopardy the very foundation of his power, and he allowed it to be raised but intermittently and surreptitiously. He had to vacillate between giving in to popular pressures with small concessions, and taking them back in part or in whole when the pressure subsided or became so strong as to endanger his regime.

Thus the destroyer of Stalinism became its victim. He could not escape the logic of the rule by which Lenin and Stalin had governed. Precluded from invoking the grace of God or the will of the people to legitimize his rule, he could only fall back upon the claim to monopolistic possession of the Marxist truth, which he himself had discredited by his attack upon Stalin.

There is, then, deep historic significance and also poetic justice in Mikhail Suslov's indictment of Khrushchev (according to the New York *Times* of October 17) before the Central Committee for the same crime Khrushchev had accused Stalin of: "cult of personality." Khrushchev was guilty of that crime. It is in the nature of Communist totalitarianism that he could not help being guilty of it.

It would be an illusion to expect that the successors of Khrushchev can escape the dilemmas to which he fell victim. The successors may patch up the conflict with China and prevent it from degenerating into an open break; they may make more or fewer concessions at home; and they may be more or less intransigent in their dealings with other nations. But they are caught in the same contradictions which were the undoing of Khrushchev. They may mitigate or aggravate them by their policies, but they cannot escape them.

The disintegration of the Communist camp will continue and so will the oscillation between harsh and moderate rule at home and abroad. Thus political life in the Soviet Union is likely to continue "nasty, brutish, and short." It is only if and when the objective conditions of Soviet politics have radically changed or a statesman of genius has transcended and thereby transformed them that the rulers of the Soviet Union will be able to rule without being stifled and in the end ruined by the inner contradictions of Communism.

43 THE POTENTIAL FOR FRIENDLY RELATIONS

Lyndon B. Johnson (1908–1973)

After being elevated to the presidency following assassination of President John F. Kennedy in November 1963, Lyndon Johnson won a landslide victory in the 1964 election only to find his administration increasingly embroiled in the domestic controversy over the Vietnam War. Born on a farm near Stonewall, Texas, Johnson graduated from the Southwest Texas State Teachers College in 1930 and later attended the Georgetown University Law School. Elected to the House of Representatives in 1937, he served as a naval officer in the Pacific during World War II, and was elected to the Senate in 1948. As majority leader of the Senate, he was a contender for the 1960 presidential nomination of the Democratic Party, and upon losing to Kennedy surprisingly accepted the latter's offer of the vice presidential nomination.

In describing his long career in public office, Johnson listed as one of his major accomplishments the Treaty of the Non-proliferation of Nuclear Weapons, signed by the United States, the Soviet Union, and representatives of more than fifty other nations at a ceremony in the White House on July 1, 1968. Johnson's views on the need for the United States to improve relations with Russia are reflected in comments he made to journalists, which were published in *America Illustrated* (1966), a magazine prepared by the United States Information Agency for distribution in the Soviet Union.

TIME AND AGAIN, in many parts of the world, we and the Soviet Union find ourselves on the opposite sides of a question. But, over the years, we've gained a lot of experience in working out many of our differences. And we've taken a few very important constructive steps together. I have in mind the Nuclear Test Ban Treaty, which forbids testing of these destructive weapons in the atmosphere or under the ocean and thus eliminates the dangerous hazard of fallout. I also think of the history of the cultural exchange program which broadened the opportunities for our best scientists, teachers, and artists to share their creativity with one another. These are positive, concrete steps. They help create a more favorable atmosphere for further steps, and further normalization of relations between countries. My prayerful hope is that they will endure and expand, despite differences of view we may have. . . .

I think there's considerable good soil for U.S.-Soviet relations to grow and prosper with the right cultivation and care. We have more in common than we sometimes realize. I have considerable faith in the people of the Soviet Union. We are both large countries. We both possess an incredible variety of natural resources. Our people are energetic, generous, and talented. We Americans really came to know and to admire the Russian people in World War II. And, I hope, they share some of the same feelings for us. So, I would say that our people are more naturally friends than enemies. I would like to see us exchange goods and ideas and technology—all of the means to achieving common progress and prosperity.

This decade of progress has undermined the goals of those who have preached that the ideological differences between America and the Soviet Union must inevitably lead to war. We see now that we can both prosper in spite of the differences. The two nations have never gone to war with one another. The fact is that no two nations have more to lose in war than the United States or the Soviet Union.

Think of what the Soviet people have accomplished after experiencing a most destructive war in which they lost 20 million people. They have not only rebuilt their country, but they also have achieved splendid technological and scientific accomplishments. Neither country would like to see all these advances go up in smoke. . . .

There is no question but that the American people and the Russian people are absolutely opposed to war. I wish I could say that nuclear war is impossible. The United States, as I said before, will never start any war, nuclear or otherwise. But this world of ours is filled with dangers. We can never know what may suddenly erupt to bring new tensions and threats to the peace. . . .

And so, I believe we must pursue avenues of cooperative effort and agreement with the Soviet Union wherever they are to be found. We've got to get into the habit of peaceful cooperation. The Test Ban Treaty was a significant step. There have been others since 1963. We have agreed not to put bombs in orbit, we are working together on a number of other important ventures—in desalination, weather information, exchanges of scientists, artists, and yes, magazines. . . .

I think both sides must realize that neither is going to convert the other. The United States has no interest in remaking the Soviet Union in our image. And I don't see any evidence that America will go Communist. I think that the real interests of nations transcend the ideological differences. For instance, some of the nations with which we work closely have moved toward planned economies. But this makes no difference to us—or to them. We work together out of mutual trust and respect and because we share many of the same ideals and aspirations. . . .

The United States and the Soviet Union still have an agenda of unresolved differences, some of them quite serious. I believe we can settle these disputes, honorably and peacefully. We in the United States are determined to try. What has changed in recent years is not the size of our problems, but the means for solving them. The United States and the Soviet Union now possess—for the first time in history—the technology and productive capacity for extending mankind's benefits to all men. The alternative, of course, is that the world can fall victim to its fears and antagonisms and plunge humanity into the nuclear abyss. I happen to prefer the positive way. . . .

I think that cultural exchange between our two countries is

extremely important. We must get to know each other better. The political realities are such that we too often dwell on one another's mistakes and weaknesses. Let's admit that every nation has its infirmities. We all make mistakes, and injustice is not the product of any one geographic area. That's why I value this magazine exchange: "America Illustrated" and "Soviet Life" show what both countries are doing in constructive social and cultural ways. Here, both nations put their best foot forward, show their best products, their finest accomplishments, their creative ability. This is a most positive step toward better understanding. And understanding is essential to the quest for peace.

As I said earlier: If you take an objective look at our two countries—not just at the issues which divide us—you see the two most powerful nations on earth with every reason to want peace and no rational reason to want war. I am an optimist about mankind. I believe men, with enough effort, can get what they want. And so I believe that the good soil will prevail over the rocks and weeds. The responsibility for the future rests in large part on the United States and the Soviet Union. We differ on many things. The Soviet leaders are often convinced of the rightness of their actions when we think they are wrong. And they sometimes think we are wrong when we feel strongly that our cause is just. As great powers, our two nations will undoubtedly have commitments that will conflict. But there is one commitment I hope we both share: the commitment to a warless world. However you define it, this is mankind's age of greatest promise. We must move toward it—not toward war. We must find ways toward disarmament and an international rule of law strong enough to take the place of arms.

44 TECHNOLOGY AND THE IRON CURTAIN

Hubert H. Humphrey (1911–1978)

In over twenty-five years as an important political figure in the United States, Hubert Humphrey was widely known for his liberal principles and for his opposition to communism. A native of Wallace, South Dakota, he attended the Denver College of Pharmacy before obtaining a B.A. degree from the University of Minnesota in 1939 and an M.A. degree from the Louisiana State University the following year. Elected mayor of Minneapolis in 1945, he went on to win a seat in the United States Senate three years later. After running unsuccessfully for the Democratic Presidential nomination in 1960, he was chosen by Lyndon Johnson to be his Vice President from 1965 to 1969. After losing to Richard Nixon in the 1968 Presidential election, Humphrey was returned to the Senate by the people of Minnesota in 1970 and reelected in 1976. His death early in 1978 was mourned by people of all political persuasions.

Temperamentally an optimist, Humphrey frequently expressed the hope that political and social evolution in the Soviet Union would lead that country toward closer ties with the United States. The following speech, delivered at Westminster College in Fulton, Missouri, on March 5, 1967, reflected Humphrey's belief that Moscow might be in the process of easing restrictions that stand in the way of improved Russian-American relations.

319

EXACTLY 21 YEARS AGO TODAY, Winston Churchill spoke these well-remembered words:

"From Stettin in the Baltic to Trieste in the Adriatic, an Iron Curtain has descended across the continent."

"The continent," of course, was Europe.

When Churchill spoke here, a new phase in history had begun —that post-war conflict, centered in Europe, which was to become known as the cold war.

It is my belief that we stand today upon the threshold of a new era in our relations with the peoples of Europe—A period of new engagement.

And I believe that this new period, if we do not lose our wits or our nerve, or our patience, can see the replacement of the Iron Curtain by the Open Door.

When Churchill spoke here on March 5, 1946 there were many in this country—and elsewhere—who would not accept his stark characterization of the state of affairs in Europe.

But Churchill was right. And he was right to speak out.

The beginning of wisdom, the foundation of sound policy and action, is to face the facts.

What were the facts in March 1946?

Western Europe lay helpless and prostrate after terrible war— literally dependent for her survival on the protection and goodwill of the United States. The political institutions, the economies, the peoples of Western Europe stood helpless—save for the United States—in face of the imperialist impulses emanating from the East.

There, Stalin had literally erected an Iron Curtain between the nations and peoples of Eastern Europe and those of the West. On his side of that curtain he saw all as occupied territory . . . the spoils of war. And his further intentions were declared and clear.

What are the facts of March of 1967?

Western Europe stands today second only to the United States as a free and powerful center of economic and social well-being. Because of their brave initiatives—and with our help—the nations of Western Europe stand able once again to assert their own role in the world.

In eastern Europe the captive states of 21 years ago are once again reaching toward *their* own identities. The monolithic control which smothered and held them in the grip of terror is today diminishing.

The Iron Curtain itself—although firm and impenetrable in many places, as in Berlin—has become increasingly permeable in others. Goods, ideas and people have begun to criss-cross the European continent.

There is reason to believe that the new leadership of the Soviet Union finds the Iron Curtain not only a crude barrier to the West, but also a costly impediment to their own well being and progress. The Soviet Union of 1967 is a powerful, productive and modern nation. There is a growing realization that a closed society is an admission of weakness—that a closed society inhibits progress. Surely a system that can produce Sputnik-missiles and satellites must find an Iron Curtain a relic of the pre-computer, pre-scientific mentality.

Perhaps then we are right when we observe that the Iron Curtain is as antique and obsolete to the modern Soviet Union as the armored suit of the Feudal Baron of the Middle Ages.

Science and technology have pierced the eroding Iron Curtain. It is being replaced by a web of communication—the transistor, the computer, the space satellite—these are the building-blocks of modern communications.

Scientists, engineers, and technicians flew back and forth—overleaping the old barrier with the jets of contemporary air travel.

The arteries of East-West trade fled over stronger and faster.

All of these physical changes, all of these profound economic changes may well be the precursors of political change.

The essence of the situation today is this: The European family—long-separated . . . long set against each other, yet still a family—is becoming reacquainted and is moving toward more normal relationships.

The Soviet Union, recovering by heroic effort from the frightful loss of human life and resources which it suffered in the war, has grown greatly in its capacity and its inclination to satisfy the material needs of the Russian people. No one who cares about the human condition can fail to rejoice at this fact. And its aggressive behavior has been tempered.

All these things have happened. Yet they did not happen by accident.

They have happened because we followed the course Winston Churchill counseled 21 years ago at Westminster College.

They have happened in large part because, in the face of Stalinist tyranny, we in America brought our power and protection to rebuilding the European continent.

They have happened because we helped and encouraged our European partners in their unceasing efforts toward self-renewal.

They have happened because—in Berlin, in Greece and Turkey, yes, and in Cuba—the Soviet Union was brought to recognize that brute force—or its threat—could no longer be an acceptable means of attaining political goals.

If today the Soviet Union takes a more prudent and cautious course, it is—for more than any other reason—because together we and our Western partners have in these two decades stood firm and fast. . . .

There are a small few in other countries who conclude that the "realistic" next step toward a settlement of European problems can therefore only be by bilateral agreement between the Soviet Union and the United States—over the heads of our Western partners.

I do not believe this is "realism".

Neither do I believe a realistic settlement of European problems can be achieved by European nations without *our* participation, and that of the Soviet Union.

It is precisely now—at the time when new opportunities lie ahead—that we must retain cohesion with our Western partners —and they with us. If the cold war is to end . . . if the Iron Curtain is to be lifted, we shall need them and they shall need us . . .

. . . we must encourage the continued evolution of Soviet policy beyond the ambiguities of "peaceful coexistence" toward more substantial forms of cooperation.

We have negotiated a treaty banning nuclear weapons from outer space.

We are working with others to bring about a treaty banning the proliferation of nuclear weapons—a treaty acceptable and beneficial to the nuclear and non-nuclear powers alike.

We have concluded an air agreement with the Soviet Union and have just signed a new U. S.-Soviet cultural agreement.

Through liberalization of credit, and easing of travel restrictions, we hope to accelerate the exchange of goods and people.

We seek early Senate ratification of the United States—Soviet consular agreement.

We shall actively work toward closer cooperation between the Soviet Union and the nations of the West in space, in medicine, in peaceful technology.

We have not responded to the Soviet deployment of a limited antiballistic missile system by immediately beginning to build one of our own. Instead, we seek to convince the Soviet leaders that this would merely mean yet another costly round in the arms race. After the expenditure of many billions of dollars, neither of us would be more secure than when we started. . . .

Churchill said aptly, that "Jaw, Jaw is better than War, War."

Most important of such institutions is the United Nations.

The United Nations, among other things, is an unmatched buffer zone between conflicting interests and ideologies. It is a place where reason and compromise may interpose themselves before major nations reach the point of no-return.

It is the invaluable "middle man" . . . the honest broker necessary when normal contacts fail.

And it is also an invaluable instrument of peace-keeping in places around the world where major powers might otherwise feel it necessary to inject themselves.

There is no denying that the Soviet Union, as our Western partners and ourselves, has a vital interest in the strength and health of an institution which may serve as a force for order and restaint among us.

Let us examine these things:

—Greater exchange at all levels with the nations of Eastern Europe;

—Active pursuit and encouragement of "peaceful coexistence" with the Soviet Union;

—A European settlement including the reunification of Germany;

—Joint efforts with our former adversaries in helping the developing countries;

—Building a system of international order in which these same former adversaries are our partners.

Would any of these things have been at all imaginable when Winston Churchill stood here 21 years ago?

When the final realization sank in on the last doubter that an Iron Curtain indeed *was* being erected across the heart of Europe, how many of us had reason for hope that in 1967—so short a time later—it might be possible to begin replacing it with an Open Door?

In the center of free Berlin there stands today a stark ruin— the skeleton of a church, preserved to symbolize eternally the depravity of war.

It is our hope that the Iron Curtain may one day, too, lie in ruins—its remnants a symbol of a time that mercifully ended.

45 PITFALLS IN TRADE WITH MOSCOW

Glenard P. Lipscomb (1915–1970)

While most recent presidents have stressed the need to expand Russian-American trade, this policy has not been without opponents in the United States. One of the best presentations on the need for caution in handling trade agreements with the Soviet Union was made by Glenard P. Lipscomb, a Republican Congressman from California, in a talk to the American Management Association in New York on March 8, 1967. A native of Jackson, Michigan, Lipscomb attended the University of Southern California and was a public accountant before entering politics. Elected to the California legislature in 1947, he became a congressman in 1953 and served in that post until his death.

———————

IT IS FULLY RECOGNIZED that our nation needs to trade, that we need to constantly probe for new vistas in the field of trade in terms of new markets, new sales, and new products to sell. In short, continuing expansion in our overseas commerce is essential. . . .

But at the same time, it is evident that there exist strong feelings that there are certain dangers in East-West trade . . .

East-West trade simply cannot be viewed as a matter of normal commercial negotiations and transactions. It does not mean private individuals or firms dealing with other private individuals or firms. In the Communist countries you deal with Government agencies who carry out the orders and policies of their government.

This is vitally important since we know that to Communist nations, by the very manner of their existence, political considerations are often paramount to economic considerations. Khrushchev commented meaningfully on this in 1955 when he stated: "We value trade least for economic reasons and most for political reasons."

The props may have been moved around a bit since then, or some of the dialogue and characters changed, but I see no indications that this is not still the overriding doctrine of the USSR and East European nations. . . .

What are the basic motives behind the Communist drive to expand trade with the West? It is not enough to quote Lenin who in 1921 said it was necessary to bribe capitalism with extra profit so as to get the machines with which to defeat it economically. To be sure, this was the heart of Premier Khrushchev's peaceful coexistence maxim, which has since been repeated by Premier Kosygin. But it is not all. To get the answer, you must take a closer look at the Soviet and East European economies and the serious problem confronting them in the mid-sixties.

A fundamental change has occurred in the tempo of economic growth in the Soviet Union. Before, in the period 1956–1960, the gross national product was expanding at an average rate of 8.2%. The stride of expansion has now shortened to at least 6% in the last five years. Nor is this a temporary slowdown. It has become very evident to economists both within and outside of the Soviet Union that a serious adjustment in the economy is now being experienced. It is serious enough to challenge the long-term objectives of the Communist Party.

It is remembered that it was the signs pointing to the economic problems ahead that helped to cause Khrushchev's downfall. The difficulties, of course, continue. . . .

Mr. Kosygin discussed this problem when the twenty-third Congress met in April last year. It had been expected that he might call for an overthrow of the still prevailing Stalinist approach in favor of a new "market socialism," based on realistic costing and broad reaching decentralization. Such an adjustment in the opinion of most economists is required to help solve the underlying fallacy of the quota system which places premium value on how much is produced rather than on a realistic assessment of how much they really need.

The Soviet economy has depended in the past on larger doses of labor and investment to prop up industrial operations otherwise suffering difficulties due to use of uneconomic physical and management techniques, but this makes for more troubles.

For instance, when products are consistently inferior, this is compensated simply by allocating more workers to repair services. In the West we could not afford such gross extravagance. But in Russia it has become a fact of life, as is attested to by the high proportion of labor so engaged—29 percent of the workers in machine building and metalworking. That is not to say labor is an inexhaustible resource, for today 70% of the women in the Soviet Union are employed or in training. The limit of labor flexibility and intensification has been reached. Eventually you run out of compensating adjustments and must face up to fundamental defects.

This situation has been brewing for some time. Khrushchev's answer was to turn on more computers, but it is clear that serious problems continue. As documented in both the Soviet and Western press, the growth of unconsumed stocks and uninstalled capital equipment continues, notwithstanding haphazard information and decision-making adjustments. Today it is estimated by the Director of the Central Institute of Mathematics, USSR that 12 million people are engaged in the sphere of administration. A Soviet mathematician estimates that if things continue as they are, by 1980 the entire adult population would be employed in administration.

We might have expected that the Soviets, faced with this growing calamity, would undertake drastic overhaul measures toward decentralization and realistic costing.

But here is the rub. This would have a devastating impact on the Communist Party and the control it exercises. But the Party faithful need not have worried. Kosygin said that the solution would lie in buying more Western technology. In furtherance of this premise he stated:

"In the past 5 years foreign trade helped us solve a number of important economic problems . . . The time has come for us to reappraise the role of foreign trade."

In the satellite nations some remedial steps have been taken to try to ease some of the built-in shortcomings of the command economy, but here as in the Soviet Union the Communist Party has not let loose the strings of control. And, we must note that the combined gross national product of those six nations is less than that of West Germany alone. So notwithstanding the binding economic ties constructed through years of built-up interdependence within the Soviet economic sphere, there are compelling economic demands to import Western machinery and to cultivate export markets elsewhere.

From this brief analysis of the Soviet economic sphere, it is clear that the West is in a commanding position.

But having realized the fruits of advantage from the inherent superiority of our free enterprise economy, we now find the Administration in effect cooperating with Premier Kosygin's party line, clearing sales to the USSR and other Communist countries of items that totalitarian society has not been able to produce.

For those who say "It's worth a try at least," I remind you that it has been tried before and found wanting. It is often overlooked that U.S. technology was instrumental in helping to build the industrial base for the Soviet Union during the first five-year plan between the years 1929 and 1933. The greatest single undertaking in that plan was construction of the Magnitogorsk blast furnace, still the world's largest. Twenty million dollars worth of U.S. technology was obtained for the building of an entire city at Gorki, the Molotov Works, and the Kim Works in Moscow. These and other plants built by U.S. companies still produce almost all Soviet automobiles, tractors, and trucks. The Dnieper Dam was built by an American firm and this was only a small part of the total contribution made to the electrification of the Soviet Union. To assist in repayment for these large projects, it was a U.S. engineer who overhauled the gold mining industry from top to bottom raising what had been previously negligible production to second rank in the world. And so it goes.

The second generation of U.S. technology made available to

the Soviets was in the form of lend-lease aid. That it was and still is of great value today is attested to by reports heard time and again from industrial engineers returning from the Soviet Union. These experts find, much to their amazement, that 25-year-old American machine tools are still much in use.

Now, it should be asked, where did these bridges get us? Unknowingly, years ago we were helping to build an industrial base that now produces weapons which are killing and maiming our men in Vietnam, weapons that find their mark on leaders who fail to serve the Communist interests, and I am sure scores of other people throughout the world whose only guilt is that they stand in the path of Communism.

That we should seriously contemplate once again upgrading the Communist bloc technology is incomprehensible to me.

It is *not* good business to unlock the door merely because our adversary has emptied his gun. Nor is it sensible to try to win his friendship by handing him more ammunition when he's still shooting, so to speak. This is a danger in the current "Bridges to the East" policy.

If we were now to act in unity toward restraining exports to the Bloc, then this could pressure them from the path of international aggression and subversion which so threaten everyone's peace and freedom. Why should we bail out the Communist regimes when their actions and philosophy are at odds with peace and harmony throughout the world.

I see no change in Soviet objectives when leaders like Marshall Sokolosky declare, and I quote him directly, "In the present epoch, the struggle for peace and the fight to gain time depend above all on a unremitting increase in Soviet military power and that of the entire socialist camp, based on the development of productive forces and the continuous growth of its material technological base." Note that he stresses that military power is based on the material technological base, a fact which seems to escape many here in the U.S.

No matter how high the profit, it can never be commensurate with the risk when our material assistance, no matter how indirectly, contributes to the Soviet arsenal of weapons. . . .

Where does all this leave us? I am compelled to the conclusion that to a large extent the move to increase trade with the Soviet Union and Eastern European countries is a matter of grave concern.

We know that the Communist buyers do not seek the usual types of raw materials and consumer products. Nor do they come to the West in the spirit of finding true trading partners. Rather they come with shopping lists carefully drawn up by centralized governments. They seek shortcuts—ways to use the West to expand their own capacities and advance bloc goals.

What are these goals? Clearly an immediate goal is to help bring about a Communist victory in Vietnam. This is however only part of a broad, continuing campaign to advance the cause of Communism throughout the world by whatever means possible, be it by subversion, through so-called wars of liberation, by economic warfare, or other means.

Regrettably, at a time such as this when Communist leaders recognize the deep difficulty their economies face, we are failing to recognize that through a proper use of trade, we and other Western nations should be able to compel the Communist bloc to work to restore peace to the world rather than support aggression. . . .

It is a very serious matter that we discuss here. "Peaceful detente" is still a condition of wishful judgment, not fact. We must be realistic therefore and weigh carefully the significance of trade with the bloc. In so doing we must give full consideration to the meaning of trade to our security and welfare. If the situation is such that restraints and controls are needed, and I believe they are, then we must act accordingly.

46 THE LACK OF FREEDOM IN RUSSIA

I. F. Stone (1907–   )

I. F. Stone, one of the best-known journalists of the American left, was at the same time a perceptive critic of the flaws in the Soviet system. A native of Philadelphia, he went to work for the *Philadelphia Inquirer* while still attending the University of Pennsylvania. Before starting his own publication, *I. F. Stone's Weekly*, he was a reporter for the New York *Post, PM* and the *Compass*. In 1948 he assisted in the campaign efforts of Henry Wallace's Progressive Party. His description of the lack of political freedom in Russia appeared in *I. F. Stone's Weekly* on November 13, 1967.

THE HISTORIC TASK which faces the best of the new youth in the Soviet Union is how to establish free institutions under socialism. This will require a double revolution, first in thought and then in action. The first must scrap all the evasive banalities of Communist party talk since the Twentieth Congress about "cult of personality"—and embark instead on a reexamination of the Soviet system and its past which spares neither Lenin nor Marx. All idols must be overthrown, all sacred dogmas exposed to criticism, the windows thrown open, the cobwebs swept away. This task will have the value of separating Soviet accomplishments from those cancerous malformations which, fifty years after the Great October Revolution, still keep the Soviet system a dictatorship in which neither worker nor peasant dares speak freely. . . .

For the Russian peasant, the Revolution was indeed a dictatorship of the proletariat. The capital the Soviet Union needed for

331

its industrialization was sweated out of the peasantry—by the huge expropriations which accompanied the liquidation of the *kulaks* and the middle peasantry, by the work extracted from them in the huge labor camps to which they were driven in Siberia and the North, and by the low prices at which the poor peasants were forced to deliver their products from the collectives and state farms into which they were forced. The *mujik* was Bolshevism's internal empire.

The Revolution was consolidated first by letting the peasant keep the lands he had seized and then by taking back the land in order to get the capital for industrialization. The basic fault of the new peasant proprietors was that they were eating well for the first time in their lives and selling less. By 1927 Russia's global production of wheat had recovered to the prewar level, but it produced only half as much for the market and exported only five percent as much for the war. The problem was how to get more out of the peasant. The right opposition, led by Bukharin, suggested the carrot. He was impressed by American agriculture. He wanted to stimulate greater farm production by offering the peasant more consumer goods and expanding industry on the basis of a prosperous agriculture. The left opposition, led by the Trotskyists, suggested the stick. Stalin adopted the program of the left, but in practice it took on a ferocity not even he had foreseen; it became a new civil war against the majority of the peasants and it was carried out with the clumsy and wasteful brutality characteristic of Russia's past.

The worker as well as the peasant suffered. The war against the peasant brought on a famine. The Russian worker as well as the peasant had to be subjected to Draconian discipline to keep the economy going. The symbol of the change was the internal passport. This was established by Peter the Great to keep the serf tied down on the farm and in the state factories. It had been abolished by the Revolution as "a police instrument of oppression of the masses." At the end of 1932 internal passports were reestablished to keep workers from changing their jobs and peasants from fleeing to the cities. Soviet citizens must still carry them. In America the passport was used—until the Supreme Court ended the practice—to restrict the movement of suspected citizens abroad; in the Soviet Union it is used to keep police control of everybody's movements at home.

This relic of the past is a reflection, like so much else, of the fundamental if disagreeable fact that the collectivization campaign, like the Bolshevik Revolution from the very beginning, was impressed by a minority of the revolutionaries themselves from above and by terror. All those terrible crimes, "distortions of socialist legality" and "departures from Leninist norms" which the Twentieth Congress attributed to Stalin and the cult of personality flow from this fundamental fact. Until it is recognized no fundamental reform can be achieved. The backwardness of the country led the Bolsheviks to deal with it by the backward methods to which it was habituated—reform from above, an omnipresent secret police system, suppression of dissent, denial of the freedoms of press and speech. . . .

Every regime must take a choice of risks—the risk of freedom with the danger of popular rejection, even misunderstanding, or the risks of a dictatorship which must increasingly, however well-meaning its founders, become rigid, despotic and encrusted with careerist barnacles. The Bolsheviks chose the latter, and so it is that 50 years after the Revolution, there is still neither free discussion nor free press in the Soviet Union. It has become a gigantic caricature of what socialism was meant to be.

The work of the Twentieth Congress has been aborted because the Party and its leaders fear that full discussion of the "cult of personality" must become a menace to their own monopoly of power and to their habits of ruling by coercion rather than persuasion. The bourgeois state borrowed from feudal experience Magna Charta principles which were developed into a means of protecting the individual from oppressive state action. There is no reason why the proletarian state should not borrow from bourgeois experience. There is no reason why habeas corpus should not exist under socialism as under capitalism, why a man's lawyer may not get him out of jail and force the state to explain why he is being held and subject its accusations to public trial. Had this right existed in the Stalin period some of the best Communists might have been saved—for it was the lickspittles who survived, the brave and the concerned who were liquidated. The only reason for denying so fundamental a right is to retain over the heads of the masses and the intellectuals the shadow of the old terror, the fear that arbitrary arrest is still possible.

The most important change of all, if the Soviet Union is to evolve toward a good society, is freedom of the press. I well remember thirty years ago how the Communists boasted that freedom of the press in Russia under the Constitution newly promulgated by Stalin was broader than in the United States because it not only guaranteed freedom of press and assembly but also ensured these rights "by placing at the disposal of the working people and their organizations printing shops, supplies of paper, public buildings, the streets, means of communication and other material requisites for the exercise of these rights." Thirty years later this is still a bitter hoax.

The Soviet regime's vast apparatus for propaganda serves today as in Stalin's time to hide these realities from the outside world and from many of its own people. All that is worst in the practice of the "bourgeois" states exists in magnified form within the Soviet Union. Despite all the promises of law reform since Stalin died, the law of counter-revolutionary crimes—many times worse in its sweep and vagueness than our Smith Act—is still on the statute books and can still be used to stifle any real discussion. It is only in the worst of the "bourgeois" states—in those of a Fascist character like Spain, Greece, South Vietnam, Brazil and Portugal—that writers are exiled, silenced or imprisoned as Sinyavsky and Daniel are in the Soviet Union. Eleven years after the Twentieth Congress, fourteen years after the death of Stalin, "corrective labor" camps are back in operation and two gifted writers are serving savage sentences of seven and five years respectively in them. Characteristically, no one can find out from the bureaucracy whether or not these sentences have been shortened by the limited amnesty declared in commemoration of the Revolution.

It is for a new generation in the Soviet Union to change these realities. Hegel declared the dialectic had ended in the creation of the despotic Prussian state; the Communists say it ended with the creation of the despotic Soviet state. But truly understood the dialectic goes on forever, and the synthesis of the contradiction between socialism and freedom must be a new state which combines the advantages of both. The Great Western tradition which comes down from Spinoza and Milton and Jefferson is fully applicable to socialist society and must be combined with it if Soviet man is to be free and if the socialist ideal is to regain its attraction for youth. The Soviet people who have suffered so much and created so much, who in 50 years have made such giant strides, owe it to themselves and the world to strike out boldly on this new road to the freedom which has so long been denied them.

47 SOVIET INTRANSIGENCE

Richard M. Nixon (1913–   )

Until his unprecedented resignation from the presidency in August 1974, Richard Nixon played a leading role in the political life of our nation following the end of World War II. Born in Yorba Kinda, California, Nixon graduated from Whittier College in 1934 and attended Duke University Law School. After serving as a naval officer in the Pacific, he was elected to the House of Representatives in 1946 and to the Senate four years later. Nixon occupied the office of Vice President for eight years under President Dwight D. Eisenhower and, after losing the 1960 presidential election to Kennedy he was successful in his second bid for the presidency in 1968. Although he was known as an outspoken foe of communism and as a "cold warrior" during his early political career, Nixon moderated his public image after reaching the White House and came to be identified as a sponsor of the policy of détente with the Soviet Union. The following comments on Russia from Nixon's second annual report to Congress on U. S. foreign policy on February 25, 1971, generally reflect his views of the Soviet Union while President.

———————

IDEOLOGY CONTINUES TO SHAPE many aspects of Soviet policy. It dictates an attitude of constant pressure toward the external world. The Soviet Government too frequently claims that the rationale for its internal and external policies is based on universalist doctrines. In certain fundamental aspects the Soviet outlook on world affairs is incompatible with a stable internation system.

The internal order of the USSR, as such, is not an object of our policy, although we do not hide our rejection of many of its features. Our relations with the USSR, as with other countries, are determined by its international behavior. Consequently, the fruitfulness of the relationship depends significantly upon the degree to which its international behavior does not reflect militant doctrinal considerations. . . .

The nature of nuclear power requires that both the Soviet Union and we be willing to practice self-restraint in the pursuit of national interests. We have acted on this principle in our conduct of the SALT negotiations, in our diplomatic initiatives in the Middle East, and in our proposals to improve the situation in Berlin. We are prepared to apply it to all legitimate Soviet interests.

Such a policy of restraint, however, requires repicrocity— concretely expressed in actions.

By virtue of its size and geography, the USSR has traditionally had important security interests in Europe and East Asia. Her undoubted status as a global power obviously creates interests in other areas where Russia has not traditionally been a factor. But the natural expansion of Soviet influence in the world must not distort itself into ambitions for exclusive or predominant positions. For such a course ignores the interests of others, including ourselves. It must and will be resisted. It can, therefore, lead only to confrontation. . . .

We do not suggest that the starting point—or, indeed, the culmination—of our negotiations with the USSR be the acceptance of our views and positions. Nor do we expect to resolve issues by cajoling the Soviet leaders into solutions damaging to their national interests. We cannot be expected, however, to accept the Soviet definition of every issue, to agree automatically to the Soviet order of priorities, or to accept every aggrandizement of Soviet positions abroad as a "new reality" no longer open to challenge. The principle of mutual accommodation, if it is to have any meaning, must be that both of us seek compromises, mutual concessions and new solutions to old problems. . . .

The last two decades witnessed the transformation of the Soviet Union from a Eurasian power to an intercontinental one. The

USSR now possesses military capabilities far beyond those at the command of previous Soviet leaders.

In earlier periods our strategic superiority gave us a margin of safety. Now, however, the enormous increase in Soviet capabilities has added a new and critical dimension to our relationship. The growth of Soviet power in the last several years could tempt Soviet leaders into bolder challenges. It could lead them to underestimate the risks of certain policies. We, of course, continue to weigh carefully Soviet statements of intentions. But the existing military balance does not permit us to judge the significance of Soviet actions only by what they say—or even what we believe—are their intentions. We must measure their actions, at least in part, against their capabilities. . . .

Mutual restraint, accommodation of interests, and the changed strategic situation open broad opportunities to the Soviet Union and the United States. It is our hope that the Soviet Union will recognize, as we do, that our futures are best served by serious negotiation of the issues which divide us. We have taken the initiative in establishing an agenda on which agreement could profoundly alter the substance of our relationship:

—*SALT.* Given the available resources, neither of us will concede a significant strategic advantage to the other. Yet the temptation to attempt to achieve such advantage is ever present, and modern technology makes such an attempt feasible. With our current strategic capabilities, we have a unique opportunity to design a stable and mutually acceptable strategic relationship.

We did not expect agreements to emerge quickly, for the most vital of interests are engaged. A resolution will not be achieved by agreement on generalities. We have put forward precise and serious proposals that would create no unilateral advantages and would cope with the major concerns of both sides.

We do not yet know what conclusions the Soviet Union will draw from the facts of the situation. If its leaders share our assessment, we can unquestionably bring competition in strategic weapons under control.

—*Europe.* With our allies, we have entered into negotiations

Another summit—the meeting between President Richard M. Nixon and Communist Party General Secretary Leonid Brezhnev, and the press, at the Kremlin in Moscow, 1974.

with the USSR to improve the Berlin situation. Arrangements which in fact bring an end to the twenty-four years of tension over Berlin would enable us to move beyond the vestiges of the postwar period that have dominated our relationship for so long. A broader era of negotiations in Europe then becomes possible.

Progress toward this goal also could be obtained through a successful agreement on mutual reduction of military forces, especially in Central Europe where confrontation could be most dangerous.

—*The Middle East* is heavy with the danger that local and regional conflict may engulf the Great Powers in confrontation.

We recognize that the USSR has acquired important interests and influence in the area, and that a lasting settlement cannot be achieved unless the Soviet Union sees it to be in its interest.

We continue to believe that it is in the Soviet interest to support a reasonable settlement. The USSR is not, however, contributing to that end by providing increasingly large and dangerous numbers of weapons to the Arab states, or by building military positions for its own purposes.

We are prepared to seek agreement with the USSR and the other major powers to limit arms shipment to the Middle East. . . .

An assessment of U.S.-Soviet relations at this point in my Administration has to be mixed. There have been some encouraging developments and we welcome them. We are engaged in a serious dialogue in SALT. We have both signed the treaty to prohibit nuclear weapons from the seabeds. We have both ratified the treaty on non-proliferation of nuclear weapons. We have entered negotiations on the issue of Berlin. We have taken the first step toward practical cooperation in outer space.

On the other hand, certain Soviet actions in the Middle East, Berlin, and Cuba are not encouraging. Taken against a background of intensive and unrestrained anti-American propaganda, these actions inevitably suggest that intransigence remains a cardinal feature of the Soviet system.

48 MALTREATMENT OF THE JEWISH MINORITY

Gerald R. Ford (1913–)

As the first non-elected President of the United States, Gerald Ford made no major shifts in the foreign policies of previous administrations. Born in Omaha, Nebraska, he attended the University of Michigan and then graduated from Yale University Law School in 1941. After twenty-five years in the House of Representatives as a Republican Congressman from Michigan, he was elevated to the vice presidency in December 1973 following Spiro T. Agnew's resignation. In August 1974, when President Richard M. Nixon resigned, Gerald Ford became the thirty-eighth president of the United States.

On December 13, 1971, Congressman Ford was invited to address a rally at Madison Square Garden in New York City to protest the treatment of Jews in the Soviet Union. His comments, very critical of the Soviets, reiterate similar pronouncements made by American political figures of both major parties on this issue.

I SEE NO POINT in elaborating on or repeating the facts of which you are so painfully aware. You know that there are more than 40 Jews in prison in Russia merely because they sought the right to join co-religionists in Israel. You know that Sylva Zalmonson is dying in captivity. You know about the deprivation of cultural and religious rights, the scapegoating of Jews, the anti-semitic propaganda, the discrimination in education and employment.

341

You know about the cruel obstructions placed in the way of those who seek to emigrate.

The real reason I came here from Washington is to discuss what the United States Government can do to help Soviet Jewry.

Some of our diplomats and experts on the protocol of statesmanship have, in the past, insisted that we have no business as a Government to comment on the internal and domestic affairs of another nation. But that has not stopped the Soviet Union from intervening in the internal and domestic affairs of Czechoslovakia, of Hungary, of Poland, of Romania, of Lithuania, of Latvia, and of other nations. They—the Russians—have certainly not hesitated to intervene in the affairs of the peoples of the Middle East. They certainly showed no sense of propriety in intervening in the India-Pakistan dispute when they vetoed the United Nations' efforts to stop the bloodshed!

Since the Soviet Union uses its veto at the United Nations and asserts itself through the U.N. when it suits Russian convenience, I feel that it is now very appropriate for the United States to remind the Russians of the United Nations Declaration of Human Rights. And I speak specifically about the right of the Jews of the Soviet Union to live as normal human beings with all the rights and freedoms enjoyed by others—and especially the freedom to leave the U.S.S.R. if they want to. . . .

The Jewish people of the Soviet Union have been singled out for special restrictions. They are denied the consideration accorded other minorities. The Kremlin is very sensitive to this issue. It has undermined the Communist pretensions of human equality and social justice. Indeed, there are some indications of minor concessions by the Moscow authorities to the rising outcry of world public opinion. This year more than 7,000 Jews were permitted to emigrate to Israel in response to the pressures exerted by men of good will. 1971 has been a record year.

But this is not the moment to relax our efforts. Too many lives are at stake. Too many men, women, and children are waiting. Too many people are in jeopardy.

The President has a very clear mandate from the Congress. Our Congress has adopted many resolutions and other expres-

American public opinion was aroused by the Soviet's treatment of its Jewish citizens. Two hundred thousand people attended the 1974 Solidarity Day for Soviet Jewry, sponsored by the Greater New York Conference on Soviet Jewry.

sions requesting and authorizing the President to act on behalf of those subjected to religious discrimination by the Soviet Union. During the Eisenhower Administration, as far back as 1953, the Congress condemned the persecution by the U.S.S.R. of all minorities. In 1954 the Congress asked the churches and synagogues of America to set aside a portion of their services on Easter Sunday and Passover for special prayers for deliverance of all those behind the Iron Curtain who are denied freedom of worship. Perhaps it would be wise to repeat this in 1972.

Even now there is new legislation pending before the Congress. I have offered my support for a House concurrent resolution that calls for the free exercise of religion in the Soviet Union and asks that country to permit its citizens to emigrate to countries of their choice. . . .

I might mention at this point the fact that the Voice of America has increased the amount of its broadcasts in Russian, on Jewish subjects, beamed at the Soviet Union. This is significant but I personally believe there should be Voice of America broadcasts in Yiddish. Not only would this tend to enhance the Jewish cultural heritage among Soviet Jews, but it also would be a symbol of U.S. support for Jews in the Soviet Union.

I would like to reassure you that President Nixon has been carefully following the cause for which you have assembled. As far back as 1959, when he served as Vice-President, Mr. Nixon inaugurated a practice of presenting to Soviet leaders lists of names of Soviet residents, including many Jews, who were denied exit permits to join relatives in the United States. In fact, Mr. Nixon innovated this approach on a visit to Moscow in that year, 1959.

I would make a particular point with the President that he place high on his agenda the liberation from Siberian labor camps of all persons jailed for Jewish activities. Also, there is no reason that a government which pretends to be civilized cannot for humanitarian considerations notify Israel, whether or not Israel is diplomatically recognized at this time by that government, of numbers and dates of departure of Jews to be released from Russia. Then the Jewish Agency and the Israeli Government Ministry of Absorption would be in a better position to make adequate preparations for housing, feeding, jobs, education, health and so forth. Now there is no notice whatever until the trains arrive in Vienna from Russia.

It was with a sense of horror that I read of the Soviet policy of confining to mental institutions as psychiatric cases those persons with courage enough to speak out against the Government. I was shocked that Russian doctors would lend themselves to a policy of declaring insane those individuals whose views trouble the authorities. When the World Psychiatric Association met last week in Mexico the association refused to condemn the Soviet's use of psychiatry as a tool for political repression.

In this country we have an American Psychiatric Association. I would recommend to the A.P.A. that it adopt a suitable resolution condemning the Russian psychiatrists when the association meets at its coming convention.

Perhaps educators, clergymen, scientists and people of various other professions in the public sector of American life could do likewise when Soviet policies involve a particular profession. This struggle must be waged on a people-to-people basis as well as a government-to-government basis.

49 A REVISIONIST VIEW OF POSTWAR RELATIONS

J. W. Fulbright (1905–   )

As a U.S. Senator from Arkansas and as Chairman of the Senate Committee on Foreign Relations, J. W. Fulbright exercised a significant influence on American foreign policy. Born in Sumner, Missouri, he graduated from the University of Arkansas in 1925. Subsequently, he attended Oxford University in England and received a law degree from George Washington University in Washington, D.C., in 1934. Prior to his election to the Senate in 1945, he served as an attorney with the U.S. Department of Justice and as a member of the House of Representatives from Arkansas.

During his early years in the Senate, Senator Fulbright supported U.S. foreign policy as initiated by the White House, and worked closely with Presidents Truman, Eisenhower, and Kennedy. His break with President Johnson, however, resulted from the prolongation of the Vietnam War, and in his later years in the Senate he differed sharply with President Nixon over U.S. policies toward the Soviet Union and American support for anticommunist forces abroad. In his book *The Crippled Giant* (1972), Senator Fulbright gives a somewhat revisionist view of U.S. policy toward Russia since the end of World War II and suggests that America bears a major responsibility for the deterioration in Soviet-U.S. relations after 1945.

UNTIL FAIRLY RECENTLY I accepted the conventional view that the United States had acted in good faith to make the United

Nations work but that the Charter was undermined by the Soviet veto. In retrospect, this seems less certain, and one suspects now that, like the League of Nations before it, the United Nations was orphaned at birth. Whereas Woodrow Wilson's great creation was abandoned to skeptical Europeans, Franklin Roosevelt's project was consigned to the care of unsympathetic men of his own country. President Roosevelt died only two weeks before the opening of the meeting in San Francisco at which the United Nations was organized. The new and inexperienced President Truman was naturally more dependent on his advisers than President Roosevelt had been; among these, so far as I know, none was a strong supporter of the plan for a world organization. . . .

Disdaining the United Nations, the framers of the Truman Doctrine also nurtured an intense hostility toward communism and the Soviet Union. Stalin of course did much to earn this hostility, with his paranoiac suspiciousness, the imposition of Soviet domination in Eastern Europe and the use of Western Communist parties as instruments of Soviet policy. All this is well-known. Less well-known, far more puzzling and also more pertinent to our position in the world today is the eagerness with which we seized upon postwar Soviet provocations and plunged into the cold war. Even if it be granted that Stalin started the cold war, it must also be recognized that the Truman Administration seemed to welcome it.

By early 1947—a year and a half after the founding of the United Nations—the assumptions of the cold war were all but unchallenged within the United States government and anti-communism had become a national ideology. It was *assumed* that the object of Soviet policy was the communization of the world; if Soviet behavior in Europe and northern China were not proof enough, the design was spelled out in the writings of Lenin and Marx, which our policy makers chose to read not as a body of political philosophy but as the field manual of Soviet strategy. It is true of course that by 1947, with the United States virtually disarmed and Western Europe in a condition of economic paralysis, the Soviet Union might plausibly have tried to take over Western Europe through the manipulation of Communist parties, military intimidation, economic strangulation, and possibly even direct military action. The fact that Stalin could have done this, and might well have tried but for timely American counteraction through the Marshall Plan and the formation of NATO, was quickly and uncritically taken as proof of a design for unlimited conquest comparable to that of Nazi Germany. Neither in the executive branch of our government nor in Congress were more than a few isolated voices raised to suggest the possibility that Soviet policy in Europe might be motivated by morbid fears for the security of the Soviet Union, and by opportunism, rather than a design for world conquest. Virtually no one in a position of power was receptive to the hypothesis that Soviet truculence reflected weakness rather than strength, intensified by memories of 1919 when the Western powers had intervened in an effort—however half-hearted—to strangle the Bolshevik "monster" in its cradle. Our own policy was formed without the benefit of constructive adversary proceedings. A few brave individuals like former Vice President Henry Wallace offered dissenting counsel—and paid dear for it. . . .

We came to see the hand of "Moscow communism" in every disruption that occurred anywhere. First, there was the conception of communism as an international conspiracy, as an octopus with its body in Moscow and its tentacles reaching out to the farthest corners of the world. Later, after the Sino-Soviet break, sophisticated foreign policy analysts disavowed the conspiracy thesis, but, at the same time they disavowed it, they said things which showed that the faith lingered on. Secretary Rusk and his associates professed to be scornful of the conspiracy thesis, but they still defended the Vietnam war with references to a world "cut in two by Asian communism," the only difference between the earlier view and the later one being that where once there had been one octopus, they now saw two.

If you accepted the premise, the rest followed. If Moscow and Peking represented centers of great power implacably hostile to the United States, and if every local crisis from Cuba to the Congo to Vietnam had the Communist mark upon it, then it followed logically that every crisis posed a threat to the security of the United States. . . .

Psychologists tell us that there is often a great difference between what one person says and what another hears, or, in variation of the old adage, that the evil may be in the ear of the hearer. When Khrushchev said, "We will bury you," Americans heard the statement as a threat of nuclear war and were outraged accordingly. The matter was raised when Chairman Khrushchev visited the United States in 1959, and he replied with some anger that he had been talking about economic competition. "I am deeply concerned over these conscious distortions of my thoughts," he said. "I've never mentioned any rockets.". . .

Now, in retrospect, one wonders: why were we so sure that Khrushchev did not mean what he said about peace? The answer lies in part, I believe, in our anti-Communist obsession, in the distortions it created in our perception of Soviet behavior, and in the extraordinary sense of threat we experienced when the Russians proclaimed their desire to catch up and overtake us economically. In our own national value system competition has always been prized; why then should we have been so alarmed by a challenge to compete? Perhaps our national tendency to extol competition rather than cooperation as a social virtue and our preoccupation with our own primacy—with being the "biggest," the "greatest" nation—suggests an underlying lack of confidence in ourselves, a supposition that unless we are "Number 1," we will be nothing, worthless and despised, and deservedly so. I am convinced that the real reason we squandered $20 billion or more getting men to the moon in the decade of the sixties was our fear of something like horrible humiliation if the Russians got men there first. . . .

Perhaps if we had been less proud and less fearful, we would have responded in a more positive way to the earthy, unorthodox Khrushchev. Whatever his faults and excesses, Khrushchev is recognized in retrospect as the Communist leader who repudiated the Marxist dogma of the "inevitability" of war between Communist and capitalist states. Recognizing the insanity of war with nuclear weapons, Khrushchev became the advocate of "goulash" communism, of peaceful economic competition with the West. During his period in office some amenities were restored in East-West relations; the Berlin issue was stirred up but finally defused; and, most important, the limited nuclear test-ban treaty was concluded. These were solid achievements, though meager in proportion to mankind's need for peace, and meager too, it now appears, in proportion to the opportunity that may then have existed. One wonders how much more might have been accomplished—particularly in the field of disarmament—if Americans had not still been caught up in the prideful, fearful spirit of the Truman Doctrine. . . .

With a decade's perspective—and without the blinders of the Truman Doctrine—it even seems possible that the Cuban missile crisis of 1962 was not so enormous a crisis as it then seemed. Khrushchev in the early sixties was engaged in an internal struggle with the Soviet military, who, not unlike our own generals, were constantly lobbying for more funds for ever more colossal weapons systems. Khrushchev had been cutting back on conventional forces and, largely for purposes of appeasing his unhappy generals, was talking a great deal about the power of Soviet missiles. President Kennedy, however, was applying pressure from another direction; unnerved by Khrushchev's endorsement of "wars of national liberation," he was undertaking to build up American conventional forces at the same time that he was greatly expanding the American nuclear-missile force, even though by this time the United States had an enormous strategic superiority. Khrushchev's effort to resist the pressures from his generals was of course undermined by the American build-up. It exposed him to pressures within the Kremlin from a hostile coalition of thwarted generals and politicians who opposed his de-Stalinization policies. In the view of a number of specialists in the Soviet field, the placement of missiles in Cuba was motivated largely if not primarily by Khrushchev's need to deal with these domestic pressures; it was meant to close or narrow the Soviet "missile gap" in relation to the United States, without forcing Khrushchev to concentrate all available resources on a ruinous arms race. . . .

Cold-war tensions have abated in Europe—partly as the result of deliberate acts of policy on the part of the Soviet Union, the Western European countries and the United States; partly, too, because of the "benign neglect" necessitated by American involvement in Vietnam; finally—and most important—because of general acceptance of the results of the Second World War, tacit until 1972, made all but explicit in the Moscow summit. . . .

The agreement reached at Moscow in May 1972 limiting ABM sites and the deployment of offensive weapons was more important as an act of mutual commitment to coexistence than for the actual arms limitations it imposed. Indeed, giving up the ABM— except for each side retaining the option to two sites—is probably the single most significant commitment the two super powers have made to the principle of coexistence. Insofar as each side abandons the effort to make itself invulnerable to attack or retaliation by the other, it also commits itself to peace and to the survival of the other's power and ideology. The Russians in effect abandon the Marxian dream of a world communized by war; we in turn lay to rest the last vestiges of the old idea of a global crusade for freedom.

These are the symbolic implications if not the immediate fact of the Moscow agreements. The immediate situation is still conditioned by vestiges of the cold-war spirit. Both sides remain capable of destroying each other many times over and, in the wake of the Moscow agreements, the Nixon Administration hastened to call for an increase of over $1 billion for offensive strategic weapons, citing the need for "bargaining chips" in the next round of SALT talks. The Secretary of Defense indeed hastened to make known his doubts as to the wisdom of the Moscow agreements unless we accompanied their ratification with an accelerated program for the development of a missile-launching submarine called Trident, the new B-1 supersonic bomber to replace the giant B-52, and other offensive weapons not covered by the Moscow agreements. The possibility, therefore, arises that, in our ambivalence as between the new coexistence and the lingering spirit of the Truman Doctrine, we may engage the Russians in an accelerated arms race at the same time that we have mutually conceded the survival of each other's power and political system.

With or without an intensified arms race, the balance of nuclear power now, however, seems likely to remain about as stable as so tenuous an equilibrium can be. Despite the continuing enormously costly arms race, the proxy conflict in Southeast Asia, and recurrent tensions in the Middle East, the Soviet Union and the United States have achieved something of the kind of peaceful coexistence advocated by Nikita Khrushchev a decade ago. The basis of that coexistence is fear, the continuing receptiveness of both sides to the warning of Albert Einstein, the man whose formula first made the nuclear bomb possible, that "at the end, looming ever clearer, lies general annihilation."

50 DÉTENTE—WHAT IT IS AND WHAT IT ISN'T

Arthur A. Hartman (1926–   )

One of the best descriptions of Russia as affected by the policy of détente was provided by Arthur Hartman, a career Foreign Service Officer who served as Assistant Secretary of State for European Affairs from 1974 to 1977. Hartman was born in New York City and graduated from Harvard in 1944. After serving in the army during World War II, he became an official of the Economic Cooperation Administration in 1948 prior to his post as Foreign Service Officer. Secretary Hartman's comments were made in a speech at Rice University in Houston, Texas, on March 4, 1976. Along with Kissinger's address (see p. 367), the speech represented an effort by the administration to defend the policy of détente from domestic criticism. In June 1977 Hartman was sworn in as Ambassador to France.

MY ANNOUNCED THEME TONIGHT IS DÉTENTE—what it is and what it isn't. The word "détente" has aroused strong emotions among Americans—in some, a favorable reaction; in many, an unfavorable one. In some cases the meaning of "détente" has been misunderstood; in other cases it has been misrepresented. Indeed, several days ago President Ford said he found the word so unhelpful that he has stopped using it altogether.

Tonight, therefore, I would like to bring the debate on the subject down to specifics. I ask you to put the *word* "détente" out of your mind and join me in taking a sober look at the fundamental and sometimes intractable aspects of our policy toward the Soviet Union. It is a policy of unique importance for all of us because it relates to the only other superpower existing today or likely to exist for many years to come. . . .

Mistakes have been made in our policy toward the Soviet Union. All history is a record of opportunities gained and opportunities lost. But I am convinced that the basic lines of our present policy are the only ones we can reasonably pursue. And I invite each of you to ask yourself at every point in our discussion tonight the same questions I consistently ask myself. Are there feasible alternatives to what we are trying to do? And is it possible to summon a national consensus around those alternatives?

Let me begin our discussion by asserting that the basic international problem of our time—perhaps of this whole half-century —is dealing with the consequences of the fact that the U.S.S.R. has become a superpower with the ability to project its military strength in global terms. The growth and expansion of Russian continental power began long before the Bolshevik Revolution brought the Communists to power. But this thrust has been accelerated by the Soviet regime, which has taken a country with a large and talented population, given it an ideology that pretends to universalism, and ruled it with an authoritarian devotion to the acquisition and retention of power.

This historical drive to superpower status is not a process which was or is in our power to stop. Let us recall that the Soviets exploded their first nuclear bomb in 1949, during the Administration of President Truman, and that they launched the first vehicle which could deliver it to intercontinental targets in 1957, during the Administration of President Eisenhower. Neither Administration was "soft" on communism or on the Soviet Union. The fact is that no U.S. Administration could have stopped this development of Soviet strategic power short of using our preponderant nuclear strength to try to wipe out the Soviet Union and most of its people—an option which I trust no responsible American leader would ever seriously consider.

Having developed the two essential strategic weapons, it was only a matter of time before the Soviet Union reached the military status of a great power. Today we Americans must cope with the implications of this inevitable accretion of Soviet strength. It is perhaps the most complex task we have ever faced in our foreign policy, because we must deal with a state which has the strength to destroy us, just as we have the power to destroy it. Today the Soviet leaders have the capacity to refuse to make concessions to us simply because we demand them, just as we have always had the capacity to refuse to accept any demands they make of us.

I ask you to ponder the implications of one simple statement which applies to all relationships between adversaries who are equals or near-equals—whether they be individuals or political groups or states—and which describes the reality of our current problem with the Soviet Union. The statement is this: We can get nothing that we want from the Soviets except by taking account, in one way or another, of Soviet interests. This means that our policy toward the Soviet Union—to a far greater degree than in earlier periods—must often proceed by a balancing of interests, which will mean accommodation or compromise by both sides. This new imperative may seem obvious. Yet it is ignored by many people who express themselves on U.S.-Soviet relations—people who concede on the one hand that the U.S.S.R. is now a superpower but seem to expect, on the other hand, that we can pursue negotiations with the Soviets as if they had just lost a war and were about to sign a document of surrender.

Soviet power has developed unevenly, with large gaps, disparities, and weaknesses. The Soviets' new military status should not obscure in our own minds the many problems they still face. The Soviet commitment to defense priorities has exposed and exacerbated the economic difficulties which have dogged them ever since the Bolshevik Revolution. Their agriculture is singularly unproductive; their consumer sector is stunted; and their gross national product is only half of ours though their population is greater. They have a continuing nationality problem, which will increase now that non-Russian nationalities are a majority, and a growing one, of the population. Externally, their control of Eastern Europe to the west is inherently unstable since it is based not on affinities but on force. They confront a hostile China to the east. Their authority in the Communist movement is being further eroded as the rift with parties in Western Europe widens. And their recent victory in Angola is balanced by setbacks over the past few years in countries like Egypt and Portugal.

The Soviet Union is thus not a fully developed superpower in every sphere of its national activity. This uneven development of Soviet power offers us opportunities as well as problems. But Soviet military strength still confronts us with the need to deal with the U.S.S.R. in different ways than we have before.

This is not a problem which confronts this Administration only. It will be a problem for the next Administration and the next one after that. Indeed, I think that it will be a problem for Americans for at least the lifetime of every person in this room.

Thus the importance of our military relationship with the Soviet Union, the first aspect of our relationship I want to discuss tonight. How do we deal with this new Soviet power? History offers us no precedents. In the past the rise of a major new military power—Napoleon's France, Bismarck's Prussia, Hitler's Germany, Tojo's Japan—has usually led to full-scale war. But war is not an option for us anymore, because of the destructive power of nuclear weapons.

Surely the only sane course in today's conditions is to try to preserve our security and promote our national interests in a way that minimizes the risk of nuclear conflict. That, in our view, is the first and most vital objective of our policy toward the Soviet Union. And we must pursue it regardless of uncertainties in the other aspects of our bilateral relations.

This Administration is not the first to reach that conclusion. President Truman in 1946 advanced a plan to put under international control the entire process of producing atomic weapons. President Eisenhower in 1955 proposed to the Soviet Union flights by planes of one nation across the territory of the other to prevent surprises in military preparations. The Soviets rejected both proposals. It was Eisenhower who 21 years ago said that "Since the advent of nuclear weapons, it seems clear that there is no longer any alternative to peace. . . ."

The first major arms control agreement we reached with the Soviet Union—the treaty banning nuclear testing in the atmosphere, in space, and under water—was signed in 1963 during the Kennedy Administration.

Ever since, successive American Administrations have steadfastly pursued additional agreements to limit the strategic arms race. To have done otherwise would surely have meant accepting the inevitability of a never-ending arms race with all its destabilizing implications.

Would Americans have accepted this? I do not think so. And that is why I profoundly disagree with those who say we should be prepared to withhold a SALT agreement from the Soviets until they improve their behavior in areas of tension or on human rights or on some other unquestionably important issue. Such an attitude assumes that SALT agreements are somehow a concession we make to the Soviet Union, that they benefit Moscow but don't benefit us. On the contrary, while the Soviets see the limitation of strategic arms to be in their interest—for otherwise they would not enter into a negotiation—it is surely also in our own interest and, above all, in the interest of peace.

Remember what I said about the necessity of balance and accommodation in achieving our objectives. Remember, too, that we cannot expect the Soviets to consent to an arms control agreement which creates a net military disadvantage for them. Arms control agreements must contain a balance of advantages, or they cannot be negotiated. . . .

Surely it is both safer and cheaper to make our best efforts to reach an agreement. And those who disagree, it seems to me, owe the American people an explanation of just how they would deal with the inevitable consequences of the failure to reach a SALT agreement.

Before I leave the security aspect of our relationship with the Soviet Union, I want to stress the importance of keeping both our strategic and our conventional forces strong enough to deter Soviet aggression. That means second to none. We cannot afford to base our relationship with the Soviet Union on blind faith, in view of the continuing massive Soviet military buildups and of statements such as General Secretary Brezhnev [Leonid I. Brezhnev, General Secretary of the Central Committee of the Communist Party of the Soviet Union] made last week that "relaxation of tensions does not in the slightest way abolish, and cannot abolish or change, the laws of the class struggle."

Preponderant Soviet military power could quickly translate itself into political pressures which could have a destabilizing effect on Europe and perhaps even on ourselves. When Stalin asked Churchill how many divisions the Pope had, he was expressing a view that only military power is ultimately translatable into political influence. Moreover, Soviet military superiority would make arms control far more difficult, since we would never agree to a treaty enshrining an actual Soviet superiority and the Soviets would never agree to a treaty dismantling that superiority. Thus, the preservation of an equilibrium of power is not contradictory to our policy of seeking arms control measures with the Soviets. On the contrary, it is vital to that policy.

Let me now turn to the second aspect of our relationship with the U.S.S.R.—to the aspect of bilateral cooperation, in which the most important factor is trade.

Imagine a mythical country with a strong interest in trade with the United States. We begin a trading relationship with it, which burgeons quickly to an annual trade of $2.1 billion a year. Furthermore, the balance of trade results in a large export surplus to the advantage of the United States. Indeed, in one year we export $1.8 billion and import only $0.3 billion, for a trade surplus of $1.5 billion, or about 15 percent of our overall trade surplus worldwide for that year. Moreover, the prospects for the year to come are even better, due largely to a new trade agreement which guarantees U.S. exports in the value of $1 billion a year for the next five years.

Would such a trade situation be generally acclaimed in the United States as an unmitigated asset for us? Logically it would. In fact it is not, because the country is of course not mythical. It is the Soviet Union; those are the trade figures for last year; and the agreement is the grain agreement we negotiated last fall. Let us look at the facts on that grain agreement.

In 1971 the Soviet Union imported 2.9 million tons of grain from the United States—literally chickenfeed. In 1972, in an uncontrolled U.S. market, it imported 13.7 million tons—over four times as much. You remember what happened. The price of bread and the price of meat rose. As consumers we all had to pay more at the supermarket for basic foodstuffs. The objective of the U.S. negotiators in the 1975 grain negotiations was to prevent this from happening again—to guarantee a market in the U.S.S.R. for our farmers' grain while safeguarding the interests of consumers like you and me. And that is exactly what we did.

The current grain agreement stipulates that the Soviet Union must buy at least 6 million tons of grain a year—about a billion dollars' worth—and that it must transport at least a third of it on American ships. It cannot buy over 8 million tons without consulting us so we have a chance to assess the potential effect on U.S. food prices. And if our own grain stocks run low, we can reduce the amount of grain the Soviets buy. This helps our farmers. It helps the makers of farm machinery. It helps our shippers. It helps our trade and payments balance. And it should considerably moderate effects on food prices.

Moreover, there is a political value which, indeed, applies to our whole trading relationship with the Soviet Union. In creating incentives for the Soviet economy to move from its historical emphasis on self-sufficiency, we are creating a pattern of Soviet economic dependence on ourselves and on other Western countries. This pattern does not in itself totally preclude the possibility of war; after all, the two World Wars of this century were between major trading partners. But it does make it necessary for Soviet policymakers to consider the potential costs in economic terms of expansionist or aggressive policies. In effect we are introducing—for the first time—a major Western economic factor into their decisionmaking process. The larger the economic relationship, the larger the factor. In time it could become a major incentive for Soviet political restraint.

Thus, while we support an increase in emigration from the Soviet Union—a subject I will want to discuss a bit later—for both economic and political reasons we have opposed the action of Congress to link trade with Soviet emigration policy. Congress has made improved Soviet performance on letting people leave the U.S.S.R. a condition of substantial Export-Import Bank credits—credits which are designed to stimulate U.S. exports. It has also made emigration a condition of granting most-favored-nation treatment to Soviet exports to the United States—treatment which 100 other countries get. Every economic tool at our disposal is a potential asset in both our political and our economic relationship with the U.S.S.R. It is a misfortune that, even for the best of motives, we have denied ourselves the use of such tools.

Other aspects of our bilateral cooperation with the Soviet Union, principally the 11 bilateral cooperation agreements we signed at summit meetings, also have a long-term purpose from the U.S. point of view. The idea is to create patterns of cooperation in a society which for hundreds of years has been suspicious of, and resistant to, Western influences. We are not sanguine about sweeping early results, but the process seems to us a useful one as long as its importance is not exaggerated. We now have over 150 joint projects underway with the Soviets—on space, health, energy, environment, transportation, and many other problems.

It is sometimes argued that in strictly technological terms the Soviets are benefiting more from these agreements than we are. Obviously it is impossible to draw an overall balance sheet. But we carefully vet every project to make sure it does not involve the export of U.S. goods or technology which could make a significant contribution to Soviet military potential in a way detrimental to our national security. And remember that the Soviets made the major military breakthroughs of the 1940's and 1950's, which I have already described, at a time when there was virtually no trade or technological exchange with the West.

Moreover, we ourselves are gaining a great deal from these programs. For example, in the field of energy, which is of such concern in the United States, the Soviets are doing important work in developing efficient ways to burn conventional fossil fuels; to transmit electricity over long distances; and to use, by way of controlled thermonuclear fusion, heavy hydrogen—of which there is a plentiful supply in ordinary water—to generate electric power. The United States is plugged into all of these developments through our joint agreements on energy and on atomic energy.

The Guatemala tragedy has reminded us of the destructive

dangers of earthquakes. The Soviets are ahead of us in the theory of earthquake prediction; using Soviet expertise available through the environmental agreement, we were able to predict earthquakes in New York State and California in 1974. . . .

These are long-range programs of bilateral cooperation whose effectiveness as an element for political restraint will develop only over time. Of course we have it in our power to suspend or cancel them at any moment, and in any case the Soviet Union certainly knows that the programs would not survive a period of intense hostility. But, considering their long-term purposes and possibilities from the point of view of U.S. interests, we would certainly want to weigh the pros and cons carefully before we tried to use them to advance shortrun or immediate goals.

I come now to the third aspect of our relationship with the Soviet Union, and the most difficult to assess. It is our relationship with Moscow in areas of possible political confrontation. At the Moscow summit of 1972 the United States and the U.S.S.R. pledged to do all they could to keep situations from arising which would increase international tensions and pledged not to seek unilateral advantage at the expense of one another.

We could not expect Moscow to set aside immediately and completely its radically different concept of the world, its global policies which are often in conflict with ours, or its ideology. But we *can* expect the Soviets to initiate a process of moderating their international conduct, and we *can* expect to use our broadening relationship with them to offer rewards for moderation and exact penalties for aggressive behavior. Realistically, progress will only be slow. But we have made clear to the Soviets one overriding reality: that the American people could not support a long-term cooperative relationship with the Soviet Union if it did not employ restraint in its international behavior.

The Soviet record has been mixed. A large plus was the Berlin Agreement, which was negotiated in 1971 before the first Moscow summit and came into force in 1972, just after it. Many of you do not remember the attempt by Stalin in the 1940's to starve out the people of West Berlin by closing the access routes across East Germany and the threats by Khrushchev in the 1950's and 1960's to turn West Berlin and its 2 million free citizens over to the Communist rule of Walter Ulbricht's East Germany. Those of us who do remember those crises know how close we may have come to war over Berlin.

Today Berlin is no longer a flashpoint of East-West tension. The four-power agreement commits the Soviet Union to see that traffic along the access routes from West Germany to West Berlin is unimpeded and even facilitated and that the ties between West Germany and West Berlin are maintained and developed. Since the signing of the agreement, there has not been a major incident on the access routes.

The Middle East, another major potential area of U.S.-Soviet confrontation, illustrates clearly the need for a U.S. policy of carrot and stick. During the Middle East war of October 1973, the Soviet Union put three of its divisions in Eastern Europe on airborne alert—potentially for use in the conflict area—and then informed us that it might send Soviet troops unilaterally into the Middle East. We felt we had to make a strong response, considering the potential consequences for peace of the intrusion of Soviet troops for the first time in the Middle East. Our own alert, which was criticized at the time as overreaction, seems to me entirely justified. As it happened, no Soviet troops were sent.

But it has been necessary to mix firmness with restraint. We could not have ended Soviet influence in the Middle East had we wanted to. It has genuine interests in the area, as do we, and a close relationship—though a rather unstable one—with a number of Arab countries and movements. We have therefore encouraged the Soviets to use their ties in the area to assist the political process, or at least not to impede it. In 1974 and 1975, when the United States took the lead in mediating negotiations between the Israelis and the Arabs, the Soviets, though not having a direct role in that process, accepted the process with relatively good grace. . . .

I don't argue that we should necessarily try to contain the Soviets automatically at every place on the globe where they choose to press. But we must make clear to them—and actions speak louder than words—that they cannot expect to use their power with impunity to seek unilateral advantage. This is a challenge which will face future American Administrations. And they will need the understanding and support of the American people and Congress, just as this Administration does.

Think for a moment of how secure we in America, and our friends in Western Europe, would feel if the Soviets felt that they could push their power outward without any risk of resistance. In my view, a policy of moderating Soviet behavior and lessening the dangers of conflict must include a readiness to let the Soviets know that we have the means and the will to protect our interests anywhere in the world. . . .

The Soviet regime consistently asserts that, whatever the state of our bilateral relations, the ideological struggle will continue. I believe that Americans have nothing to fear from such a struggle. For, while we don't have—and don't want—an ideology, the power of ideas expressed in our Declaration of Independence, Constitution, and Bill of Rights is far stronger and more durable than the doctrines of Lenin or the thoughts of Mao. So our answer to the Soviets is: "Let the struggle of ideas go on; we will continue to let your ideas into our country and we challenge you to let our ideas into yours."

Realistically, however, we can expect at best only slow and meager progress from the Soviet Union in this area. Ever since the 16th century, foreign travelers to Russia have noted and described the degree to which individual rights have been subordinated to the all-powerful interests of the state. There is nothing distinctly Soviet about this approach to government and society. It is profoundly Russian. And the forces for change are contending with half a millennium of Russian tradition.

This means, it seems to me, that we must put the great weight of our policies on objectives where we *can* have a real effect, such as advancing our security interests and moderating Soviet international behavior. In areas which the Soviets assert to be their internal affair, we must do what we can—but in the sober realization that our efforts will meet stubborn resistance, even to the point of being counterproductive if pushed too far too fast.

Let me cite an example. In a significant incident, the American Congress called on the Administration to severely restrict the U.S. trading relationship with the Russian Government because of the way that government treated Jews. The vote was almost unanimous. The one Congressman who voted against the legislation complained that such pressure would not benefit the Jews and would harm American business.

I have not just described the passage by Congress in 1974 of legislation to tie the U.S.-Soviet trading relationship to Soviet emigration policy; I have described a resolution passed by the House of Representatives in 1911 to terminate a bilateral trade treaty with the Russian Government of Czar Nicholas II. The point—as drawn by our wisest expert on the Soviet Union, George Kennan, who has told this story in one of his books—is that some differences between Russia and the United States may never be reconciled.

The modern counterpart of that story is perhaps even more poignant. In 1972 and 1973, when there were strong behind-the-scenes pressures on the Soviet Union from the United States, Jewish emigration from the U.S.S.R. averaged 2,600–2,900 per month. In 1974, when the claim became more explicit that congressional trade legislation was a potent tool to force internal changes in the U.S.S.R., the rate dropped to 1,700 per month. In 1975, following the passage of legislation to restrict trade, the rate fell further, to 1,100 per month. Those figures tell the story. By trying to force the Soviets to take actions—however important in moral terms—which they considered within their sovereign competence, we repeated the mistake of 1911.

If the lesson to be learned is that we cannot expect overnight change from the Soviets in the human rights field, it is nevertheless also true that, besides the 1972 and 1973 emigration figures, we have made some progress in other areas touching on human rights.

I refer, for example, to the Conference on Security and Co-operation in Europe—the so-called Helsinki Conference—which ended at summit level last July. Since this conference has been misunderstood by many in the United States, let me take a minute to make clear what it did and did not do.

The Helsinki Conference—or CSCE, as we bureaucrats perversely call it—began as a Soviet initiative in 1969 designed to confirm the territorial and political status quo in Europe, which would mean confirming also Soviet hegemony over its Eastern

European neighbors. That is not how the conference ended, however. Indeed, for simply agreeing to go to the CSCE negotiation at all, the West exacted a price from the Soviets which *already* altered the status quo in Europe in human terms.

The price was the Berlin Agreement, whose conclusion NATO made a precondition to starting the CSCE talks. Apart from the guaranteed access I have already described, the agreement made it possible for the people of West Berlin to make visits to East Berlin and East Germany, often to see relatives, friends, former homes—something which the East German government had not allowed them to do before. Since the Berlin Agreement went into effect in June 1972, some 12 million visits have been made by West Berliners to East Berlin and East Germany through the infamous Berlin Wall—a dramatic change of the status quo and one with a direct effect on several million people whose isolation had been one of the most tragic remnants of the cold war.

Even when CSCE began, the Soviets found the ground had shifted under them. They had hoped for a fuzzy declaration that would create a sense of euphoria in the West and ignore the real reasons for division in Europe. Instead, the NATO members, aided in certain instances by pressures from neutrals and even Eastern Europeans, introduced a list of resolutions to promote freer contacts between peoples in the Eastern and Western halves of Europe and freer exchanges of ideas and information. The Soviets didn't want any of this, but in the end they had to take some of it.

In the process of compromise, the West did not get all the Soviet concessions we wanted. But we *did* get explicit Soviet admission that Europe would not have to be locked into a territorial status quo but that frontiers could be changed by peaceful means and by agreement. We *did* get the establishment of a principle that there should be freer East-West contacts. And we *did* get the Soviet Union to admit—for the first time ever—that its internal policies, and those of the Eastern European Communist countries, which affect those contacts are a legitimate subject for East-West discourse.

This, then, is an account of our complex relationship with the Soviet Union. In describing it, I have not once used the word "détente." That word can only get in the way of understanding the problems involved. Let me conclude by summing up what our policy of improving relations with the Soviet Union is and what it is not:

—It is not a luxury which we can choose to pursue or not pursue. It is a necessity brought about by the fact that the Soviet Union has become a superpower in military terms.

—It is not the pursuit of summit meetings or joint communiques or paper agreements. It is the pursuit of a long-term relationship with the Soviet Union which will reduce the threat of war.

—It is not a profit-and-loss sheet in which a plus for one side is necessarily a minus for the other. It is a recognition that there must be a mutual U.S. and Soviet interest in the primary objectives of arms control agreements and political restraints to make the world safer in a nuclear age.

—It is not based on a pleasant atmosphere or good will or trust. It is based on a U.S. defense second to none, on the preservation of an equilibrium of power, and on verifiable agreements which must be in our national interest.

—It is not a matter of being tough for the sake of toughness or being soft for the sake of not offending Moscow. It is a necessary combination of incentives for Soviet restraint and penalties for Soviet aggression.

—It is not a blind eye turned to human rights and liberties. It is a desire to advance those rights and liberties within the limits of the possible and in the understanding that the major influence we can exert on the Soviet Union is in moderating its international, not its internal, behavior.

—It is, finally, not a short-term or a partisan policy. It is, and must be, a national policy which will have to continue for a generation or longer—for as long, in fact, as the Soviet Union remains a military great power.

The problem of the Soviet Union, then, is a problem for all of us and will be a problem for a long time to come. I, for one, am confident that we can manage it successfully, though perhaps it will never be really solved.

51 NUCLEAR DÉTENTE

Henry A. Kissinger (1923–   )

Probably no other man has so personified American foreign policy as did Henry Kissinger in his eight years of service, beginning in 1969 as Assistant to President Richard M. Nixon for National Security Affairs and subsequently as Secretary of State. Born in Germany in 1923, Kissinger moved to the United States with his family in 1938. He became a citizen in 1943, while serving with the U.S. Army. After studying and teaching at Harvard University, he first won public recognition in 1967 with the publication of his book *Nuclear Weapons and Foreign Policy.*

Kissinger won the Nobel Peace Prize in 1973 for his efforts to bring about a peace settlement in Vietnam. Earlier, he had played a key role in arranging President Nixon's headline-making trips to China in February 1972 and to the Soviet Union in May of the same year. Following Nixon's resignation from the presidency in August 1974, and particularly with the approach of the 1976 presidential campaign, Kissinger became the target of considerable criticism from groups in the United States who believed that his policy of détente with the Soviet Union was working to the disadvantage of this country. In March 1976 he used the forum provided by a luncheon of the Boston World Affairs Council to make the following comments in defense of his policies toward the Soviet Union and to stress that a measure of cooperation with them was essential if war was to be avoided.

TODAY THE SOVIET UNION is a superpower. Nothing we could have done would have halted this evolution after the impetus that two generations of industrial and technological advance have given to Soviet military and economic growth. But together with others we must assure that Russian power and influence are not translated into an expansion of Soviet control and dominance beyond the U.S.S.R.'s borders. This is prerequisite to a more constructive relationship. . . .

Since the dawn of the nuclear age, the world's fears of catastrophe and its hopes for peace have hinged on the relationship between the United States and the Soviet Union.

In an era when two nations have the power to visit utter devastation on the world in a matter of hours, there can be no greater imperative than assuring that the relationship between the superpowers be managed effectively and rationally.

This is an unprecedented task. Historically, a conflict of ideology and geopolitical interests such as that which characterizes the current international scene has almost invariably led to conflict. But in the age of thermonuclear weapons and strategic equality, humanity could not survive such a repetition of history. No amount of tough rhetoric can change these realities. The future of our nation and of mankind depends on how well we avoid confrontation without giving up vital interests and how well we establish a more hopeful and stable relationship without surrender of principle.

We therefore face the necessity of a dual policy. On the one hand, we are determined to prevent Soviet military power from being used for political expansion; we will firmly discourage and resist adventurist policies. But at the same time, we cannot escalate every political dispute into a central crisis; nor can we rest on identifying foreign policy with crisis management. We have an obligation to work for a more positive future. We must couple opposition to pressure and irresponsibility with concerned efforts to build a more cooperative world. . . .

There is no question that peace rests, in the first instance, on the maintenance of a balance of global stability. Without the ultimate sanction of power, conciliation soon becomes surrender.

Moderation is a virtue only in those who are thought to have a choice.

No service is done to the nation by those who portray an exaggerated specter of Soviet power and of American weakness, by those who hesitate to resist when we are challenged, or by those who fail to see the opportunities we have to shape the U.S.-Soviet relationship by our own confident action.

Soviet strength is uneven; the weaknesses and frustrations of the Soviet system are glaring and have been clearly documented. Despite the inevitable increase in its power, the Soviet Union remains far behind us and our allies in any overall assessment of military, economic, and technological strength; it would be reckless in the extreme for the Soviet Union to challenge the industrial democracies. And Soviet society is no longer insulated from the influences and attractions of the outside world or impervious to the need for external contacts.

The great industrial democracies possess the means to counter Soviet expansion and to moderate Soviet behavior. We must not abdicate this responsibility by weakening ourselves either by failing to support our defenses or refusing to use our power in defense of our interests; we must, along with our allies, always do what is necessary to maintain our security.

It is true that we cannot be the world's policeman. Not all local wars and regional conflicts affect global stability or America's national interest. But if one superpower systematically exploits these conflicts for its own advantage and tips the scales decisively by its intervention, gradually the overall balance will be affected. If adventurism is allowed to succeed in local crises, an ominous precedent of wider consequence is set. Other nations will adjust their policies to their perception of the dominant trend. Our ability to control future crises will diminish. And if this pattern is not broken, America will ultimately face harder choices, higher costs, and more severe crises.

But our obligation goes beyond the balance of power. An equilibrium is too precarious a foundation for our long-term future. There is no tranquillity in a balance of terror constantly contested. We must avoid the twin temptations of provocation and escapism. Our course must be steady and not reflect momentary fashions; it must be a policy that our adversaries respect, our allies support, and our people believe in and sustain.

Therefore we have sought with the Soviet Union to push back the shadow of nuclear catastrophe—by settling concrete problems such as Berlin so as to ease confrontations and negotiating on limitation of strategic arms so as to slow the arms race. And we have held out the prospect of cooperative relations in the economic and other fields if political conditions permit their implementation and further development.

It goes without saying that this process requires reciprocity. It cannot survive a constant attempt to seek unilateral advantage.

. . . If the Soviet Union is ready to face genuine coexistence, we are prepared to make every effort to shape a pattern of restraint and mutual interest which will give coexistence a more reliable and positive character making both sides conscious of what would be lost by confrontation and what can be gained by cooperation.

And we are convinced that when a vigorous response to Soviet encroachment is called for, the President will have the support of the American people—and of our allies—to the extent that he can demonstrate that the crisis was imposed upon us; that it did not result from opportunities we missed to improve the prospects of peace.

No policy will soon, if ever, eliminate the competition and irreconcilable ideological differences between the United States and the Soviet Union. Nor will it make all interests compatible. We are engaged in a protracted process with inevitable ups and downs. But there is no alternative to the policy of penalties for adventurism and incentives for restraint. What do those who speak so glibly about "one-way streets" or "preemptive concessions" propose concretely that this country do? What precisely has been given up? What level of confrontation do they seek? What threats would they make? What risks would they run? What precise changes in our defense posture, what level of expenditure over what period of time, do they advocate? How, concretely, do they suggest managing the U.S.-Soviet relationship in an era of strategic equality?

It is time we heard answers to these questions.

In short we must—and we shall—pursue the two strands of our policy toward the Soviet Union: Firmness in the face of pressure and the vision to work for a better future. This is well within our capacities. We owe this to our people, to our future, to our allies, and to the rest of mankind.

52 HUMAN RIGHTS AND THE COLD WAR

Jimmy Carter (1924–   )

Following his inauguration as the thirty-ninth president in March 1977, Jimmy Carter moved rapidly to re-invigorate American policy toward the Soviet Union. He not only continued to emphasize prior efforts toward nuclear disarmament, but also actively sought to direct attention to the relatively neglected field of human rights in Russia. The first "southern" president since the Civil War, Jimmy Carter was born in Plains, Georgia, and graduated from the United States Naval Academy in 1947. After eight years as a naval officer, he returned to his family's agricultural interests in Plains. He served as Democratic Governor of Georgia from 1971 to 1974 and two years later went on to defeat President Gerald R. Ford in the November 1976 national election. Faced with criticism that his administration's emphasis on human rights was leading to strained relations with Moscow, President Carter defended his policy toward the Soviet Union in a speech at Charleston, South Carolina, on July 21, 1977.

FOR DECADES the central problems of our foreign policy revolved around antagonisms between two coalitions, one headed by the United States, and the other headed by the Soviet Union.

Our national security was often defined almost exclusively in terms of military competition with the Soviet Union.

This competition is still critical, because it does involve issues which could lead to war. But however important this relationship of military balance, it cannot be our sole preoccupation, to the exclusion of other world issues which also concern us both.

Even if we succeed in relaxing tensions with the USSR, we could still awake one day to find that nuclear weapons have been spread to dozens of other nations who may not be as responsible as are we. Or we could struggle to limit the conventional arsenals of our two nations to reduce the danger of war, only to undo our efforts by continuing without constraint to export armaments around the world.

As two industrial giants, we face long-term worldwide energy crises. Whatever our political differences, both of us are compelled to begin conserving world energy and developing alternatives to oil and gas.

Despite deep and continuing differences in world outlook, both of us should accept the new responsibilities imposed on us by the changing nature of international relations. . . .

Both the United States and the Soviet Union have learned that our countries and our people, in spite of great resources, are not all-powerful. We have learned that this world, no matter how technology has shrunk distances, is nevertheless too large and too varied to come under the sway of either one or two superpowers. And, what is perhaps most important of all, we have, for our part, learned, all of us, this fact, these facts in a spirit not of increasing resignation, but of increasing maturity.

I mention these changes with which you are familiar because I think that to understand today's Soviet-American relationship, we must place it in perspective, both historically and in terms of the overall global scene.

The whole history of Soviet-American relations teaches us that we will be misled if we base our long-range policies on the mood of the moment, whether that mood be euphoric or grim. All of us can remember times when relations seemed especially dangerous, and other times when they seemed especially bright.

We have crossed those peaks and valleys before. And we can see that, on balance, the trend in the last third of a century has been positive.

The profound differences in what our two governments believe about freedom and power and the inner lives of human beings, those differences are likely to remain. And so are other elements of competition between the United States and the Soviet Union. That competition is real and deeply rooted in the history and the values of our respective societies. But it is also true that our two countries share many important overlapping interests. Our job—my job, your job—is to explore those shared interests and use them to enlarge the areas of cooperation between us, on a basis of equality and mutual respect.

As we negotiate with the Soviet Union, we will be guided by a vision—of a gentler, freer, and more bountiful world. But we will have no illusions about the nature of the world as it really is. The basis for complete mutual trust between us does not yet exist. Therefore, the agreements that we reach must be anchored on each side in enlightened self-interest, what is best for us, what is best for the Soviet Union. That is why we search for areas of agreement where our real interests and those of the Soviets coincide.

We want to see the Soviets further engaged in the growing pattern of international activities designed to deal with human problems—not only because they can be of real help, but because we both should be seeking for a greater stake in the creation of a constructive and a peaceful world order.

When I took office, many Americans were growing disillusioned with detente. President Ford had even quit using the word, and by extension people were concerned with the whole course of our relations with the Soviet Union. Also, and perhaps more seriously, world respect for the essential rightness of American foreign policy had been shaken by the events of a decade—Vietnam, Cambodia, CIA, Watergate. At the same time, we were beginning to regain our sense of confidence and our purpose and unity as a nation.

In this situation, I decided that it was time for honest discussions about international issues with the American people. I felt it was urgent to restore the moral bearings of American foreign policy. And I felt that it was important to put the U.S. and Soviet relationship, in particular, on a more reciprocal, realistic and ultimately more productive basis for both nations.

It is not a question of "hard" policy or of "soft" policy, but of a clear-eyed recognition of how most effectively to protect our own security and to create the kind of international order that I have just described. This is our goal.

We have looked at the problems in Soviet-American relations in a fresh way, and we have sought to deal with them boldly and constructively with proposals intended to produce concrete results. I would like to point out just a few of them.

In the talks on strategic arms limitations, the SALT talks, we advanced a comprehensive proposal for genuine reductions, limitations, and a freeze on new technology which would maintain balanced strategic strength.

We have urged a complete end to all nuclear tests, and these negotiations are now underway. Agreement here could be a milestone in U.S.-Soviet relations. . . .

But none of these proposals that I have outlined to you involves the sacrifice of security. All of them are meant to increase the security of both sides. Our view is that a SALT agreement which just reflects the lowest common denominator that can be agreed upon easily will only create an illusion of progress and, eventually, a backlash against the entire arms control process. Our view is that genuine progress in SALT will not merely stabilize competition in weapons, but can also provide a basis for improvement in political relations as well.

When I say that these efforts are intended to relax tensions, I am not speaking only of military security. I mean as well the concern among our own individual citizens, Soviet and American, that comes from the knowledge which all of you have that the leaders of our two countries have the capacity to destroy human society through misunderstandings or mistakes. If we can relax this tension by reducing the nuclear threat, not only will we make the world a safer place but we will also free ourselves to concentrate on constructive action to give the world a better life.

We have made some progress toward our goals, but to be frank, we also hear some negative comments from the Soviet side about SALT and about our more general relations. If these comments are based on a misconception about our motives, then we will redouble our efforts to make our motives clear; but if the Soviets are merely making comments designed as propaganda to put pressure on us, let no one doubt that we will persevere. . . .

Increased trade between the United States and the Soviet Union would help us both. The American-Soviet Joint Commercial Commission has resumed its meetings after a long interlude. I hope that conditions can be created that will make possible steps toward expanded trade.

In southern Africa we have pressed for Soviet and Cuban restraint. Throughout the non-aligned world, our goal is not to encourage dissension or to redivide the world into opposing ideological camps, but to expand the realm of independence, economically self-reliant nations—and to oppose attempts at new kinds of subjugation.

Part of the Soviet Union leaders' current attitude may be due to their apparent—and incorrect—belief that our concern for human rights is aimed specifically at them or is an attack on their vital interests.

There are no hidden meanings in our commitment to human rights.

We stand on what we have said on the subject of human rights. Our policy is exactly what it appears to be: The positive and sincere expression of our deepest beliefs as a people. It is addressed not to any particular people or area of the world, but to all countries equally, yes, including our own country.

And it is specifically not designed to heat up the arms race or bring back the Cold War.

On the contrary, I believe that an atmosphere of peaceful cooperation is far more conducive to an increased respect for human rights than an atmosphere of belligerence or hatred or warlike confrontation. The experience of our own country, this last century, has proved this over and over again.

We have no illusions that the process will be quick or that change will come easily. But we are confident that if we do not abandon the struggle, the cause of personal freedom and human dignity will be enhanced in all nations of the world. We are going to do that.

In the past six months we have made clear our determination

—both to give voice to Americans' fundamental beliefs, and to obtain lasting solutions to East-West differences. If this chance to emphasize peace and cooperation instead of animosity and division is allowed to pass, it will not have been our choice.

We must always combine realism with principle. Our actions must be faithful to the essential values to which our own society is dedicated, because our faith in those values is the source of our confidence that this relationship will evolve in a more constructive direction.

I cannot forecast whether all of our efforts will succeed. But there are things which give me hope, and in conclusion I would like to mention them very briefly. . . .

Although there are deep differences in our values and ideas, we Americans and Russians belong to the same civilization whose origins stretch back hundreds of years.

Beyond all the disagreements between us—and beyond the cool calculations of mutual self-interest that our two countries bring to the negotiating table—is the invisible human reality that must bring us closer together. I mean the yearning for peace, real peace, that is in the very bones of us all.

I am absolutely certain that the people of the Soviet Union who have suffered so grievously in war feel this yearning for peace. And in this they are at one with the people of the United States. It is up to all of us to help make that unspoken passion into something more than just a dream—and that responsibility falls most heavily on those, like you, of course, but particularly like President Brezhnev and me, who hold in our hands the terrible power conferred on us by the modern engines of war.

Index